Hijacked Nation

Donald Trump's attack on America's greatness.

From the pages of Not Fake News

Volume 1

BOB GATTY

&

C J WALDRON

DEDICATION

Hijacked Nation is dedicated to all those who are
fighting to save our nation from the tyrant who occupies
the White House and whose actions are jeopardizing the
futures of generations still unborn. #resist

CONTENTS

About the Authors

Bob Gatty

Not Fake News is the brainchild of Bob Gatty. Together with a talented team of writers, Bob and many others set the record straight on what would otherwise be labeled "Fake News".

Bob's career has included reporting for newspapers, managing a state capital national wire service bureau, and covering Washington for several national business publications.

His company, G-Net Strategic Communications, assisted numerous national trade associations with their publications and communications needs. He is a journalist, editor, scriptwriter, speechwriter and photographer.

Bob now lives in Myrtle Beach, SC, where he launched Not Fake News in September 2017. NFN's blogs now reach readers across the U.S. and numerous foreign countries. Bob also is volunteer communications director for the Horry County, SC, Democratic Party.

Chris (C J) Waldron

Chris is from Upstate New York. He has earned degrees in English and Political Science from the University of New York. For almost 30 years, he taught in Schenectady, NY as an English and Special Education teacher. He has continued his career as an educator, currently as an adjunct instructor at Horry Georgetown Technical College.

Always active in politics, Chris has served as a poll reporter and worked on the campaigns of NYS Representative Paul Tonko as well as several local elections. He assisted the presidential campaigns of Bill Clinton, John Kerry, Hillary Clinton and Barack Obama with "Get Out the Vote" efforts, passing out leaflets, making phone calls and seeking campaign contributions.

An astute political analyst, Chris continues to be active in politics, supporting local, state and national Democratic candidates.

Chris writes with knowledge, insight and perspective as he analyzes important developments and shares his thoughts with Not Fake News readers. "Our job, he says, "is to preserve American ideals until America comes to its senses.

Contributing Authors

Stacy Fitzgerald

Stacy Fitzgerald is a full-time marketing and communications pro and part-time freelance writer using her considerable experience in living-while-black to engage in conscious storytelling.

She enjoys politics, traveling, reading, wine and dogs and abhors arrogance, aggressiveness and anything fake. When she's not working or writing, she also loves spending time with her family and practicing her considerable sarcasm skills.

Stephen Hamelman

With degrees from the University of Maine and Brandeis, Steve is an English professor at Coastal Carolina University, Conway, SC. His publications range from essays on early American writers to studies of rock music.

Long active as a rock drummer in the bar-band circuit, Steve is a member of the Waccamaw Dreadnoughts, whose other members include fellow university administrators and teachers. Steve is a lifestyle cyclist (i.e., bikes more than he drives), is the father of two radiant daughters, and is devoted to his dog Yuri, whom he adopted from the Waccamaw Animal Rescue Mission.

Susan Hutchinson

Susan Hutchinson is a retired Medical Technologist who spent over 18 years working in the clinical diagnostics industry where she learned technical writing and marketing.

In 2005 she accepted a position in England as regional product manager and spent the next six years working with colleagues from various European countries as well as Israel and South Africa. This gave her first-hand knowledge of how healthcare is managed in other countries. Her hope is that this healthcare model will be implemented in the United States. Susan is currently the Secretary of the Horry County, SC, Democratic Party.

Stacie Pearman

Stacie earned degrees in Behavioral Science and Criminal Justice. Her background is in Social Work, predominantly focusing on underserved and at-risk populations.

In her free time, Stacie is an avid World of Warcraft player, loves to fish but is terrible at it. She often can be found on the beach just off the Garden City Pier near her home in Murrells Inlet, SC, where she recently moved after having bounced around the country with her military husband and three sons. Stacie is a frequent traveler, returning often to her hometown of Wilmington, Delaware or going to Wingate University to watch her son play football.

Stacie is passionate about opposing the conservative movement and loves to wear edgy t-shirts to proclaim it!

Cover Art -- Michael Pearman

Stacie Pearman's military husband, Michael, also a talented graphic artist, created the cover for Hijacked Nation.

With an AAS degree in Advertising and Graphic Design, Michael is in the Army Reserves after serving two overseas deployments with the United States Army.

He is now reconnecting with the design world and hopes to grow and learn more about what this unique world has to offer.

We are grateful to Michael for his outstanding work and assisting

Foreword

By Bob Gatty

It was September 2017 and Donald J. Trump, the 45th President of the United States, was attacking the mainstream media with increasing intensity, claiming that any newspaper, magazine, or television news story that called him out for his regular exaggerations and lies constituted "fake news."

Journalists, he famously said in the summer of 2019, are the "Enemy of the People." But long before that, I decided to use whatever talent I have and platform that I could find to somehow resist this constant harangue of the media – except, of course, for his committed followers, Fox News, Breitbart and the like.

So, I decided to launch a blog to comment on the day's news and, when appropriate, call out Trump for his lies and distortions. Who was I to do this? I was not famous, just a retired former journalist, freelance writer and communications guy. But, I thought, why not? Even if nobody pays attention, at least you won't be standing by, silently letting this liar and demagogue go unchallenged.

Why "Not Fake News"?
What to call it? That was an important question. I decided it would be "Not Fake News" – because my intention was to challenge Trump's own fakery from my platform.

Soon, I invited some of my colleagues to contribute articles to Not Fake News. That's how my co-author, Chris Waldron, entered the picture. Chris is a prolific contributor bringing excellent writing, terrific analysis and perspective to our content. We rarely miss a day, and we often publish two, even three blogs in one day.

Now, after more than 1,000 blogs since the inception, our audience is worldwide, with readers – and members – from as far away as China, Thailand, Ireland, Pakistan, Great Britain, German, the Netherlands, Spain, Malaysia, the Philippines, and several other countries. We have a growing following of members and subscribers from across the U.S., some of whom offer invaluable suggestions for topic for us to cover.

Also included are blogs by several other talented writers: Stacy Fitzgerald, with whom I worked in Washington, and Stacie Pearman, Susan Hutchinson, and Steve Hamelman, all that are members of the communications team that I lead for the local Democrats. Several other talented writers also have contributed, but less frequently.

Hijacked Nation includes blogs that provide a contemporary history of important national developments since September 2017, developments that will leave an indelible mark on the history of our nation. We do this, of course, "with a little lean to the left."

Volume 2 in this two-volume set covers:

- Immoral Immigration
- An Impeached President
- Politics in the Age of Trump.
- The Coronavirus Pandemic

◆◆◆

Not Fake News is published under the website:  *https://www.notfakenews.biz/ You can also listen to Not Fake News podcasts from this page and connect with our YouTube channel.*

Contact Not Fake News at info@notfakenews.biz.

1

ATTACKS ON THE MEDIA

Throughout his presidency, Donald Trump has viciously and unrelentingly attacked the news media, blaming it for his many difficulties and threatening and belittling journalists who have the courage to call him out.

WHO is the ENEMY of the PEOPLE?

August. 5, 2018

By Bob Gatty

President Trump continues his war against the news media calling journalists "the Enemy of the People," a tactic that might whip up his loyal 30 percent base, but one that I believe is dangerous and totally irresponsible.

Actually, one might turn that label around, because if anybody truly is the "enemy of the people," it is Donald Trump, the would-be dictator who with the help of the GOP is endangering our country in untold numbers of ways.

Trump simply cannot stand it when media outlets call him out on his lies, his exaggerations, his misstatements. He cannot abide the fact that his relationship with Russia is being slowly and methodically unwrapped in the Mueller investigation. He is turning on his friends, including his former bagman who once said he would "take a bullet" for Trump.

So, Trump keeps going to these rallies where he can suck up the adulation from his supporters. The more he whips them up with his hateful rhetoric, the more they cheer, the better he likes it, and the more dangerous he becomes.

Today, even his former and very temporary communications director Anthony Scaramucci said on TV that Trump was wrong to continue his war against the media. He made the comment just hours after this tweet by Trump:

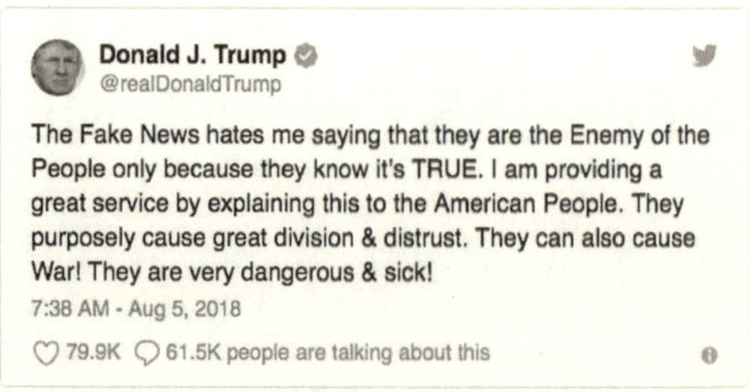

"I've said that consistently that they're not the enemy," Scaramucci said on CNN's "Reliable Sources". "You can have an adversarial relationship; you can disagree with people in the press ... But I don't like the war declaration because it will lead to something that none of us really want."

National reporters and commentators are receiving death threats from Trump's true believers. What if one of them actually follows through and shoots somebody?

Trump is playing a dangerous, irresponsible game.

Trump's War Against the Free Press Must End

August 12, 2018
By Bob Gatty
Newspapers across the country will publish editorials Thursday, August 16, calling out President Trump for his vicious and dangerous attacks against the news media, including individual reporters, whom he repeatedly calls "the enemy of the people."

It's an effort organized by The Boston Globe, and as of today, more than 100 newspapers have signed up to participate.

"We propose to publish an editorial on August 16 on the dangers of the administration's assault on the press and ask others to commit to publishing their own editorials on the same date," The Globe said in its appeal to newspaper editors.

"We have more than 100 publications signed up, and I expect that number to grow in the coming days," Marjorie Pritchard, the Globe's deputy editorial page editor, told CNN. The American Society of News Editors, the New England Newspaper and Press Association and other groups have helped spread the word, she said.

"The response has been overwhelming," Pritchard said. "We have some big newspapers, but the majority are from smaller markets, all enthusiastic about standing up to Trump's assault on journalism." Instead of printing the exact same message, each publication will write its own editorial.

The consistent message that is expected to be included in all of these editorials is the importance of a free and independent press, said Pritchard.

Trump's diatribe against the press has been going on since his 2016 campaign, when he launched his attacks about "fake news" every time a reporter wrote a story he didn't like. But his anti-media campaign has escalated and in February, he sent out this tweet:

Since then, reporters have received death threats from nutcase Trump supporters and angry Trump rally attendees have shouted obscenities and made obscene gestures at reporters. Who knows if the deadly June attack on the Capital Gazette in Annapolis, MD that claimed five lives was emboldened by Trump's rhetoric?

This has got to stop. The First Amendment of the U.S. Constitution guarantees the right to free speech and provides protection for a free press. No public official, including the president, has the authority to abridge those rights and protections.

The Partisan Divide in Media Trust

January 29, 2018

By Stacy Fitzgerald

A report released this month shows that although most Americans believe the news media is important for democracy, there's a partisan divide in Americans' trust of the media.

The report, published by The Knight Foundation and Gallup, concludes that 33 percent of the public has a very or somewhat favorable view of the media, 23 percent are neutral, and 43 percent have a very or somewhat unfavorable view of the media.

More troubling is that confidence in the media is starkly different depending on one's political affiliation, with 54 percent of Democrats having a favorable opinion and 68 percentage of Republicans having an unfavorable opinion. How did that happen, given that facts are firm, not fluid?

How We Got Here

A short explanation of how we got to this point is the Internet.

While technology has made sharing news and information much easier, it's also made it possible to rapidly share misinformation or "fake news," presenting both an opportunity and a challenge for the public and their faith in the media.

Today, 67 percent of American adults get all or most of their news from social media, which is also highly susceptible to fake news. Moreover, while 80 percent of Americans feel the news media are critical to our democracy, most also believe that knowing portrayal of false information as if it were true constitutes fake news. Interestingly, 40 percent of Republicans consider accurate news stories that cast a politician or a political group in a negative light always constitutes fake news.

Generally, perceptions of the news media are negative, and the perception of bias has increased sharply compared to a generation ago.

Today, 66 percent of Americans say most news media do not do a good job of separating fact from opinion and less than half (44 percent) say they can think of a news source that reports the news objectively.

Also, the media may have as much potential to reinforce existing views as they do to persuade, with most Americans claiming to rely on a mix of liberal and conservative news sources, but one in four admitting to getting news from only one perspective. Republicans who could name an accurate source of news overwhelmingly mentioned Fox News, while Democrats' responses were more varied.

Responsibility for Credibility

At a January 23 Washington Post Live event, various members of the media as well as representatives of the sponsor companies dissected and discussed the research and potential solutions to address the mistrust in the media.

Jennifer Preston, vice president of Journalism for the Knight Foundation, called the scale of the problem with Americans' distrust in the media immense. "Polarization heightens the responsibility of journalists to do a better job in their communities," noted Preston.

Another panelist, PBS NewsHour Anchor and Managing Editor Judy Woodruff, agreed and added that the media bears tremendous responsibility in the digital age. "Are we contributing to people getting a better understanding of what's really going on and what's right for them and their families?" she asked.

Veteran White House Reporter and Urban Radio Network Correspondent April D. Ryan said there's no simple solution to changing perception and trust of the media but added that integrity matters in securing credible sources for stories and reporting facts are vital to ensuring credibility.

In the age of information overload, Ryan advised that the media "bury them with facts," and operate with integrity and accountability in reporting those facts.

Ryan remarked that finding credible sources for stories can be a challenge for members of the media, but there are ways to gain access to those people. "If you work with integrity and you're accountable, people will find out and help you out," Ryan said.

Integrity and accountability. Those are core principles of journalism and they must always be kept in mind by every journalist reporting the news today – especially in this age of distrust.

Study: Fake News Spreads Faster & Farther Than Truth

March 10, 2018

By Bob Gatty

According to a just published study by Science, Twitter postings from 2006 to 2017 show that false news spreads faster and farther than the truth, a phenomenon that may well have influenced the 2016 Presidential election and may threaten the coming 2018 Congressional elections.

"About 126,000 rumors were spread by ~3 million people," the report says. "False news reached more people than the truth; the top 1% of false news cascades diffused to between 1000 and 100,000 people, whereas the truth rarely diffused to more than 1000 people. Falsehood also diffused faster than the truth."

In other words, falsehoods, lies and fake news spread on Twitter are up to 100 times more powerful than the truth -- or "not fake news."

"The degree of novelty and the emotional reactions of recipients may be responsible for the differences observed," the study observed.

I guess that tells us that we are suckers for sensational stories and rumors that we want to believe or find salacious or fit into the mindset into which we have been indoctrinated by whatever influences we prefer.

As the study said, "Falsehood diffused significantly farther, faster, deeper, and more broadly than the truth in all categories of information, and the effects were more pronounced for false political news than for false news about terrorism, natural disasters, science, urban legends, or financial information."

"We found that false news was more novel than true news, which suggests that people were more likely to share novel information. Whereas false stories inspired fear, disgust, and surprise in replies, true stories inspired anticipation, sadness, joy, and trust."

Perhaps that explains the success of Fox News, for example, which habitually broadcasts falsehoods and half-truths to support their political bias. Fox News fans and other conservatives might say the same goes for the "mainstream" media, which President Trump continually derides as "fake news." But most of that, truth be told, is because Trump doesn't like the fact that the real media reports the facts that he, Donald Trump, has created.

"Contrary to conventional wisdom, robots accelerated the spread of true and false news at the same rate, implying that false news spreads more than the truth because humans, not robots, are more likely to spread it," the study reported.

Looks like the Russians have figured this out, given the stories about their use of social media to influence the U.S. electorate. It's scary that the Trump administration has done nothing to protect the coming Congressional elections from similar tampering.

Guess fake news will continue unabated in Twitter-world, and our elections -- our democracy -- may well be affected much to the detriment of us all.

◆◆◆

Slain Journalists - Unsung Heroes

June 29, 2018

By Bob Gatty

In Washington, DC, there is a wall that contains the names of 2,323 people who should be considered heroes to all freedom loving people. Rising for two stories in Washington's Newseum, this wall honors journalists who have lost their lives reporting the news.

Soon, five more names will be added to that wall. They are the men and women murdered at The Capital Gazette yesterday in Annapolis, MD, when the man suspected in the massacre fired a shotgun through the glass front door of the newspaper's office, killing five and injuring two others.

According to published reports, the man, Jerrod Warren Ramos, was angry with the Capital Gazette because of its coverage of his criminal case, a matter of public record. That's what hometown newspapers do every day: write about crime, courts, local government, sports, schools, police and fire, community activities.

Their job is to inform. To help readers understand by providing facts and putting them into context. They usually are little heralded, but their work is incredibly important.

The Los Angeles Times recounted the history of journalists who have been killed doing their job. It hasn't happened to a newspaper journalist in the United States in more than 10 years, The Times reported.

In 2007, Chauncey Bailey, who edited the weekly Oakland Post, was gunned down to shut down his reporting about Oakland's Your Black Muslim Bakery, who's financial and personnel problems Bailey had been covering, the Times wrote.

A Personal Experience

Years ago, when I was in my 20s covering state politics in New Jersey for United Press International, I was threatened by right-wing protestors outside the State House in Trenton. They were supporting the late Dr. Carl McIntire, a fiery fundamentalist evangelist whose Shelton College was prohibited by the state Department of Education from granting degrees.

My reporting was partially responsible for this, as I had discovered, and reported that the McIntire-selected academic dean, Richard Coulter, had never graduated from college and that the degrees he claimed to have personally were false. Coulter, who McIntire publicly claimed had the experience and academic credentials to help Shelton College meet state standards, eventually was fired.

During this controversy, McIntire led a protest rally in Trenton against the state's action that I covered. "There, he is, the left-wing liberal press," a woman in the crowd screamed, pointing at me. "He did this."

Fortunately, no harm came from her tirade and the protest, while rowdy, was generally peaceful. Although unnerved, I was unharmed.

It was a scary moment, however; one of just a few that occurred during my career as a local community newspaper, and then UPI, reporter and bureau chief. But it's not uncommon, especially today.

The Trump Effect

The LA Times article pointed out that "every day, and now more and more each year, newspaper reporters and radio, TV and online news reporters across this country get hate mail, hate email, even death threats. Some are preposterous; some are all too plausible. Within hours of Thursday's murders, Buzzfeed writer Anne Helen Petersen tweeted, "I've had people email death threats, threaten to cut my dog's throat, tell me I'd pay for my fake news."

The First Amendment of the Constitution is supposed to protect freedom of speech and a free press. But under Donald Trump's presidency, it is under attack. And when he calls journalists "the enemy of the people," it only emboldens bitter and dangerous people like the Capital Gazette shooter.

It also encourages Trump supporters and idiots in the media, too. The other day I was listening to music on a local Myrtle Beach, SC classic rock station and the DJ said a listener had called in to say that "Fake News reporters should be strung up."

"I'm OK with that," the DJ said.

Thanks Trump. You like walls, go visit the one in the Newseum.

Stupid Headlines Crack Me Up

July 23, 2018

By Bob Gatty

With all of the nastiness going on in the world today, Trump playing kissypoo with Putin, Trump playing macho man with the nutcase president of Iran, little immigrant kids being caged like dogs, on and on...here are a bunch of actual stupid headlines that will make you laugh.

They come to us courtesy of one of our friends, Hermey Schlesinger, who lives in Florida and apparently has nothing better to do than paste together stuff like this. Here ya go:

Rangers get whiff of Colon

Homicide victims rarely talk to police

Barbershop singers bring joy to school for deaf

Miracle cure kills fifth patient

Bridges help people cross rivers

Girls' schools still offering 'something special' – head

City unsure why the sewer smells

Starvation can lead to health hazards

Man Accused of Killing Lawyer Receives a New Attorney

Parents keep kids home to protest school closure

Hospitals resort to hiring doctors

Federal Agents Raid Gun Shop, Find Weapons

DIANA WAS STILL ALIVE HOURS BEFORE SHE DIED

Meeting on open meetings is closed

Tiger Woods plays with own balls, Nike says

Lady Jack off to hot start in conference

Republicans turned off by size of Obama's package

New sick policy requires 2-day notice

Statistics show that teen pregnancy drops off significantly after age 25

Bugs flying around with wings are flying bugs

Study Shows Frequent Sex Enhances Pregnancy Chances

Marijuana issue sent to a joint committee

Worker suffers leg pain after crane drops 800-pound ball on his head

I have two questions: Where are the editors? What are they teaching these days in journalism school?

Yikes!

America the Beautiful

September 1, 2018

By Bob Gatty

It was a remarkable, in today's atmosphere of hatred, vitriol and division, to see two former adversaries of the late Sen. John McCain, both former presidents, join together with hundreds of others in the Washington Cathedral to sing "America the Beautiful."

It was a solemn ceremony, filled with touching anecdotes and humorous recollections as well as statements of deep admiration for McCain, who died just a week ago from brain cancer -- his last battle lost, but with courage and grace.

But there was more.

Sen. McCain's daughter, Meghan, pulled no punches even as she honored her father for all of his pursuits in life -- sailor, Congressman,

Senator, Presidential candidate, husband. But the most important, she said, was just being her dad.

Clearly, though, she -- like her father -- has no tolerance for those who bully, taunt, and try to diminish others only to make themselves feel more important.

"The America of John McCain has no need to be made great again, because America was always great," she said drawing a ripple of applause through the cathedral from an audience that included President Trump's daughter Ivanka and son-in-law, Jared Kushner, who sat seemingly unmoved. Trump was not invited to the service.

But Meghan McCain was not alone in speaking out against the actions of Donald Trump, without ever uttering his name.

There was his predecessor, Democrat Barack Obama.

"John understood that part of what makes our country great is that our membership is based not on our bloodline, not on what we look like . . . but on our adherence to a common creed that all of us are created equal, endowed by our Creator certain unalienable rights," he said.

Obama noted that McCain "championed a free and independent press that's vital to our democratic debate," clearly referencing Trump's repeated attacks on the news media, which he calls "the enemy of the people."

"So much of our politics can seem small and mean and petty," Obama added. "Trafficking in bombast and insult, phony controversies and manufactured outrage. It's a politics that pretends to be brave and tough but is instead born of fear. John called on us to be bigger than that, to be better than that."

There was Obama's predecessor, Republican George W. Bush, a bitter rival for the 2000 GOP presidential nomination.

Said Bush, McCain "detested the abuse of power and could not abide bigots and swaggering despots."

"He respected the dignity inherent in every life, a dignity that does not stop at borders and cannot be erased by dictators," said Bush. Lest we as a nation forget who we are, he added, "John's voice will always come as a whisper over our shoulder: 'We're better than this, America is better than this.'"

America the Beautiful.

Bad Day at the White House

September 4, 2018
By Bob Gatty
Today, President Trump awakened to a blitzkrieg of rotten news and it had to send him around the bend. I'm willing to bet it was a really bad day at the White House.

It wasn't enough that a new Washington Post/ABC poll came out saying that 60 percent of Americans believe Trump and the GOP do not represent the interests of most people and that Democrats are on a roll, heading to a huge victory in the mid-term elections.

And it wasn't enough that the Senate Judiciary Committee hearing on the Brett Kavanaugh nomination for the Supreme Court turned into a sideshow with Republicans looking sleazy, angry, nasty and defensive.

What really had to frost Trump was reports of renowned Washington Post journalist Bob Woodward's new book, Fear, which said a frustrated Defense Secretary Jim Mattis compared Trump to "a fifth or sixth grader" and Gen. John F. Kelly, the White House Chief of Staff, labeled Trump "unhinged," an "idiot" and "off the rails." The White House under Trump, he said, is "crazy town."

Well, folks, the prez wasn't real happy with all of that. Can you imagine being Mattis and Kelly today? This evening, Trump fired off this tweet:

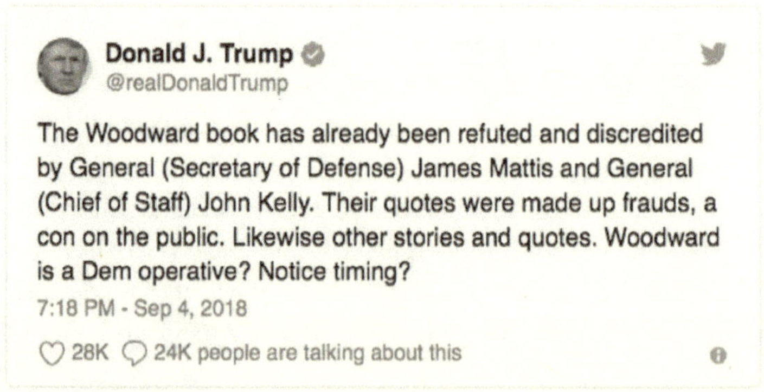

So, it's more fake news, right?

Bob Woodward, along with his sidekick Carl Bernstein, uncovered the depths of the Watergate scandal, which led to the eventual resignation of President Richard M. Nixon in the face of certain impeachment. He has written detailed, highly respected books about every president since Nixon.

There is little doubt about the accuracy of Woodward's work. Trump can scream "fake news" and "enemy of the people" all he wants, but the fact is that he is in deep doodoo...to say it gently.

And the mid-term elections are just two months away. And Woodward's book has already rocketed to the top of Amazon's best seller list.

A Look Ahead: Will it be War?

November 7, 2018

By Bob Gatty

With the 2018 mid-term elections now in the history books, it's time to look ahead and it would be nice if that could rationally be done with at least some semblance of unity and optimism.

Now, with Democrats controlling the U.S. House of Representatives and Republicans increasing their margin in the Senate, the potential for absolute gridlock going into the 2020 elections is very real. Despite the early offers for bipartisan initiatives on such issues as infrastructure, trade and healthcare, the deep partisan divisions can be expected to dominate and only worsen in the months ahead.

After presumed House Speaker Nancy Pelosi (D-CA) called for bipartisan approaches to key issues that affect us all, Trump, in his news conference today, essentially said, "That's fine, but if you guys try to investigate me, there will be war."

In fact, at that news conference, Trump went to war with reporters, one of whom he called "The Enemy of the People."

Who doesn't expect House Democrats to launch new investigations into Trump's activities? That is sure to happen. Many of the new members of Congress come from the liberal wing of the party and they can be expected to encourage efforts to impeach the president.

That would certainly enrage him and given the GOP's now wider margin of control in the Senate would most likely be doomed. It, in fact, could backfire and be used by Trump as a weapon against Democrats in the 2020 election campaign.

Investigations? If the House investigates him, Trump said today the Senate would investigate members of the House. "They can play that game, but we can play it better, because we have a thing called the United States Senate," Trump said. "I could see it being extremely good for me politically because I think I'm better at that game than they are, actually, but we'll find out."

Trump claims to have the power to fire Special Counsel Robert Mueller and end the investigation into Russia's influence in the 2016 election and how, if at all, Trump and his campaign might have been involved. But he reiterated today that he would be better off politically to let the investigation run its course.

But that is hanging out there and can be expected to add fuel to the fire once it is completed.

Pelosi said the Democratic party's takeover of the House was about "restoring the Constitution's checks and balances to the Trump administration."

We'll see how that works out. It would be nice if Republicans and Democrats could learn to work together once again in Washington, that's for sure. We would all benefit. But, realistically, I expect Trump will get his war with the Democrats and the months leading up to the 2020 election will not be pretty.

The Enemy of the People? Does Trump Have a Mirror?

December 7, 2018
By Bob Gatty
Yesterday, shortly after a bomb threat forced evacuation of CNN headquarters in New York, President Trump sent another vitriolic Robert Mueller investigation tweet, "FAKE NEWS - THE ENEMY OF THE PEOPLE!".

It was yet another attack on journalists who are doing their job, reporting to the American people on important developments that affect their lives and the nation at large. And as he continues these attacks, he puts more lives in danger as he encourages the nut jobs out there to physically attack journalists because they either buy into their hero's views or they will do just about anything to please him.

In so many ways, this president reminds me of the actions of real dictators, who I am convinced Trump seeks to emulate. A Washington Post article pointed out that Adolf Hitler, Joseph Stalin and Mao Zedong all regularly used the term to attack domestic enemies — particularly scholars and reporters whose only offense was to tell the truth.

But, says the article, "That hasn't stopped the president from regularly trotting out the slur on the campaign trail to thunderous applause from supporters and mounting concern from journalists covering his rallies."

I can tell you that, as a journalist, it is a scary thing to be threatened by an angry mob. It happened to me many years ago when I was working for United Press International. "That's him," evangelist Dr. Carl McIntire yelled through his bullhorn to demonstrators in the streets of Trenton, NJ, as he pointed to me. "That's the left-wing liberal reporter who's called all this trouble."

But being threatened by little old ladies with umbrellas, as I was that day, is nothing compared to the danger facing today's journalists as rabid Trump supporters are encouraged by the terrorist-in-chief. Crazies with guns and bombs are just a bit more dangerous.

Yesterday's bomb threat to CNN, one of Trump's favorite "enemy of the people" targets, is just the latest such incident.

Last June, five journalists were murdered in a mass shooting at the Capital Gazette in Annapolis, MD, when a gunman barged into the newsroom and started shooting. Jarrod Ramos, who has been charged with five counts of murder in the case, reportedly was intent on wiping out as many journalists as possible.

"This person was prepared today to come in, this person was prepared to shoot people," Anne Arundel County Deputy Police Chief William Krampf said. "His intent was to cause harm."

Why did he do it? Was he encouraged by Trump's constant labeling of the media as the "enemy of the people"? Who knows? But such irresponsible rhetoric by the man who is supposed to set an example for Americans could not have helped.

When CNN's Jim Acosta was temporarily stripped of his White House credentials by Trump because he did not like his news conference questioning, Acosta worried that the president's rhetoric toward him "will result in somebody getting hurt." Looks like they are still out there, those wackos who continue to be inflamed by Trump.

Who really is "the enemy of the people?" Trump should look in the mirror.

2018: The 'Year of Lies'

December 31, 2018
By Bob Gatty
For President Trump, 2018 was a lot of things, but one label stands out above the rest. For the purported leader of the free world, the person we are supposed to hold in the highest esteem, it was the year of lies.

It's so bad that today even many of his most ardent supporters don't believe what he says, at least some of the time.

According to The Washington Post's Fact Checker, throughout the year Trump has averaged more than 15 falsehoods -- either outright lies or exaggerations -- every day. Not only is that remarkable, it is disgusting and dangerous.

Here are some key points from The Post:

When 2018 began, the president had made 1,989 false and misleading claims, according to The Fact Checker's database, which tracks every suspect statement uttered by the president. By the end of the year, Trump had accumulated more than 7,600 untruths during his presidency — averaging more than 15 erroneous claims a day during 2018, almost triple the rate from the year before.

Even as Trump's fact-free statements proliferate, there is growing evidence that his approach is failing.

Fewer than 3 in 10 Americans believe many of his most-common false statements, according to a Fact Checker poll conducted this month. Only among a pool of strong Trump approvers — about 1 in 6 adults in the survey — did large majorities accept several, though not all, of his falsehoods as true.

Similarly, a November Quinnipiac poll found 58 percent of voters saying Trump wasn't honest, compared with just 36 percent who said he was honest. The same poll found 50 percent saying he is "less honest" than most previous presidents, tying his own record for the highest share of registered voters saying so in Quinnipiac polling.

I would like to point out that the Quinnipiac poll is one that Trump most likes to cite, as its results are often more to his liking than other national polls.

"What is it that schoolchildren are taught about George Washington? That he never told a lie," presidential historian Michael R. Beschloss told The Post. "That is a bedrock expectation of a president by Americans."

Not anymore.

The Post pointed out that Trump began 2018 on a similar pace as last year, generally averaging about 200 to 250 false claims a month.

"But his rate suddenly exploded in June, when he topped 500 falsehoods, as he appeared to shift to campaign mode." The Post reported. "He uttered almost 500 more in both July and August, almost 600 in September, more than 1,200 in October and almost 900 in November. In December, Trump drifted back to the mid-200s."

Trump's midsummer acceleration came as the White House stopped having regular press briefings and Trump met repeatedly with reporters, held events, staged rallies and tweeted constantly.

Here's more directly from The Post:

The president misled Americans about issues big and small. He told lies about payments that his now-convicted attorney says Trump authorized to silence women alleging affairs with him. He routinely exaggerates his accomplishments, such as claiming that he passed the biggest tax cut ever, presided over the best economy in history, scored massive deals for jobs with Saudi Arabia and all but solved the North Korea nuclear crisis.

He attacks his perceived enemies with abandon, falsely accusing Clinton of colluding with the Russians, former FBI Director James B. Comey of leaking classified information and Democrats of seeking to let undocumented immigrants swamp the U.S. borders.

The president often makes statements that are disconnected from his policies. He said his administration did not have a family separation policy on the border, when it did. Then he said the policy was required because of existing laws, when it was not.

On and on. Trump's lies never stop. He is called out in the media. Then he lies again, all the while lambasting the media for reporting the truth.

One day this will catch up with him. There is an old adage, "Lies will always come out." Richard Nixon found this to be true. Bill Clinton found this to be true. And, so will Donald Trump.

Recently, I designed a T-shirt for Not Fake News readers. It reads, "All Those Lies & Democracy Dies."

That's the truth.

Journalist Killings Reach 53 in 2018

January 1, 2019

By Bob Gatty

In a year in which President Trump repeatedly labeled the news media as "the enemy of the people," the number of journalists killed on the job around the world reached at least 53 in 2018, with 34 of them singled out for murder because of their work.

According to an analysis by the Committee to Protect Journalists (CPJ), the total of journalists killed on duty was the highest in three years, while the number of those killed in conflict fell to its lowest level since 2011.

CPJ said 11 journalists were killed in combat or crossfire, while eight died working on dangerous assignments, such as covering protests that turn violent. In 2017, a total of 47 journalists were killed, 18 of whom were pinpointed for murder. In 2016, a total of 50 were killed.

According to CPJ, jailing of journalists hit a sustained high, which the group said adds up to a "profound global crisis in press freedom." Changes in technology, including social media, has made journalists expendable to political and criminal groups who once needed them to spread their message.

"Another significant factor is the lack of international leadership on journalists' rights and safety," said CPJ.

The murder of Washington Post columnist Jamal Khashoggi in Saudi Arabian consulate in Istanbul in October by Saudi agents was the most gruesome and widely publicized murder worldwide. Khashoggi was a vocal critic of Saudi Crown Prince Mohammed bin Salman (MBS), who the Central Intelligence Agency has said likely ordered the execution.

President Trump, however, has equivocated on blaming MBS and said the U.S. "intends to remain a steadfast partner of Saudi Arabia," citing that country's purchase of military equipment and opposition to Iran.

"Essentially, Trump signaled that countries that do enough business with the United States are free to murder journalists without consequence," wrote CPJ.

Just days after four journalists and a sales associate were murdered by a gunman at the Capital Gazette in Annapolis, MD, Trump resumed his attacks on the press, labeling the media "fake news" and journalists as "enemies of the people." He did so on social media and at his campaign style rallies, where he whips up his frenzied supporters and sometimes even pinpoints specific reporters whom he dislikes.

Trump's vicious and irresponsible attacks on reporters who are simply doing their jobs apparently is catching on in other countries, such as Turkey, where President Recep Tayyip Erdogan's government has effectively shut down the independent media, according to CPJ, and is jailing more journalists than any other country.

Meanwhile, CPJ reported that 13 journalists were killed in Afghanistan in 2018, the most in any year since 2001, when the U.S. attacked the country and nine journalists were killed.

So the next time you hear Trump label reporters as "the enemy of the people," think about the work they are doing to keep us all free by reporting the news, including Trump's actions and activities, so we can be informed and form our own opinions free of influence by Trump's lies and embellishments.

So, I ask again. Who is the enemy of the people?

Trump on Media: 'It's a Beautiful Thing'

February 1, 2019

By Bob Gatty

So, President Trump has gone from calling the news media "The Enemy of the People" to "a very, very beautiful thing." Well, not exactly.

What he actually said yesterday in an Oval Office interview with The New York Times' publisher and two reporters was this: ""And if it (the media) describes it (news events) accurately and fairly, it's a very, very important and beautiful thing."

Notice the caveat. If events are described "accurately and fairly," then it's fine, says the single most powerful man in the entire world who has lied more than 8,000 times since taking office two years ago.

So, it all depends on whether Trump thinks media reports are accurate and fair, not whether they really are. And you know how he feels about stories that reflect upon him negatively: "Fake News!" "The Enemy of the People."

When asked what he thinks a free press actually does, Trump told The Times that it "describes and should describe accurately what's going on anywhere it's covering, whether it's a nation or a state or a game or whatever."

Yea, that's one thing the media does, Mr. President. Journalists go out and cover events and speeches and political developments and sporting activities and human-interest stories and all of that, and they report on those events telling readers what happened.

But what Trump was missing in that response is that reporting what happens at various events is only the beginning. The news media is also responsible for looking below the surface to find the truth, and then to accurately report when people in positions of power, like, say, the president, misstate the facts or are found to be abusing their position. Good reporting includes more than simply being a parrot. It includes uncovering and reporting the truth.

That is what Donald Trump either does not understand or chooses to ignore.

He said in The Times interview that Fox News "treats me very well" as do the local media. Well, of course he would say that since Fox News simply parrots his line and goes out of its way to aggrandize the self-aggrandizer-in-chief.

And the local media? Certainly, how often do local reporters get to report on the president of the United States firsthand? Hardly ever. So, when they do, it's often with a little bit of awe that Trump would appreciate.

Yes, Mr. President, a free press is "a very, very important and beautiful thing."

Especially today with you sitting behind the Resolute Desk in the Oval Office with the fate of our nation in your hands.

Cameraman Attacked; Trump Whips Up Anti-Media Hate

February 12, 2019
By Bob Gatty

Last night at President Trump's Build-a-Wall Rally in El Paso, TX, a red-MAGA hatted supporter tried to violently attack a cameraman from the British Broadcasting Co. after Trump, as usual, complained about the "fake news" media, which he frequently labels "The Enemy of the People."

As he was restrained, the man screamed "F**k the media! "F**k the media!"

Eleanor Montague, the BBC's Washington News Editor, said in a tweet that the El Paso crowd had been "whipped up into a frenzy against the media by Trump and other speakers all night."

The BBC's Washington correspondent Gary O'Donoghue described the incident as "an incredibly violent attack."

Apparently aware the incident had occurred, Trump looked towards the press pen and asked if everybody was OK. Nice. Kind of him to show such concern.

This is just the latest anti-media attack that can be directly attributed to Trump's hateful and irresponsible rhetoric. He apparently won't be satisfied until some reporter or camera person is seriously injured or even killed simply because they were doing their job.

The Media IS NOT THE ENEMY OF THE PEOPLE
The media's job is to report what is happening and to find the truth, not to be Trump's puppet or PR arm. That becomes increasingly difficult considering the truth is a foreign commodity to this president.

If anyone is "the enemy of the people," it is the orange buffoon who masquerades as the president of the United States and whips up divisions, fear and hate like no president in the history of our country.

Fear Factor and Ignorance

April 8, 2019
By CJ Waldron
When there is an issue that Trump wants to attack, he will invariably use fear to motivate his base. He will mark the most distorted views and explain them in terms that reflect the wildest conspiracy theories. From the Paris Accords to the Green New Deal, they are explained in the simplest terms, in a way that will instill the most fear.

From the start of his campaign, Trump sought to use fear of illegal immigrants to awaken the racist underbelly of a twisted segment of the population. Calling Mexicans rapists who were bringing drugs over the border was his introduction to the world political stage. He continued this tactic, including the pledge to build a wall for which he promised Mexico would pay.

He also vilified the Muslim community, insulting the parents of a Gold Star soldier, who was killed in action. He also promised to ban all Muslims from entering the country, insinuating that they were all terrorists. This oversimplification and fear mongering further incited the racist nature of his base, who were more than happy to stand behind these vague accusations.

Trump's inauguration speech, invoking "American carnage", had the same fear inducing tone. His bizarre choice of Frank Sinatra's "My Way", a song about dying, evoked more of a macabre element into the launch of this administration, which made its first acts an attempt to undo any strides made by President Obama, such was his hatred of the former president.

The campaign promised Muslim ban was also an early act of the administration. The ensuing chaos it caused through its inept attempts at enforcement led to it twice being struck down, yet it still appealed to the basest elements of his followers. In the end, a proposed 180-day travel ban has evolved into a permanent one.

Throughout it all was the issue of illegal immigration and the promised Mexican paid-for wall that became a major campaign issue during the midterms. Largely ignored was the administration's policy of separating families. Claims of caravans of criminals resurfaced, as did renewed calls for a border wall. When Democrats won the House of Representatives, Trump used the issue of the border wall and illegal immigration to shut down the government for the longest period in its history. It ended without a wall, but with the threat of yet another shutdown.

Once in control of the House, progressive members of the newly anointed Democratic leadership proposed a Green New Deal, aimed at converting the United States from a nation dependent on fossil fuels to one that uses renewable energy. Again, Trump stoked fear, claiming that the Green New Deal would eliminate air travel, automobiles and even, yes, farting cows.

Backed by anti-abortion Evangelicals, Trump seized upon the New York law that was passed, removing abortion from the criminal statutes of the state. He spread the claim that babies would be murdered moments after they were born. This ludicrous assertion was spread from church pulpits to the bully pulpit, with many seemingly rational adults believing this fantastical lie.

Trump's lies were not limited to minorities and the opposition party. The media, other than his propaganda network, Fox, have been, and currently are, living under constant threats of violence. Bombs have been mailed to news agencies that have criticized the administration, reporters covering Trump rallies are berated and threatened. At his latest rally, a BBC reporter was attacked, all egged on by shouts of Fake News at any coverage that Trump dislikes.

Where will it end? Even the deaths of children didn't stop the hate.

Even when faced with facts, fear is still the primary motivator.

Lies and misinformation are the primary avenues.

When will enough be enough!?

◆◆◆

Tuning Out the Spin

May 5, 2019

By CJ Waldron

Like death and taxes, there is another unavoidable issue we all face; that's the undeniable influence of media on our lives. Is there any way we can avoid it? Probably not, but I'd like to offer an out-of-the box suggestion.

As the election draws closer, we are bombarded with noise on all sides. Our inboxes are filled with requests for contributions as policies are becoming clearer and candidates jockey for position. Meanwhile, there is the incessant droning of 24-hour cable news networks, as each side takes on the other.

Democrats have the additional burden of a primary battle that sees them fighting each other while each maintains they are the best choice to beat Trump. Being an incumbent has decided advantages because resources can be focused on the opposition and not those within their own party. Arrows flung during the primaries can be used to weaken an opponent during the general election campaign.

Then there is the issue of foreign intervention, which, despite this administration's denials, played a major role in the 2016 election. This is something that will definitely become an issue in the 2020 election, yet in a recent phone call between Trump and Putin, Trump refused bring up the topic of the 2020 election and even joked with Putin about the Mueller investigation. Presumably, Trump is expecting the same kind of "support" for the 2020 campaign.

How is this even legal?

How can we tune out the noise and focus on the issues? Is it time to unplug, turn off the news and listen to the candidates without the spin? Can it even be done in this age of 24-hour news and social media? It's worth a try, but highly unlikely.

The spin doctors of the media, both regular and social, will seek to influence opinions. Despite efforts to silence those on both the far right and the far left, there undoubtedly will be new sources of misinformation to be addressed.

And, despite past history, there are those who will believe the lies and conspiracy theories while calling the facts "Fake News". And there will be candidates who will continue to spread these theories, no matter how outlandish they are, and no matter what facts are uncovered to refute them.

It's time to unplug. Turn off the television. Abandon social media. Listen to the candidates and make your choice based on their words and not some media interpretation. Go to rallies (yes, even THOSE rallies, if it helps). Speak directly to the candidates, if possible. Look at their websites to clarify their positions. Find a way to get through the smoke and mirrors of the media.

Can it be done? It's highly unlikely. We are far too attached to our devices. We are too connected to one side or the other. Getting our news only from those sources we agree with doesn't help. As difficult as it may be, speak to the other side to get their views.

It may help in shaping an informed decision. Anyway, it's an idea, and one worthy of consideration.

Don't Feed the Trolls

May 11, 2019
By CJ Waldron

They are the villainous creatures of J K Rowling and J R R Tolkien. They are the nemeses of fairy tales. They are the cute, bed-headed toys of a bygone era. They are also the agents of chaos on social media. They are trolls.

Read any post and they are there, infesting the comments section with their claims of Fake News and ratings. Their goal is to incite anger and gather attention. When anyone responds to a troll, as I have on numerous occasions, trying to correct their false narratives, they respond with "Triggered", meaning they have achieved their desired intent. The more responses they get to their incendiary comments, the more they feel justified.

I follow several sites that would be considered "mainstream media". I avoid the fringe sites, both on the left and the right, and when I find the ideas expressed by a certain site, Facebook page or Twitter account, I stop following them. I also do not follow the right-wing propaganda networks such as Fox, InfoWars or Brietbart because I have no interest in their unsubstantiated conspiracy theories, hyper partisanship, NRA sponsored trash or endless bashing of Liberals.

Trolls have the opposite approach. They don't follow a site to gain information. Instead, they do so to sow discontent, gain attention and make lame comments about the post they are following. Trolls can be either right-wing malcontents, who feel they are doing "a public service" by attempting to discredit a story they see as unfavorable to this administration. They feel justified because that is what they hear on a daily basis from the White House.

Trolls are also agents of foreign governments. Their role is to confuse and discredit those who support the views of the media. They often dupe the malcontents into believing and even spreading outlandish stories aimed at discrediting those who oppose this administration. These are the very trolls that swayed the 2016 election results.

And they aren't done yet. There is growing suspicion that they will do the same in 2020. Why not? This administration has already made it clear they won't be making any effort to prevent it.

Are there trolls and on the left-wing sites? I'm sure there are, but I couldn't be bothered to follow them, much less comment on their twisted rhetoric.

My advice: Don't feed the trolls. This only raises their social media status.

Lies, Damn Lies & the Rumor Mill

July 2, 2019
By CJ Waldron
As we approach the 2020 election, it's sad that much of the energy will be focused on fighting rumors and false claims that are generated by a variety of sources.

For the party that shouts "Fake News" at any unfavorable coverage, Republicans have been the ones to spread false, outlandish and downright offensive stories about Democrats. From the birther issue to Pizzagate to open borders, there is no issue that the right won't seek to exploit with false narratives.

So, let's take a moment to compare fact to fiction.

Claim: Democrats are coming for your guns.

Facts: It's hard to tell when this rumor began, but its origins can definitely be traced to the NRA as a means of juicing up the anger of the right wing to oppose any candidate they don't support. Despite so many mass casualty shootings in America, the NRA and its acolytes continue to stubbornly make this baseless claim. While Democrats support stronger gun control measures, there has been no blanket call to ban all guns except by Donald Trump. He quickly backed down from this position after meeting with representatives from the NRA.

Despite this, the right continues to push this distortion of the truth.

Claim: Democrats want open borders.

Facts: This is all tied to his promise to build a wall to halt illegal immigration through Mexico. The facts are, however, that 75 percent of illegal immigrants enter the country legally, but overstay their visas. No wall can prevent this from happening.

So, what about open borders? This is another fallacy spread by the right. Instead, Democrats have sought to work with Republicans on Comprehensive Immigration Reform, which would provide asylum to those who legally need it, as well as offer a solution to those who came into the U.S. illegally, but were too young to make the choice themselves.

Claim: The press is "the enemy of the people.

Facts: It's no secret that this administration has an adversarial relationship with the press. Sadly, it has become the norm to call any criticism "Fake News". Certainly there is some bias among the various news outlets, but the cry against fair reporting in favor of those who speak favorably of administration efforts has reached a fever pitch, even to the point of a network journalists being temporarily banned from covering the White House for questioning administration policies. Instead, presidential decisions are being made based on the advice and viewpoint of a news organization that continually praises Trump and his actions.

There are so many more examples of the right, particularly the group that forms the base of support for President Trump, relying on rumor and innuendo to formulate its opinions and actions. That's what makes factual reporting of information so important.

Media Distrust

September 10, 2019
By Bob Gatty
This morning I was chatting with a couple here in Cooperstown, NY, where I'm spending a few days, and expressed relief to them that our home in Myrtle Beach, SC had been spared from any damage as a result of Hurricane Dorian.

"We were very fortunate," I said. "Our neighborhood, which is about 10 minutes from the beach, was completely spared. We didn't even lose a shingle."

"That just goes to show you how the media exaggerates," the woman said. "See, it wasn't really that bad. They always make things seem worse than they really are."

I explained that many communities along the east coast had suffered serious damage from the storm surge and winds, to say nothing of the devastation that cost untold numbers of lives in the Bahamas. "It wasn't exaggeration," I assured her.

The woman clearly is an idiot. Nevertheless, why do so many people inherently mistrust the news media these days? Yes, I know, the logical response is to blame these attitudes on Donald Trump and his constant denigration of the mainstream news media (MSM) as "Fake News," and the right-wing media echo chamber that supports and repeats such claims.

But still, should the MSM share some of the blame for such distrust?

Over the years, my observation as a journalist is that it should. Increasingly, the distinction between factual reporting and opinion-based editorials has become blurred. It's found its way into virtually every media outlet and, unfortunately, onto the news pages and newscasts of some of the most respected publications and news outlets in the nation.

When I first began as a journalist with the wire service, United Press International, the distinction was eminently clear. Stick to the facts. Don't sensationalize. Never exaggerate. Check your sources. And always report the truth. Those were just some of the standards that were supposed to guide our work as journalists.

Even as a young reporter, I became angered at what I viewed as the shallow sensationalism of television news, which increasingly seemed to be built upon drama and a never-ending chase for ratings. Now, with the advent of social media, all of this seems to have worsened. Standards of journalism do not exist on Facebook and Twitter and Instagram. And, all too often postings become the genesis of news reports, which then get shared and sent into the universe until they go viral.

Of course, the fact that we have a president who parrots such postings as fact does not help matters as his legions believe whatever he says, no matter how outrageous. And then it gets repeated on the likes of Fox News and Brightbart, and what began as fiction somehow becomes fact.

So, it's no wonder that people, like the woman cited above, distrust what they see and hear and read in the media, and that is a dangerous thing for our country -- especially in this era when even our leaders cannot be trusted to tell the truth.

The news media has a sacred trust, and that means it must always scrupulously report the truth, separate fact from fiction, and withstand the temptation to use the power of news reports to retaliate against attacks, unfair as they may be. Separate news from opinion and make the distinction clear. And stop exaggerating.

The press absolutely must remain free from intimidation and political control if it is to protect the citizenry with the most powerful weapon of all, the truth. But for that to happen, it must meet its own responsibilities, as well.

Tabloid Journalism & the Right-Wing Media

November 19, 2019
By Chris Waldron
We've seen them. Those so-called magazines that use outlandish, and often unsubstantiated claims to create banner headlines. We've glanced at them at the checkout, wondering how they can continue to stay in business.

They morphed into tabloid television, reality TV and now are becoming part of the news cycle as opinion, innuendo and conspiracy theories. This is the evolution, or should I say devolution, of how people have come to accept what they consider the truth.

Let's look at how we got here.

Tabloids

What I called "trash mags" were those with sensationalist, attention-grabbing headlines that were produced on every week for the prurient, salacious, scandal-mongering segment of the population that thrives on the suffering of others while lapping up the stories of the rich and powerful.

They thrived on rumors and innuendo. Headlines such as "Elvis Lives!", stories of alien life and tales of deformed individuals such as "bat boy" fed their curiosity for the bizarre and outlandish much as those who marveled at the machinations of P.T. Barnum from another era.

These magazines also sought to satisfy the needs of those seeking to vicariously live the lives of the rich and famous, giving rise to the paparazzi that invariably intruded upon the lives of celebrities as they tried to obtain the most unflattering images or stories of suffering so that those who led lives of quiet desperation could feel fulfilled in the knowledge that even the well-off shared their suffering despite their success.

Tabloid Television

The blaring baritone of Robin Leach ushered in a new era of tabloid journalism with his Lifestyles of the Rich and Famous. Other shows followed as the producers sought to intrude, invade and otherwise disrupt those who had the audacity to live better than us. As the media grew, so did the appetite for even the smallest tidbit of information or hint of scandal.

The hunger for more led the Kardashians, members of the Jersey Shore and "Real Housewives" to greater popularity as they became famous simply for being famous. Their vapid lifestyles only increased their viewership among those who sought to give the appearance that they too could be famous if they only caught a break.

Like the bread and circuses of the Roman era, keeping the masses entertained kept them from noticing that they were missing out on so much more, and that the truly elite were only using them as tools for their own profit.

Reality Television

As viewership increased with the multi-channel cable industry, the need for a new type of entertainment became obvious.

Enter Mark Burnett and the world of so-called reality television. It offered everyday people the opportunity to hit it big if only they could survive a variety of tests like surviving on an island, racing around the world or carrying out the day-to-day tasks of a pseudo-tycoon. People sought shortcuts to diligence and hard work the same as they did when buying endless lottery tickets.

Reality television also provided viewers with the opportunity to revel in others' failures while choosing favorites based upon superficial attributes. Like the supermarket tabloids, they want to see the ugly side of people because it flatters their own self-image.

Fake News

No, I don't mean the inaccurate attacks that Trump throws at any news item that casts him in an unflattering light. The REAL fake news can be found on largely right-wing sites, publications and broadcasts masquerading as news.

They peddle unfounded conspiracy theories, innuendo and distortion of the facts. Sadly, a large part of the audience is comprised of the very same people who believe the supermarket tabloids are factual.

These viewers equate ratings with facts, reasoning that, since so many people are like me, we must be right. Therefore, they belittle any news that goes against their beliefs. They use insults and bullying tactics in an attempt to shut down any opposing views.

This is Trump's base of supporters and they don't just stick to television. Radio is still a popular medium for their lies and distortions. Rush Limbaugh, Alex Jones and others use this to spin their yarns of "alternative facts". Other sources of misinformation include Breitbart and The Drudge Report, as well as websites like Q-Anon and 4Chan.

The Future

As the public's appetite for more of this grows, the next step will likely be using You Tube and other forms of social media, making Andy Warhol's "fifteen minutes of fame" a reality. As more and more avenues for spreading lies and misinformation become available, there will always be those who will seek to distort the facts to their advantage.

If this abuse goes unchecked, we will have more Trumps, only far worse. Attacks on the free press and reliance on conspiracy theories has been part of the American psyche trailing back to the Salem Witch Trials, which serves as the origin for the "witch hunt" claims of Donald Trump.

We survived McCarthy's Red Scare and Nixon's Watergate scandal, but each time left us more fractured and distrustful. When this current crisis ends what will be left? Will there finally be an insistence that our news is factual again; free from the spin from the left or the right? Or will we become Lincoln's "house divided", until the inevitable fall?

Spreading Fake Pics for Political Points

January 7, 2020
By Bob Gatty
Rep. Paul Gosar (R-AZ), who clearly has no compunction about spreading lies if it serves his political purpose, tweeted out a photo purportedly showing former President Barack Obama shaking hands with Iranian President Hassan Rouhani. He did this apparently to capitalize on fears of possible war with Iran, thanks to his hero, President Trump.

Only one problem. The pic was photoshopped and worse, Gosar knew it. Obama never met Rouhani and the real photo was of him greeting then-Indian Prime Minister Manmohan Singh in 2011.

As The Washington Post pointed out, His latest tweet comes as Iranian American relations have sunk to their recent nadir in the days since a U.S. airstrike killed one of Iran's top military commanders, Maj. Gen. Qasem Soleimani, in an escalation that fueled fears of another regional war in the Middle East.

Challenged by a reporter who called Gosar out for his transgression, the conservative Congressman replied in a a follow-up tweet:

"No one said this wasn't photoshopped. No one said the president of Iran was dead. No one said Obama met with Rouhani in person."

The Post also noted, It's at least the third time in two months that the lawmaker has tweeted conspiratorial messages or misinformation. In November, he posted an acrostic to his account that spelled out the phrase "Epstein didn't kill himself," an oft-memed claim referring to the death of jailed financier Jeffrey Epstein. The day after, in a now-deleted tweet, Gosar signal-boosted a conspiracy theory suggesting that George Soros's son was the whistleblower who triggered the House's impeachment inquiry into President Trump.

Obviously, Gosar's tweets that spread lies and misinformation are irresponsible at best, harmful and divisive at worst. He should be sanctioned by Congress for such actions, or otherwise punished by voters at the polls.

Unfortunately, neither of those fates are likely to befall Gosar given today's political climate in which Republican voters seem to gladly believe lies spread by politicians (see Donald Trump) so long as those politicians toe the line on such matters as gun rights and abortion. Note: Gosar's district is heavily Republican and he defeated his Democratic rival, David Brill, in 2016 with 68 percent of the vote.

What You Can Do

However, if you care about truth and avoiding mistakenly distributing fake photos on social media, here are three steps you can take as recommended by California at Berkeley professor Hany Farid, who has written a book about detecting fake images. He shared these tips with The Post, which are relayed here:

Reverse image search. Save the photo to your computer and then drop it into Google Image Search. You'll quickly see where it might have appeared before, useful if an image purports to be over a breaking news event. Or it might show sites that have debunked it.

Check fact-checking sites. This can be a useful tool by itself. Images of political significance have a habit of floating around for a while, deployed for various purposes. The fake Obama-Rouhani image, for example, has been around since at least 2015 — when it appeared in a video created by a political action committee supporting Sen. Ron Johnson (R-Wis.).

Know what's hard to fake. In an article for Fast Company, Farid noted that some things, like complicated physical interactions, are harder to fake than photos of people standing side by side. Backgrounds are also often tricky; it's hard to remove something from an image while accurately re-creating what the scene behind them would have looked like. (It's not a coincidence that both the physical interaction and background of the "Rouhani" photo were clues that it was fake.)

The Pig President Strikes Again

January 28, 2020
By Bob Gatty
The other day Secretary of State Mike Pompeo excoriated a female reporter who asked him a question about Ukraine he didn't like, then President Donald Trump, male chauvinist pig-in-chief, commended him for it.

"That was very impressive, Mike," Trump said at a White House event after Pompeo was introduced to applause. "That reporter couldn't have done too good a job on you yesterday, huh? I think you did a good job on her, actually."

The incident Trump was referring to occurred last week when Mary Louise Kelly, host of All Things Considered on NPR, asked Pompeo about whether he should apologize to former U.S. ambassador to Ukraine, Marie

Yovanovitch, for her sudden ouster at the behest of Trump and his personal attorney, Rudy Giuliani.

Angered because the interview was supposed to be about Iran, Pompeo told Kelly, "I have defended every State Department official. We've built a great team. The team that works here is doing amazing work around the world... I've defended every single person on this team. I've done what's right for every single person on this team."

But he didn't let it go at that.

Here's how Kelly reported it, according to NPR:

"I was taken to the Secretary's private living room where he was waiting and where he shouted at me for about same amount of time as the interview itself. He was not happy to have been questioned about Ukraine.

"He asked, "do you think Americans care about Ukraine?"

"He used the F-word in that sentence and many others. He asked if I could find Ukraine on a map. I said yes, and he called out for aides to bring us a map of the world with no writing. I pointed to Ukraine. He put the map away.

"He said, 'people will hear about this.'"

On Saturday, Pompeo issued a statement saying that Kelly lied to him by saying the post-interview conversation was off the record, which she denies.

"It is shameful that this reporter chose to violate the basic rules of journalism and decency. This is another example of how unhinged the media has become in its quest to hurt President Trump and this Administration. It is no wonder that the American people distrust many in the media when they so consistently demonstrate their agenda and their absence of integrity.

"It is worth noting that Bangladesh is NOT Ukraine."

Bangladesh? That's odd, Kelly would have to be horribly geographically deprived if she mistook Bangladesh for Ukraine, considering the two countries are 3,000 miles apart -- an unlikely circumstance since she's a former national security reporter with extensive international travel and a master's degree in European studios from Cambridge University.

Perhaps it is Pompeo who is geographically deprived. She pointed to Ukraine and he mistook it for Bangladesh! Doesn't say much for our genius Secretary of State, does it?

Trump? He just looks for every opportunity to berate the media, especially when its reporting calls into question his actions, and those of his administration suck-ups -- like Pompeo.

But That's Not What I Asked!

March 16, 2020
By CJ Waldron

How many times have you watched a news conference with a member of the Trump administration only to hear the reporter complain, "But that's not what I asked!" Or "can you please address my question?"

It's no secret that politicians will answer a question by responding with a completely different issue. It's called trying to control the narrative. When asked a difficult question, it's common to hear a totally unrelated answer.

That's when you hear the reporter respond as stated above.

The Trump administration has taken this to a new level with its attempts at deflection, refusing to allow a question to be asked, or out and out distortion of the facts. Instead, they will talk over the interviewer, plow on with a seemingly endless verbal barrage and refuse to address key issues -- or respond to the question being asked.

With Trump, himself, he simply resorts to insulting reporters he doesn't like or if they are from a news organization that doesn't praise his every move. "You're fake news," he said the other day to a reporter from CNN, before calling on a friendly face from Fox News, the "Trump Fake News Network (TFNN)".

Besides Trump, the premier master of this practice of evasion is undoubtedly White House spokesperson Kellyanne Conway, who coined the term "alternative facts" to explain the paltry size of Trump's inauguration crowd. She's an expert at spewing verbal diarrhea to avoid providing answers, and her use of deflection has become the norm for any administration member being interviewed by any news outlet other than Fox.

She must be providing coaching lessons on the side.

While Fox is only too happy to allow administration spokespersons to rant on, giving credence to their distorted views, legitimate news networks and journalists seek honest answers. Despite being continually deflected, interviewers from CNN, MSNBC, CBS and other news organizations that

Trump calls "fake news" for their refusal to accept his administration's false narratives, continue to press for answers

In a recent interview, White House economist Peter Navarro was asked if he sees the US economy slipping into a recession. He responded by citing protective measures the administration is taking to combat the coronavirus. When pressed, he said he would rather "stay in his lane" and continued to comment on relief efforts.

He's an economist! Matters of the economy are in "his lane".

Although he eventually led the interview down a meandering path by citing economic measures being implemented, he still refused to answer the original question.

And, of course, no Trump administration interview would be complete without a dig at previous administrations. So, Navarro closed things out by blaming the current crisis on allowing pharmaceutical companies to move their operations offshore. He was careful not to blame Big Pharma, and instead focused his criticism on "previous administrations".

It's like the directions on a bottle of shampoo, but instead of "lather, rinse, repeat", it's "deflect, deny and drift off topic".

Round and round we go!

Ditch Twitter?

April 28, 2020
By Bob Gatty
My sidekick, Chris Waldron, believes it's time for thinking Americans to abandon Twitter and ignore Donald Trump's tweets, and for the media to stop reporting on blitzkrieg of BS. I disagree. Here's his argument. Then, mine.

Waldron: It's Time to Abandon Twitter
It's no secret that Trump's favorite social media is Twitter. It's a rare day when he doesn't bombard us with Tweets. He uses this medium to spread conspiracy theories, create misinformation, attack the media and ridicule anyone who dares to disagree with him.

What if we abandoned Twitter? What if the media refused to report his outlandish Tweets? Could this take the wind out of his sails?

If we stopped using Twitter, and the media stopped reporting on his Tweets, all Trump would have left as followers are his base and the Russian trolls and bots who populate, and re-Tweet, his lies.

This would certainly put a huge dent in his re-election chances. The Coronavirus pandemic has forced a shutdown of his rallies. Blaming the media, he is now stating he will stop the daily Coronavirus briefings.

All he would have left is Twitter.

While Twitter has explicit rules for suspending accounts for use of threatening and intimidating behavior, it has refused to suspend Trump's Twitter account despite numerous violations of this policy. Twitter execs explicitly this by stating Trump's Tweets have "clear public interest value". So, once again, Donald Trump is proving that the rules don't apply to him.

World leaders have criticized Trump for using Twitter as a means of communication. Democrats in Congress have protested Trump's use of Twitter to notify his intent to declare a National Emergency when he circumvented Congress to get money for his signature border wall.

And yet, he's allowed to keep doing it.

It's time for a social media revolution! Delete your Twitter account. Refuse to follow or acknowledge his lying Tweets.

This may be the only way we can stop this daily flow of misinformation. As his audience dwindles, he will inevitably attempt to find other ways to stay in the public eye.

Or perhaps he will diminish in relevance and slowly fade into obscurity.

Gatty: You're wrong, Chris

Deleting our Twitter accounts would be like throwing the baby out with the bathwater. (Where did that saying come from, anyway?) Or, it would be like cutting off your nose off to spite your face. (Ouch!)

Why should we let Trump's idiocy hamper our ability to otherwise communicate and to express our disagreement with, and directly to him?

There are those who advocate unfollowing @realDonaldTrump, which is the primary account the #orangeOne uses to spread his propaganda, as a way to protest while reducing his Twitter numbers, of which he is so proud.

But I disagree with that approach, too, because those who oppose him are now able to fire back, disagree with him directly, retweet his inanity with comments, and spread their criticisms and points-of-view throughout Twittersphere. That is a powerful tool for us to use because it gives us a way to vent directly to him and his supporters. It also is an extremely important way to exercise our Constitutionally guaranteed right of free speech.

I also disagree that the #mainstreamMedia should stop reporting on Trump's Tweets. If the media did that, it would leave a huge information void that would quickly be filled by rightwing outlets like #FoxNews and #Breitbart. That would further bolster their influence, which would strengthen and no doubt broaden Trump's support.

Yes, Trump misuses #Twitter and those who run that platform should tighten up. Rules should apply to him, the same as any other user. He thinks he is above the law, and he acts like he's above the law. Letting him get away with abusive violations on Twitter simply bolsters that attitude. But that's on Twitter to do, so perhaps there needs to be a campaign to encourage such action.

Finally, Chris says abandoning Trump on Twitter would reduce his audience and "perhaps he will diminish in relevance and slowly fade into obscurity."

The only way Donald Trump will fade into obscurity is if he is defeated November 3, hauled out of the White House, and sent to jail where his cellphone and laptop should be confiscated.

Then, Donald Trump's Twitter storm would go dark. And peace would reign upon the land.

Trump's Latest Attack on Free, Truthful Speech

May 29, 2020

By Bob Gatty

President Trump's executive order Thursday aimed at intimidating social media companies like Twitter, Facebook and YouTube is a blatant retaliatory attack by a would-be dictator against those platforms, which he regularly abuses with lies and disinformation.

Trump's order came just days after Twitter directed viewers of some of his tweets to fact-checking news reports with the label, "Get the facts about mail-in ballots." Trump's tweets claimed voting by mail causes voter fraud.

According to Twitter spokeswoman Katie Rosborough, Trump's tweets "contain potentially misleading information about voting processes and have been labeled to provide additional context around mail-in ballots."

And then, after the violence in Minneapolis-St. Paul Thursday night that erupted after a white police officer was shown in a video kneeling on the neck of a black suspect who pleaded that he could not breath and then died, Trump tweeted that protestors were "THUGS," adding "When the looting starts, the shooting starts."

Twitter then flagged that tweet for "glorifying violence," an action that brought more protests from Trump's right-wing supporters.

"We're here today to defend free speech from one of the greatest dangers," said Trump before signing his executive order, the legality of which is being called into question by legal experts, legislators and advocates for the tech sector. That is an ironic statement coming from Trump.

Matt Schruers, president of the Computer and Communications Industry Association, which represents major tech companies like Facebook and Google, said Trump's action sets "the wheels of law enforcement and regulation in motion against a private company for questioning the president."

Declared Jon Berroya, interim president of the Internet Association, "Based on media reports, this proposed Executive Order seems designed to punish a handful of companies for perceived slights and is inconstant with the purpose and text of Section 230. It stands to undermine a variety of government efforts to protect public safety and spread critical information online through social media and threatens the vibrancy of a core segment of our economy."

Retaliation. Punishment. Twin characteristics of this "stable genius" of a president.

The executive order could result in the Federal Communications Commission (FCC) acting against the tech companies and in the Federal Trade Commission investigating them to determine if they are upholding their pledges of political neutrality.

Trump, with his more than 80 million followers, regularly uses Twitter to promote his views, castigate and belittle adversaries and critics, and to spread lies and misinformation. It's about time Twitter acted on behalf of truthfulness, and hopefully his punitive action will be challenged and cast aside.

Here we have arguably the most powerful man in the world attempting to bully and intimidate a social media platform into allowing him to run roughshod over the truth. That must not stand.

Already, Trump is using the Justice Department to investigate the tech industry, and Attorney General William P. Barr has suggested the federal government may seek changes to rules governing such companies.

At issue is a law, Section 230, which prevents tech companies from being held liable for content posted by users, as well as for decisions to remove content. Republicans have threatened to revoke those protections complaining the social media platforms have an anti-conservative bias.

All of this is ironic, since it was Trump's prolific use of social media -- and Russia's, by the way -- that many credits for his defeat of Democrat Hillary Clinton in 2016. Now, he is complaining that those very platforms, which provide him a massive free megaphone, are being mean to him and his right-wing pals.

Complaining would be fine. But using the power of the presidency to intimidate? That is a dangerous step toward the control of free speech and a potential violation of the First Amendment of the U.S. Constitution.

◆◆◆

Spotting a Fake Executive Order

June 1, 2020
By Susan Hutchinson
After years of letting Donald Trump spread lies and hatred, Twitter finally decided to put a fact check warning on one of his Tweets. Why? Because Trump continues to spread misinformation that voting by mail opens the doors to voter fraud.

Voting? That's Twitter's breaking point? Not the thousands of hate-filled Trump Tweets over the years, his promotion of countless conspiracy theories, spreading lies that Barack Obama was not born in the U.S. or re-tweeting a video of a white supremacist who says the only good Democrat is a dead Democrat?

Well, better late than never.

Trump's Response to Twitter Fact Checking

Being Donald Trump, he was not going to take this slap back lying down. The very next day he decided to abuse his power of the Presidency to create an Executive Order. This Executive Order has the misleading title of "Preventing Online Censorship."

The actual title should be "Trump Wants Government Control of Social Media So He Can Freely Spread Lies to Get Re-elected."

Trump needs to look up the definition of censorship. Adding a link to fact check something you can still have access to is <u>not</u> censorship.

Interpreting the Executive Order

Here are some key points from the Executive Order with comments.

The freedom to express and debate ideas is the foundation for all of our rights as a free people.

Comment: Trump should be able to freely publish false information to suppress Democratic voters so he can get re-elected.

When large, powerful social media companies censor opinions with which they disagree, they exercise a dangerous power.

Comment: Trump has the right to express his opinions and pass them off as facts without question. Trump has said his supporters should not believe anything they read; they should only believe him so he needs to keep them in the dark on actual facts.

Twitter, Facebook, Instagram, and YouTube wield immense, if not unprecedented, power to shape the interpretation of public events; to censor, delete, or disappear information; and to control what people see or do not see.

Comment: Only Trump and the federal government should have the ability to control what people see or not see.

As President, I have made clear my commitment to free and open debate on the internet.

Comment: If you post something that disagrees with or criticizes him, Trump will block you from his Twitter page.

Twitter now selectively decides to place a warning label on certain tweets in a manner that clearly reflects political bias. As has been reported, Twitter seems never to have placed such a label on another politician's tweet. As recently as last week, Representative Adam Schiff was continuing to mislead his followers by peddling the long-disproved Russian Collusion Hoax, and Twitter did not flag those tweets.

Comment: He even put fake facts in an Executive Order and made it political rather than an order intended to protect the First Amendment right to free speech.

Other companies have accepted advertisements paid for by the Chinese government that spread false information about China's mass imprisonment of religious minorities, thereby enabling these abuses of human rights.

Comment: Russian bots are an exemption as they help Trump's re-election campaign. However, these are part of the "Russian Hoax" so they don't really exist, right?

The Very Next Day…
The day after signing the Executive Order intended to protect Trump's right to exercise "the freedom to express and debate ideas", he posted this response to the violence in Minneapolis, which was also posted on the official White House Twitter page.

"These THUGS are dishonoring the memory of George Floyd, and I won't let that happen. Just spoke to Governor Tim Walz and told him that the Military is with him all the way. Any difficulty and we will assume control but, when the looting starts, the shooting starts. Thank you!"

Twitter's response? They placed a "public interest notice" on both posts saying they glorify violence; however, they still allow you to click on it to read what it says. Based on Trump's Executive Order, flagging this post amounts to censorship and it should not be allowed.

After all, how can he stir up racial tension with his base if he can't incite violence?

2

TRAMPLING THE CONSTITUTION

Apparently, the United States Constitution means very little to Donald J. Trump, or he has no idea what is contained therein. His actions reflect his disdain for the rights guaranteed to the American people, especially when they get in the way of his personal agenda.

The Bill of Rights Under Donald J Trump

By C J Waldron

It is no secret that Donald Trump does not follow the Constitution, nor does he understand the limitations that it places on his office. Therefore, he has altered the Bill of Rights to meet his own purposes.

Amendment I

Congress shall make no law respecting an establishment of religion, except for those who aren't white Christians, or restricting freedom of the press, unless you disagree with Trump, then you are Fake News, or freedom of speech, unless you criticize this administration; or the right of peaceable assembly, because there are very fine people "on both sides"

Amendment II

You have the right to bear arms.

Amendment III

No soldier shall be quartered in a house during peacetime, unless a National Emergency is declared because you didn't get your way with Congress

Amendment IV

You have the right to be secure from unreasonable search and seizure, unless you are executing a legal search of Trump associates. Then it will be considered an illegal raid.

Amendment V

No person should be compelled to testify against themselves, especially when it concerns matters of foreign intervention in an election, investigation of illegal business practices or investigation of family members.

Amendment VI

You have the right to a speedy, public trial unless your knuckle-dragging lawyers refuse to cooperate and drag out the process ad nauseum.

Amendment VII

You have a right to a trial by a jury of your peers, unless you consider anyone to be beneath you, therefore making such a trial impossible.

Amendment VII

Excessive bail shall not be required, nor excessive fines levied nor cruel or unusual punishment, unless you are a person of color, LBGTQ, or Muslim. Then, all bets are off.

Amendment IX

The rights guaranteed by the Constitution shall not be construed to deny or disparage the rights of white, Evangelicals. All others are deemed fair game and will be vehemently chastised via Twitter.

Amendment X

The powers not enumerated therein shall be deemed to be the responsibility of the individual states, unless an Executive Action is made, or a National Emergency is declared. Then, all bets are off.

We Deserve Better

By C J Waldron

As any parent will tell you, the "terrible twos" are indeed trying time for many. Tantrums, unpredictable outbursts and general misbehavior are part of the territory. The displays are often public, and a cry for attention. This is what we saw in the Rose Garden after the breakdown of the infrastructure talks.

Make no mistake, this was not a bargaining ploy. Nor was it a spontaneous eruption of emotions based upon current events. This was a calculated distraction to deflect from the fact that, although 45 continues to tout infrastructure, he has no concrete plan to make it happen. Instead, he scolded the ones with a plan and then went to a podium that was already displaying the talking points he wanted to make.

Now, we have an administration that has pledged not to negotiate with Democrats until they end their investigations of the multiple indiscretions and cover-ups committed during and before his time in the White House. In other words, we have Presidential Extortion.

The administration claims, falsely, that the Mueller Report totally exonerated 45. He even had signs posted to tout this falsehood. They claim that Democrats, unhappy with the results, are demanding a "do-over". Nothing could be further from the truth, but this administration only has a tenuous grasp on the truth, choosing instead to promote "alternative facts".

The Mueller Report provided a roadmap to Congress to conduct its oversight (a Constitutionally mandated duty) into the myriad of issues this administration has presented.

Now, we have an administration that asserts that they cannot conduct business and deal with investigations. In other words, they can't walk and chew gum.

These words need to be on the lips of every American:
WE DESERVE BETTER!

Things I learned from the SOTU

January 31, 2018
By C J Waldron

- 45 equates separation of powers with "presidential harassment"
- He doesn't know when the economic recovery started or who actually started it
- His limited understanding of the new laws regarding "late term abortion" shows that he gets his information from right wing conspiracy sites
- He TOTALLY misread why women were cheering at his comments about the economy

- Nancy Pelosi would have made an excellent teacher. She was able to command obedience with "the teacher look"
- Every speech is the same campaign speech he's been making for years.
- He is willing to start a nuclear war while negotiating with terrorists in Afghanistan
- He can make the same offer to North Korea that he rejected in Iran because "the other guy made it".
- He used a child as a prop while offering less than a weekend at one of his properties
- When they sang Happy Birthday to a Holocaust survivor, he tried to make it about himself

There is so much more, but my hangover is killing me! (I took a drink every time he lied)

What If...

By C J Waldron

What if a Democratic president refused to release their tax returns? Republicans were foaming at the mouth, demanding President Obama's birth certificate and college transcripts, yet 45 is blocking the release of his tax returns and has threatened to sue his schools if the reveal his grades or SAT scores.

What if a Democratic president repeatedly praised dictators while continually insulting our allies? Yet Republicans bashed President Obama for his perceived bow to a foreign leader.

What if a Democratic president was the target of a Congressional investigation, yet refused to release the results of that investigation? The report on President Clinton was released soon after its conclusion, yet we are still waiting for the Mueller report, which, if reports are true, will be so heavily redacted it will resemble a "Cliff Notes" version with damaging information about 45 excluded.

What if a Democratic president repeatedly lied even in the face of undeniable facts? 45 has been on a pace of 22 lies a day, yet his supporters aren't batting an eyelash to call him out on these.

What if a Democratic leader in the Senate repeatedly blocked legislation even though it had bipartisan support? Mitch McConnell has routinely refused to introduce numerous pieces of legislation based on his personal beliefs or attitudes.

What if you were told that you couldn't question the mental health of a sitting president, yet you are accused of having a made-up diagnosis of "Derangement Syndrome" by someone who barely graduated high school?

Sadly, we don't need to ask "what if". We are living our own Bizarro nightmare.

Oops! NASA's Epic Spacesuit Fail

By Stacy Fitzgerald

March 28, 2018

Apparently, the National Aeronautics & Space Administration (NASA) can put a man on the moon, but <u>fitting a woman with a size medium space suit is an insurmountable challenge</u>.

Young women across America were ecstatic to learn last week that the first all-woman spacewalk would occur this month. It would be historic because while there have been women in space before, there never has been an all-female space mission.

Well, those hopes were dashed this week when NASA abruptly changed the mission and replaced one of the women astronauts with a man. Not because he was more qualified or she refused the mission, but because they had a space suit to fit more than one man, but apparently, not more than one medium-sized woman.

Admittedly, the specifications for spacesuits, which are specialized thermal protective uniforms, aren't as simple as your run-of-the-mill Target khakis and red polo. But you'd think someone would have considered that with more than one female astronaut, there might be the need for a few smaller space suits.

Astronaut Anne McClain is the woman who was replaced on the mission by a man. McClain thought initially that a large-sized suit would be fine, but after a spacewalk last week she determined that a medium-sized suit fit better and would be more comfortable on her mission to the International Space Station. The problem: Re-sizing a space suit for the mission would take longer than replacing McClain on this mission with a man who could fit a size large suit.

Well, you know what happened next. Gotta wait, Anne. We don't have your size in stock.

Despite the fact that only 11 percent of the people who have been to space have been women, you would have thought that NASA, with its decades of experience in momentous and historic space missions, would have planned for the day when multiple women would be on a mission.

Apparently, not. And it seems a little ridiculous.

What if other industries and businesses operated the same way?

Do hospitals only order large size surgical gloves and scrubs, or do they have a variety of sizes to fit medical professionals regardless of their gender?

Do shoe manufacturers only make men's sizes, or do they manufacture a variety of sizes for women as well?

Given that 47 percent of the American labor force is comprised of women and their participation in traditionally male dominated fields including science, technology, engineering and mathematics has grown exponentially in the past 30 years, it is puzzling to me that NASA can be working today on plans for a space force but can't figure out how to crank out more "girl sizes" for its female astronauts.

If you ever needed an example of the continued patriarchy in American society this is it. While I doubt, we'll see feminists take to the streets in pink pussy hats to protest, you can bet that American women won't forget that the greatest nation on Earth can put a man on a moon, but somehow forgot to order the right size spacesuits for its female astronauts.

But more importantly, I'll bet there's a woman somewhere at NASA right now working on a prototype for the next planned all-female spacewalk. And they'll be enough suits for everyone.

Supreme Court Arbitration Ruling Attacks Workers Rights

By Stacy Fitzgerald

May 22, 2018

In a stunning 5-4 ruling Monday, the Supreme Court of the United States (SCOTUS) directly attacked workers' rights, ruling that companies can use arbitration clauses that employees are forced to sign to prevent them from organizing and filing class action lawsuits, including those for unfair pay and working conditions.

The vote was a solid slap in the face of American workers by the court's Republican justices, who formed the majority in ruling against efforts by workers to organize.

The decision is also an attack on the many blue-collar workers who voted overwhelmingly for Trump, but who now will have limited legal options to resolve serious workplace grievances. Effectively, the court chose to protect corporations over workers.

The crux of the case, Epic Systems Corporation v. Lewis, was whether the Federal Arbitration Act, passed in 1947, compels two willing parties (the employer and employees), to use arbitration to resolve grievances.

The employees contended they still retain the right to pursue collective legal action against the company under the National Labor Relations Act, a 1935 law that allowed workers to organize and collectively bargain for better pay and working conditions. They argued that pursuing legal action against the employer freed them from the obligations to participate in arbitration.

The Republican majority, however, viewed it otherwise.

Writing for the majority, Judge Neil Gorsuch, Trump's appointee, said the SCOTUS' decision was dictated by a federal law favoring arbitration and the court's precedents. Gorsuch said that if workers are allowed to organize and pursue legal action, "the virtues that Congress originally saw in arbitration – its speed, simplicity and inexpensiveness, would be shorn away and arbitration would look like the litigation it was meant to displace."

In her dissent, Justice Ruth Bader Ginsberg called the decision "egregiously wrong." Ginsberg said the decision will result in "a huge under-enforcement of federal and state statues designed to advance the well-being of vulnerable employees."

Why It Matters

According one report, more than 60 million employees are forced to sign arbitration agreements as a condition of employment. If your job depends on signing an arbitration agreement – it's the only thing that stands between you and gainful employment – most people would feel compelled to do so and keep the lights on and food on the table.

But, it's only after working in the job that some of the conditions come to light for employees. Being prohibited from organizing to pursue collective legal action over unfair pay and dangerous working conditions that must now be settled through arbitration -- designed to protect the company's interest in the first place -- is unjust and will hurt American workers -- including school teachers throughout the country fighting collectively for fair pay, adequate school funding and pension protection.

Elections Have Consequences

For Democrats who sat out the last election or decided that they couldn't support an imperfect candidate in Hillary Clinton, the Supreme Court's decision is another reminder that there are consequences to the outcomes of elections.

When American workers are effectively stripped of the right to organize to fight for better pay and working conditions and instead, are forced into arbitration stacked in favor of the company, they will lose.

And when our elected officials fill judicial benches with Republican justices who believe that "corporations are people too," American workers can expect that in exchange for the ability to provide for their families, they also may have to give up the right to fight against unfair pay and working conditions.

The American labor force is in a dangerous place when corporations matter more than the rights of workers. And there's no clearer demonstration that every election matters more than the outcome of this court's epic fail--perpetrated at the expense, safety and wellbeing of the American worker.

Trump Jumps the Shark on Alternative Reality

By Stacy Fitzgerald

July 30, 2018

One would expect that the presidential administration that coined the phrase "alternative facts" would play fast and loose with realism, but this week, he may have officially jumped the shark. Speaking at a Veterans of Foreign Wars Convention this week, President Trump said the following:

"This country is doing better than it's ever done before economically…. it's all working out. Just remember: What you're seeing and what you're reading is not what's happening." (Italics added)

That's right. The president is essentially asking Americans to ignore what they're seeing and reading in the mainstream media, which he has repeatedly referred to as the "enemy of the people." The implication is that instead, we should only believe what he and the administration tell us.

Seriously?

Yes, the president for whom news outlets have a running tally of lies he's told (more than 3,200 through the end of May), is asking us to believe him instead of mainstream news.

It would be funny if it were an episode of the Simpsons, but it isn't so comical if you're an American citizen clinging to the freedoms of Democracy, fighting the spread of false news, and pushing back against the creeping signs of fascism.

If the president is to become our official news source, we're going to be awfully busy just trying to decide which of his contradictory statements and positions is the one the president would have us believe.

Did They or Didn't They, Mr. President?

Do we believe the President Trump who stood on a platform at the Helsinki summit with Russian President Vladimir Putin on July 16 and denied Russian interference in our election? Or do we believe the president's sharp reversal on his remarks the next day -- only after bipartisan condemnation of his slap in the face to U.S. intelligence agencies that have confirmed that Russia did indeed try to meddle in our presidential election?

On July 16, when asked by a reporter if he believed that Russia interfered in the 2016 presidential election, Trump said: "I have President Putin. He just said it's not Russia. I will say this. I don't see any reason why it would be." Then, 27 hours later at a meeting in the White House, Trump walked back that statement and said, "The sentence should have been, 'I don't see any reason why I wouldn't' or why it wouldn't be Russia instead of why it would.'"

Just a few days after that, Trump once more denied Russian interference, leaving the White House communications team to interpret what the president meant when he said yet again that Russia didn't interfere.

The problem is this: clear communication and information sharing is a fundamental responsibility of the presidency that shouldn't require interpretation by the White House communications team. Moreover, 'yes' and 'no' are full and complete declaratory responses. They need no interpretation.

Yet, the president's responses have vacillated from one to the other with seemingly no rhyme or reason for taking the reverse opinion. If we're to believe the president, he must be consistent and truthful with the American public, and that's proven to be difficult for him.

Consider the Source

While Americans are certainly well within their rights to believe either the media or the president, there's plenty of evidence to suggest that the former is a more reliable source for truth than the latter.

Unbiased, non-partisan, well-established and credible news outlets accurately and consistently portray the details of what happened or what exists – the facts. Yes, those outlets occasionally get the details wrong and must run corrections, but they don't intentionally aim to deceive or lie to the American public. Of course, Trump has brainwashed his true believers to believe that this exactly what the "fake news" media deliberately does.

Conversely, the president has with alarming frequency made demonstrably false statements to the American people and called them truths.

If the goal is to obtain honest information, consider the source.

The Red MAGA Hat

By Susan Hutchinson

January 24, 2019

Donald Trump's 2016 campaign slogan was Make America Great Again. He plastered the MAGA acronym on red hats that his supporters wear with pride. What could possibly go wrong with a seemingly innocent campaign prop?

Fast forward to 2019. My friends and I attended the Myrtle Beach, SC Women's March in Chapin Park on January 19. About an hour before the march ended, we noticed a young man wearing a MAGA hat.

Our radar immediately went up as we watched him move through the crowd taking photos and conducting on camera interviews with attendees. The police were also watching. Would he start trouble? Was he carrying a concealed weapon?

His presence was disturbing. Why? Because of the red MAGA hat. Wearing one elicits a visceral reaction from those of us who see Trump and his devout followers as a threat to America. For more on this phenomenon, please see this Washington Post Jan. 25 article.

On the same day in Washington DC another event took place at the Lincoln Memorial. The Indigenous People's March was ending as a small group of Black Hebrew Israelites began to spew hatred at Native Americans, other African Americans and a group of white students from a Catholic high school. The students especially were targeted. Most wore red MAGA hat.

The Native Americans and African Americans decided not to engage the religious group and simply walked away, ignoring the rhetoric hurled at them. But not the white students.

Perhaps feeling empowered by their MAGA hats, they chose to close ranks and, with the approval of their teacher, loudly sang school fight songs trying to drown out the verbal abuse. The number of students was about 200, the number of Black Hebrew Israelites was 5. The racial tension between the two groups escalated.

Nathan Phillips, an Omaha elder, began playing his drum, singing Native American songs and leading his people away from the situation. The students began making tomahawk chops, whooping and imitating Native American dances they probably picked up watching old western movies. It clearly showed their lack of respect.

One student, Nick Sandmann, chose to stand in the way and block Mr. Phillips as he tried to make his way up the steps of the memorial. He stared the elder down with a smirk on his face and an air of superiority. And he was wearing a red MAGA hat, now a symbol of racism and entitlement.

Mr. Phillips said the action he took was to try to diffuse a racially charged situation between the students and the Black Hebrew Israelites. He described the students as a mob and said he was afraid wading into the group of students, but persevered because he wanted to lead his people to safety.

Sandmann later issued his own statement saying he was the one trying to diffuse the situation, one that he and his fellow students created because they refused to walk away and ignore the taunts. He said he and his family have received death threats and blames everything on the Black Hebrew Israelites.

So, the students created a situation and then blamed someone else when it turned bad. Sounds very much like what Trump does, doesn't it?

The right-wing media now says the students are being vilified and instead we should applaud this young man's initiative. And, President MAGA has invited them to the White House.

David Hogg and his fellow students at Stoneman Douglas High School watched as their classmates were gunned down last year. They immediately decided thoughts and prayers were not enough and were compelled to become activists for gun sense legislation. The right-wing media vilified them, and they received death threats. They did not get an invitation to the White House. But then again, they don't wear red MAGA hats.

Could the media have been more objective in their reporting and more carefully analyzed the entire situation? Of course. However, upon re-evaluating what happened no one can dispute that the red MAGA hat was the trigger.

The students chose to stand and fight instead of walking away, which showed the world their ignorance and immaturity. These students feel they were unfairly targeted because of their hats. Now they've had a tiny taste of what it feels like to be a person of color in America today.

The Vague, the Cherry-picked & Outright Lies

February 8, 2019
By C J Waldron
Filled with vagaries, innuendo and outright lies, the State of the Union failed to live up to the promise of unity. The speech resembled one of his rallies, with constant applause from Republicans, who grasped at the even a hint of a possible policy change. Instead, the speech denigrated into another campaign speech for his useless wall. Claiming credit where none was due, creating facts out of thin air and misreading why Democratic women were applauding.

One of his more outlandish claims was to take credit for more women in Congress; completely neglecting the fact that they are largely Democrats who ran on a platform of opposition to this administration. The women stood, applauding their own efforts. It was badly misread as an affirmation of this administration's policies, which has the least number of women in top level positions than those past.

On the economy, he claims credit for starting the recovery that began under President Obama.   The claims of having the largest economic numbers were equally vague. While he claimed to have done more than ANY of his predecessors, he ignored how President Obama rescued the country from the Great Recession. Even while touting these tremendous economic numbers, he contradicted himself by claiming jobs and the economy were suffering because of illegal immigrants.

And then there was border security; the endless drumbeat of building a wall. Unsubstantiated claims of more caravans, more drugs and more criminals coming over the border kept with the same rhetoric that resulted in the useless shutdown. Using an unfortunate family as props, he highlighted the murder of a couple while ignoring the numerous mass shootings during his tenure.

His claim to battle childhood cancer was also a red herring. He used a child as a prop while proposing a mere $500 million over ten years while asking for billions for his useless wall.

Spouting right wing rhetoric, he spread the outlandish lie of late term abortion being permitted, even after birth. This is a dangerous stance that has caused violent attacks on those performing lawful abortions.

His proposal to reignite the nuclear arms race is extremely dangerous. It moves the Doomsday Clock closer to oblivion and his promise to build more and more weapons threatens to explode our already burgeoning national debt. He held the contradictory views of negotiating with North Korea but pulling out of the same situation with Iran.

Claims of creeping Socialism again led to campaign-like chants of "USA!" There was no offer of explanation, nor was there an option for a different approach.

Another "accomplishment" he lauded, as he proposed withdrawing from Afghanistan, was the killing of the leader of the group they attacked the USS Cole, while ignoring President Obama killed Bin Laden.

It was a rambling, unconnected speech that had little to do with unity and much to do with the smoke-and-mirrors efforts at deflecting from the issues. Instead of calling for unity, he called for an end to "partisan investigations".

His flashbacks to D-Day had nothing to do with the current state of our union. His lame attempts at making a connection were weak and showed a disconnect with everyday Americans. He attempted to paint an American image, while his actions showed anger and disdain for anyone who disagrees with him. His "America First" claim along with his claim of "greatness", at his terms, were without focus and without meaning. No new plans were presented. No great ideas were proposed.   No solutions were offered. In essence, it was a nothing-burger.

Presidential Harassment and Executive Privilege Farce

February 8, 2019
By C J Waldron
As the Democrats prepare to address the issues that were ignored by the sham investigation led by Republicans, they are being challenged with threats of "presidential harassment" and claims of Executive Privilege. Adam Schiff is opening his investigation by crossing the "red line" the administration drew when the Mueller probe began.

His committee is looking into the finances of the Trump Organization and how his family used their connections to allow access to foreign donors. They are also investigating Trump's inaugural committee and the foreign governments that made huge donations to gain the favor of the incoming administration.

These are the reasons Trump has gone on a rampage, claiming "presidential harassment". Since when was this a thing? Since when was the system of checks-and-balances that was put in place by our Founding Fathers turned into this farce? It was when an actual investigation was launched by members of Congress to rein in the illegal activities of this administration. If Trump is allowed to maintain this claim, we have abandoned the three branches of government that serve as the foundation of our democracy.

The claim of Executive Privilege is equally absurd and has been repeatedly struck down by the Supreme Court during the Nixon and Clinton administrations   I'm certain that Trump is placing his faith in the Supreme Court ruling in his favor, since two of the justices are his appointees, and he believes they will remain loyal to him rather than the rule of law. Despite this, having his sons claim Executive Privilege , the administration is gambling that they will be allowed to hide their misdeeds and potentially criminal activity. Experts don't see this as a winning strategy.

With the Executive Privilege argument, the administration hopes to avoid facing questions about its involvement in the Mueller investigation and so much more. Instead Democrats, led by California Congressman Adam Schiff, will continue to probe, question and investigate all the issues that Republicans attempted to sweep under the rug.

◆◆◆

Time for the Klan to 'Ride Again', Says Alabama Editor

February 19, 2019
By Bob Gatty
An award-winning small-town Alabama newspaper editor is calling for the Ku Klux Klan to head to Washington and deal with the politicians there, saying he'll provide the "hemp rope" so they can be hung.

The editor, Goodloe Sutton told the Montgomery Advertiser that he had written the editorial in the Linden, AL Democrat-Reporter. "If we could get the Klan to go up there and clean out D.C., we'd all been better off. We'll get the hemp ropes out, loop them over a tall limb and hang all of them," Sutton said.

Asked by the Advertiser's reporter if it was appropriate for a newspaper editor to be calling for public lynchings, Sutton replied: "It's not calling for the lynchings of Americans. These are socialist communists we're talking about. Do you know what socialism and communism is?"

In that same interview, Sutton argued that the KKK "didn't kill but a few people" and "wasn't violent until they needed to be." He compared the Klan, a white supremacist hate group, to the NAACP.

In his editorial, Sutton claimed Democrats in Congress were trying to raise taxes in Alabama and blamed Democrats for everything from "getting us into" World War I, World War II, Korea and Vietnam, and said Democrats banned the draft so their sons wouldn't have to serve.

"Seems like the Klan would be welcome to raid the gated communities up there," he wrote. "They call them compounds now. Truly, they are the ruling class."

Sen. Doug Jones (D-AL), who prosecuted two members of the Klan for their role in the 1963 Birmingham church bombing that killed four young girls, called the editorial "disgusting" and demanded Sutton's immediate resignation.

"I have seen what happens when we stand by while people-especially those with influence- publish racist, hateful views," he wrote.

Incredible. This is 2019 and this kind of stuff still happens.

America has ALWAYS Been Partisan

March 2, 2019
By C J Waldron
I heard the news today, oh boy! Partisanship is threatening to tear the country apart. The thing is, the United States was founded on a partisan compromise. The United States has always been a partisan nation and the news that partisanship is leading to the country's demise is, in a popular phrase, Fake News.

Other than history geeks like myself, most Americans assume that the country went from being a set of colonies to a democracy overnight. The victory over the British led immediately to the protections given under our

Constitution.   Many are shocked to learn that we were first governed by a set of laws known as The Articles of Confederation.   If the term "confederation" rings a bell it's because it's the very set of rules that the breakaway southern states sought to establish during the Civil War.

So what were The Articles of Confederation? They were a set of rules established to create a government that was heavy on the rights of the individual states while a weak centralized federal government had little power. They were ratified in 1781 and weren't replaced until 1787, when the Constitution was finalized. It was this rift between state's rights and a strong federal government that was the first partisan disagreement. Those disagreements continue today.

Other disagreements have threatened us throughout our history.   Big business versus government oversight, hawks versus doves, social programs versus government overreach and on and on. Partisan bickering is as old as America itself and as American as apple pie. It gives the people a choice. It helps us to correct bad decisions and replace ineffective policies.

Over our history, the roles have changed due to a changing political climate. For example, while Republicans can claim that Lincoln ended slavery, it was the Democrats who established the Civil Rights Act. And while the Republicans call themselves the party of fiscal responsibility, it has historically been Republicans who have ruled during our greatest economic calamities.

These are just a few examples of partisan divide, the greatest being the Civil War. Will partisanship again divide us to the brink of war, or will cooler heads prevail? Only time will tell.

Stuck in the Middle

April 8, 2019
By C J Waldron
The words of a popular song refer to "clowns to the left of me, jokers to the right" and ends with the refrain "stuck in the middle with you". Such is our political climate as the 2020 elections approach. There are polarized views in both parties, with many rejecting a centrist view.

But what does it all mean?

When President Obama was elected, it gave rise to the Tea Party movement, which sought to oppose every measure the administration proposed. They opposed healthcare, government regulations and virtually anything Democrats supported. This approach led them to victory in the midterms of President Obama's first term, and thus began an era of obstructionist politics.

The Tea Party movement failed largely due to the successes of the Obama administration in bringing the country back from the brink of catastrophe during the Great Recession. Nonetheless, there were still enough members of the Republican Party left to impede the progress gained during his first term.

Many in his own party publicly criticized President Obama for his centrist approach and his willingness to reach across the aisle to seek the advice of Republicans, particularly House Speaker John Boehner. Tales of their late-night conversations spread throughout the Washington establishment, despite the openly hostile opposition of Mitch McConnell and Senate Republicans.

Is this the approach we need right now? Many, on both sides, would strongly disagree.

On the right, there is the Freedom Caucus. This group, which includes current White House Chief of Staff Mick Mulvaney among its founders, rose from the ashes of the failed Tea Party. Despite the exorbitant spending of the Trump administration, they support fiscal conservatism and limited government involvement in both industry and Wall St., despite the fact these were the very factors that led to the Great Recession.

Their diametric opposite is the far-left movement of Democratic Socialists. Led by some time Democrat Bernie Sanders, this movement supports free college for all and universal, government-sponsored, healthcare. The meteoric rise of Alexandria Ocasio Cortez mirrors the rise of Tea Party Republicans during the Obama administration. Their primary purpose is the defeat of Donald Trump.

The one rare area of agreement between these groups is voter fraud. The right, led by Trump, have resurrected these claims to explain their losses in the 2018 midterms, and will undoubtedly keep these falsehoods alive if they lose the 2020 election.

On the left, many Bernie Backers are still stinging from reports the Democratic Party refused to support him. They claim he out polled Trump and should be in the White House. They remind their followers to remain vigilant as the 2020 elections approach.

So, what are our choices? Do we pick the "clowns to the left", the "jokers to the right", or are we "stuck in the middle"? The upcoming elections will tell the tale.

Who's Fooling Who?

May 22, 2019
By C J Waldron

When asked about his multiple failures in making a light bulb, Thomas Edison famously replied, "I haven't failed. I just found 10,000 ways that didn't work." Edison persevered and eventually invented the light bulb. He learned from his mistakes and perfected the process. We currently have a leader who, as a businessman, lost more money than anyone, yet continues to tout his business acumen as a reason to follow him.

Now, unlike Edison, he is compounding his business mistakes by applying them to his approach to government. Despite losing over a billion dollars his followers still believe this is a recipe for success. His Trade War with China, tax breaks for millionaires and America First, except when it comes to his own products, are policies that have failed in the past.

He refers to himself in the third person, calls himself a "stable genius", says he's "like really smart," and claimed, as a candidate, to "know more than the generals" about world affairs, yet has threatened to sue the schools he's attended if they release his grades or SAT scores. Still, his base slavishly believes every word.

We are in dangerous territory. With the rise of white supremacists, continuing questionable conduct by law enforcement and a Democratic field of presidential candidates, we risk another four years or more of the same chaos. With the strength of his base, Trump hopes to ride strong economic numbers to re-election .

And it just might work. Bickering and infighting between the huge Democratic field could be used against them in the presidential campaign. This is a recipe for disaster on the Democratic side.

One can only hope that cooler, and wiser, heads will prevail. Otherwise, we are left struggling with the question raised in Star Wars: "Who's the more foolish, the fool, or the fool who follows him?"

Memorial Day & the American Dictator

By Bob Gatty

May 25, 2019

WASHINGTON -- President Donald Trump found four federal officials guilty of "treason" Thursday — and then commissioned his intelligence agencies to help the Department of Justice prove it.

That's the lead from this article from NBC News.

The article continued:

At the same time, he is blocking Congress from executing its constitutional duty to execute oversight of his administration, not only with regard to his campaign's ties to Russia and the interference detailed in special counsel Robert Mueller's investigation but also on a host of other fronts.

He's wielding power in ways not seen in the United States in generations, if ever, and which many experts say do not resemble global norms for heads of state.

Commenting about that article on Facebook, my friend, Scott Ramminger, had this to say as we approach Memorial Day on Monday:

"The stuff of thugs and dictators. Happening right here in the United States of America.

"Memorial Day honors those who died in the armed forces defending out freedom of religion, freedom of speech, freedom of the press.

"How about we do a little better job of defending those freedoms here at home? That would be a nice way of honoring our fallen heroes."

Scott is correct. Only in totalitarian countries led by dictators like Vladimir Putin or Kim Jong-un do we see the power of the government turned against those in opposition. Now, we are living in a country where that is happening and continues to happen.

Fortunately, for now, the courts are stepping in and blocking some of Trump's totalitarian-style actions, such as using money approved by Congress for the Pentagon and using it to pay for his unapproved wall.

""The position that when Congress declines the Executive's request to appropriate funds, the Executive nonetheless may simply find a way to spend those funds 'without Congress' does not square with fundamental separation of powers principles dating back to the earliest days of our

Republic," wrote Judge Haywood Gilliam, of the Northern District of California, a Barack Obama appointee.

But Trump continues his effort to stack the federal courts with right wing judges whom he believes will do his bidding, and if he remains in power long enough even that safeguard could well be gone.

As my friend, Scott, says, "How about we do a little better job of defending [our] freedoms here at home."

To my friends who are blinded by Trump's rhetoric and false promises and care nothing about his abuses, charmed by his bravado, I encourage you to pay attention to what is happening every day under this president and stop repeating the Republicans' hateful, misleading and just plain wrong talking points about Democrats.

The question is this: Do you want to live in a free society where we are free to believe as we wish, speak our minds freely, with an unfettered press able to report on the activities and decisions of our leaders without fear of retribution? Or do you want to live in a country where one by one those freedoms are challenged, threatened and ultimately wiped away?

This is a great weekend to think about that. Remember, this is "the land of the free and the home of the brave." Let's keep it that way.

His Royal Highness

June 12, 2019
By C J Waldron
It's no secret that Donald Trump considers himself royalty. During his recent trip to England, he intimidated that his sons would be the next dynasty. He even named one of his sons Barron, as an indication that he believes his own hype.

But that's not the royalty I'm thinking about. Instead, I see Trump patterning himself after a fictional German baron, Baron Munchausen. Like the American fictional character, Walter Mitty, this character sees himself as larger than life, creating a series of fantastical stories to make them appear larger than life. No doubt Trump sees himself, and his accomplishments, that way. By calling anything he does "the greatest ever", Trump has excelled in using hyperbole.

Another quality he shares with this fictional character is Munchausen Syndrome. This is a condition where a caregiver creates a crisis only to "save" the person. The most famous case of this was an Upstate New York mother, Mary Beth Tinning, who was convicted of murdering her children as a means of seeking attention. She was convicted of smothering one of her children, confessed to murdering two others and suspected in the deaths of five other of her children. Tinning seemed to thrive on the attention she received from those who sympathized with her grief of losing a child. As a result, she repeatedly smothered her children, in order to gain this attention.

Like Tinning, Trump thrives on creating a crisis, only to come in to heroically "solve" the issue through his ability as "a master deal-maker". Most recently, we have the threat of tariffs on Mexico in order to solve the "border crisis", which he declared a National Emergency in order to circumvent Congress, which refused to provide funding for his campaign promised Border Wall. What he failed to mention was that negotiations had already been on-going, and the provisions were agreed upon long before this tariff threat. Instead, being the master showman, he created this crisis and is now claiming victory.

Like his government shutdowns, Trump has created crisis after crisis, often as a diversion from unfavorable news stories. This is equivalent to the attention sought by those suffering from Munchausen Syndrome.

Sadly, his base will continue to tout these fake accomplishments, while calling any unfavorable coverage "Fake News". The danger is in going too far. We only have to look to Iran to see the possibility of a crisis escalating into a full-scale conflict. Climate change, the border crisis, healthcare and a myriad of other issues could be the next "crisis" to be "solved" by this unstable individual.

We need this to stop!

Attacking the Four Freedoms

On January 6ᵗʰ, 1941 Franklin Roosevelt delivered what became known as "The Four Freedoms" speech. It was later illustrated by artist Norman Rockwell in a series of paintings for "The Saturday Evening Post". This series examines the threats to these freedoms as they are attacked by Donald Trump's administration and his defiant base.

Part One: Freedom of Speech

July 4, 2019

By C J Waldron

"I do not agree with what you say, but I will defend to the death your right to say it" is a quote often erroneously attributed to the French philosopher, Voltaire, but actually written in 1906 by <u>Evelyn Beatrice Hall</u>, defends freedom of speech as an absolute right, guaranteed in our Constitution. The meaning couldn't be any clearer, yet we currently have an administration attacking this right on a daily basis. The Founding Fathers wanted a debate on the foundations upon which America was established and encouraged opposing viewpoints to the status quo as a means to correct what may have been an erroneous conclusion in this "Grand Experiment" known as the United States of America.

Instead, what we currently have is an administration that stifles free speech by declaring anything that goes against their rigid dogma as "Fake News". As a major component of freedom of speech, freedom of the press is the major way that this right is expressed.

They have declared the press, or at least those news sources that offer differing views as "enemies of the people". They restrict access to the White House by refusing to press conference where they can be called out on their indiscretions. Instead, there are hastily arranged "press gaggles" on the White House lawn, or impromptu helicopter conferences, that precede any one of many junkets to a campaign rally or one of his golf courses.

In this way, they can avoid answering direct questions while framing the narrative to suit their own needs.

Meanwhile, we have a "leader" who steers a one-sided assault on this freedom via Twitter, where he can state his opinions without fear of direct confrontation. Often propelling this "Tweetstorms" is a news story that has been promoted by the decidedly right-wing Fox "News". Other times, his

Tweets are from radical right-wing propaganda sources. Sadly, these Tweets have been the basis of policy in this highly unconventional administration.

Freedom is speech is not without its flaws. It is this very freedom that permitted Russian trolls to exert their influence on the 2016 election. Using various internet sites, primarily Facebook and Twitter, these agents of a hostile foreign government spread baseless rumors, spun conspiracies and sowed distrust throughout the American populace. These attacks are being threatened for the 2020 campaign, yet this administration refuses to take steps to stop them.

While the left isn't blameless in their denial of free speech; denying the right to former Breitbart exec, Steve Bannon and ultra-right wing advocate Milo Yiannopoulos, their objections were based on a denial of the right to promote hate speech, which both speakers advocate. Like shouting "Fire!" in a crowded movie theater, these speakers attempt to instill violence and hatred of others is a right that freedom of speech should not be defending.

These threats, and insults, continue, yet Congressional Republicans are doing nothing to halt these attacks on one of our most cherished freedoms. We must make our voices heard and take a stand at the voting booth come 2020.

Attacking the Four Freedoms
Part Two: Freedom of Worship

July 11, 2019
By C J Waldron

Even before he took office, Trump announced a war on religion. As a candidate, he declared that he would have "a complete and total shutdown of Muslims entering the United States". This is a far cry from the religious freedom established by the Founding Fathers, and a direct contradiction of the freedom from religious persecution that drew so many to this country.

Sadly, the Evangelicals, who comprise a major part of his base, wholly embrace this philosophy. They condemn Sharia Law yet want to establish a nation based on "Christian values", which is exactly what the framers of the Constitution sought to avoid. Their narrow-mindedness refuses to see the parallels between their approach and the most extreme form of Islam.

They wholeheartedly support Israel, but chant "Jews will not replace us!" Again, they do not see this as a contradiction since Israel was the biblical land of Jesus. Therefore, they are not so much supporting Israel as they are carrying on a tradition as old as the Crusades by "protecting the Holy Land from Muslim infidels". Because of this, they refuse to accept a two-state solution as a viable peace plan for the region.

It would make sense that freedom of worship should extend to houses of worship, yet anti-Semitic attacks have been on the rise since this administration took office. There have been shootings at synagogues and anti-Semitic slogans painted on houses of worship and Jewish cemeteries.

Despite the massacre in New Zealand, this administration refuses to tamp down its anti-Muslim rhetoric. As election season rolls on, the hatred will undoubtedly increase. This is no way to support freedom of worship.

Meanwhile, in Louisiana, a white man has been charged with burning down black churches. He has been charged with hate crimes, which demand harsher penalties, despite the suspect being the son of a sheriff.

What is the result of all this violence? Non-white and non-Christian churches are forced to have armed personnel to prevent future attacks. How is this even what was promised in the Constitution?

More importantly, what are we going to do about it?

Attacking the Four Freedoms
Part Three: Freedom from Fear

July 18, 2019
By C J Waldron

"The only thing we have to fear is fear itself." It is a famous line from Franklin D. Roosevelt's speech which was intended to reassure Americans following the bombing of Pearl Harbor. It was also meant to prepare them for the struggles they would be facing in the war to come.

Nowadays, fear is a constant. We are in fear of losing basic rights, such as freedom of speech and the press. We are in fear of losing vital healthcare and Social Security. We are in fear that the system of checks and balances promised by our Founding Fathers is failing as Congress refuses to challenge an Executive branch run amok. We are in fear of foreign intervention in our cherished electoral process, as we once again see uncertainty in our future.

While these fears are real, they are trivial when compared to the fears faced by minorities and others. An African American lives in fear that a traffic stop might lead to their death. Immigrants, fleeing oppression in their own countries, fear being separated from their children as they seek safety in asylum. Jews and Muslims face fear in their houses of worship as gunmen target them for perceived slights. School children face fear as the threat to their schools becomes more and more a frightening reality. Even those who speak out against this administration have to live in fear as rabid supporters make threats and mail pipe bombs.

What is stoking these fears? You have to look no further than a certain Twitter feed.

Despite this administration's claims, white nationalism is on the rise. One only has to look to Charlottesville to see stark evidence of this. Chanting "Jews will not replace us!" and brandishing tiki torches, this group sought to intimidate those who were protesting a Confederate statue. Despite one of the counter protesters, Heather Heyer, being killed by a white supremacist plowing his car into a crowd, Trump famously defended the attackers, repeatedly declaring that there were "fine people on both sides".

Shouldn't Congress be calling him out on his fearful rhetoric? You would think that would be common sense. Instead, the Republicans who control the Senate, and for the first two years of this administration, the House, cower in fear as they worry their actions could result in a career-ending Tweet. They value their precious jobs over the needs of the citizens they are supposed to represent.

It's time to stop living in fear. It's time to take back our country.

Attacking the Four Freedoms
Part Four: Freedom from Want

July 26, 2019
By C J Waldron

"It's the economy, stupid!" was a phrase coined by Bill Clinton campaign strategist , James Carville, as a means of focusing the Clinton campaign on the important issues. With the rosy economic numbers, one would think that would be what this administration would want to do.

When challenged on a myriad of other issues, the White House talking heads are quick to deflect with these "facts", yet Trump just can't stay on message. Perhaps there's a reason for that.

During the campaign, Trump called economic numbers under Barack Obama fake. In his first year, he repeatedly pointed to a rising stock market and jobs numbers as proof of his economic success. He touted his "tax reform" as a boon to the middle class, and has continually pledged to repeal and replace Obamacare, which provides health insurance to millions.

These are all supposed to be signs that America is doing better (according to Trump, "the best in history), yet there are troubling signals that these are indeed fake numbers. While unemployment is down, many working class families find themselves having to take on multiple jobs just to make ends meet. Meanwhile, the poorest of Americans are being tossed into the streets as programs are cut to support various illegal expenses and golf outings.

Education is supposed to be the great equalizer. All one has to do is to work hard and get a good education. This is supposed to lead to a good job and higher economic status. Unfortunately, this administration, headed by Betsy DeVos, is focused on funneling money into for-profit charter schools, in which she has a financial stake.

The so-called "middle class tax reform" is anything but. Instead, it is a boon to the wealthy as several tax loopholes opened to allow them to hide their wealth. The middle class saw a slight boost in their weekly wages only to be stunned by a bill when it came time to file their annual income taxes. This was but a smoke-and-mirrors stunt from someone who still refuses to release his own tax returns to dispel any notions of conflicts of interest or violations of the Emoluments Clause of the Constitution.

Partly as a result of this "tax reform", we are seeing the gap between the rich and poor widening. So, there is indeed a great deal of want in our supposedly egalitarian country.

When it comes to taking care of its citizens, America ranks last among civilized countries when it comes to healthcare. Yet, we have an administration that has repeatedly stood behind failed efforts to take this valuable right away from those with the most need. Yet, in a 60 minutes interview, candidate Trump vowed to repeal and replace Obamacare "simultaneously".

Despite this promise, and several efforts to repeal Obamacare, there has yet to be any proposed replacement. The latest strategy is to postpone any healthcare initiatives until he is re-elected.

Meanwhile, there are suggestions that a way to fund the monumental deficit is to privatize Social Security. This is money that many have allowed to be taken from them for years, and now the government wants to put this money at risk.

Is any of this making us free from want or is it a widening of the gap between the haves and have-nots. You decide.

Follow the Bouncing Ball

August 17, 2019

By C J Waldron

For those of us old enough to remember, there was once a television show where viewers were encouraged to sing along as a bouncing ball appeared over the lyrics so viewers could stay on beat, much like karaoke today.

In our present context, the "bouncing ball" is the ever-changing stock market, which has experienced so many ups and downs, the Dow Jones resembles a roller coaster.

Up 300 points one day, down 800 points the next, back up by 350 points -- and that is just within a single week. It's enough to have investors reaching for oxygen, or a defibrillator. This is the new normal on Wall St. as we have a trade deal one day and tariffs the next. A random Trump Tweet sends the markets scrambling, sometimes even before the president is out of his bathrobe.

For those who follow history, these extreme gyrations in the stock market were exactly what preceded the Stock Market Crash of 1929, which led to the Great Depression. But President Trump and his administration lackeys choose to ignore history. Given their erratic behavior, they choose to ignore science, English and math, as well.

Meanwhile, those who follow the volatile markets as they worry about their pension plans and various investments, are left looking on helplessly. What were once considered to be comfortable "Golden Years", have turned into anxiety and outright terror that they will lose everything they spent years earning.

And what is this administration doing? Trump is golfing, Tweeting and holding rallies where he is further stoking fear by telling the crowd they have "no choice" but to vote for him, or their investments will disappear.

What is the average person to do?

As for me, I plan on continuing to invest in the stock market. My suggestion is to buy stock in companies that supply alcohol and anti-anxiety medication. Or since it's legal in many states, pot.

Good luck as we keep following the bouncing ball. Sing along with me…here are the words (Add your own tune):

Trump, Trump, Trump
 You've got to go
We can't afford you any mo…

You lie, you cheat,
you play the field
And all the while,
We have no yield.

Trump, Trump, Trump
You've got to go…
We can't afford you any mo…

You've killed my savings
With your tariffs, and now
The fight with China's
Sent stocks way down.

Trump, Trump, Trump
You've got to go
We can't afford you any mo!

The Deficit and the Bully

By Steve Hamelman

August 22, 2019

With the national budget nearing the trillion dollar mark and fears of recession rising daily, the government of the United States, these days not much more than an emblem of monumental dysfunction, lurches toward the next election under the "leadership" of President Donald Trump, whose understanding of political economy is as deficient as his diplomatic skill.

Readers: rub your eyes all you want. When you open them again, the same number still will be staring back. An $800 billion deficit. What's being done about it?

Washington Post business reporters Jeff Stein and Jonnelle Marte are sufficiently professional to avoid subjective asides, but the rest of us are free to express our opinions about what they reveal in their August 21 article, where they discuss the national debt as well as strategies to stave off a recession, such as whether or not the Fed should cut interest rates. The President thinks they should be cut "sharply."

For non-experts trying to make sense of the situation, two things jump off the page.

The $800 billion Deficit

First, there's that deficit, which, according to the nonpartisan Congressional Budget Office, is "on track to push the nation into levels of debt unseen since the end of World War II."

Republicans, Democrats, and Independents alike: Do the math. 2019 minus 1945 equals 74 years—a measure of how badly we're doing.

Someday someone will have to settle that debt. As long as our government dithers and politicizes the issue, the more certain that that "someone" will be our posterity—children, grandchildren, and onward unto generations cursed by our folly.

Second, although national economies are enormously complex entities whose health is shaped by countless domestic policies and codes and by international financial conditions either competing against or collaborating with our self-interests, we Americans must accept the fact that the Republican tax breaks of 2018 are a key reason for the pessimistic forecast.

You get what you pay for. If you "pay" for Republican leaders, and if they give you tax cuts (cuts, it must be said, that disproportionately benefit corporations and wealthy individuals), then you get soaring deficits and threats of recession—not to mention everyday things like stagnant wages, underfunded social programs, and crumbling infrastructure.

At a time when strong, sane leadership of all parties and all Americans is bottoming out, what else do we get?

The Bully

We get Donald Trump blathering on in the same old reductive way, contradicting himself at every turn, and ultimately, on cue, turning to personal affront: "The only problem we have is Jay Powell and the Fed. He's like a golfer who can't putt, has no touch," Trump tweeted Wednesday. "Big U.S. growth if he does the right thing, BIG CUT—but don't count on him!

So far, he has called it wrong, and only let us down."

Not incidentally, just last year Donald Trump nominated this same "bad putter," Jerome H. Powell, to chair the Federal Reserve.

Trump's tweet is standard fare from the most powerful bully in the land. Shout down or demean someone sarcastically, the bully intuitively believes shifting the blame to that person will take the heat off the bully himself, around whom weak-minded and/or loyal individuals will rally, thereby propping up the bully's self-esteem.

All well and good—the psychology of a bully, whether of the playground or the presidential variety, and his supporters is easy enough to understand.

But look where it goes next. The same day, with the American economy facing upheaval, the President busied himself accusing the Prime Minister of Denmark for being "nasty and inappropriate." Her characterization of his idea of buying Greenland (!) as "absurd" offended him.

Why is it so hard to be "patriotic" by backing up our president in spats like this?

Because forever ringing in our ears are his own nasty and inappropriate words about Jews who vote Democratic, about Muslims, about immigrants, about Mexicans, about journalists, about overweight people, about Democratic congresswomen, about Michael Cohen (remember him?), about—well, the list goes on.

Bullies—quick to offend and to be offended.

As everything unravels, unpredictability reigns—except for that something nasty is sure to come, any second now, from the mouth or the tweeting fingers of the President of the United States of America.

Protected by the Bill of Rights

By Susan Hutchinson

October 3, 2019

Some 230 years ago when the U.S. Constitution was being written, the Anti-Federalists insisted on the inclusion of The Bill of Rights. We should be forever grateful, because it is the Bill of Rights that will eventually save America from the ravages of the 45th President of the United States, Donald J. Trump.

In The Fate of the Revolution, author Lori Glover explains how that went down.

The United States Constitution was sent to the 13 states for ratification in 1787. The Federalists, who supported the document as it was originally written, felt it was complete and needed no further changes. But the Anti-Federalists were hesitant to approve a Constitution that gave more power to the federal government, the opposite of the Articles of Confederation, which was state focused.

Where were the rights of the people and the states in this new document?

Federalists argued that if you specifically itemize individual rights it would mean only those rights would be protected. Better not to include any and assume that all rights would be protected. The Anti-Federalists had serious concerns with a document that did not have a Bill of Rights, which were included in several state Constitutions.

Anti-Federalists were fearful that the transition of power to a federal government, now with a President, might not protect people from government over-reach or suppression. In addition, they worried that an autocratic minded president might become a new king. Anti-Federalists wanted assurances the new democracy would not become another oppressive monarchy.

Then Comes Trump

Enter Donald Trump 230 years later; an egotistical, power-hungry president out to destroy democracy in the United States.

Trump has admitted he doesn't read, so it is a given that he has never read the Constitution of the United States. As proof of this, he insists the Constitution lets him do whatever he wants.

It doesn't.

It's this belief that he is all powerful that has led to an impeachment investigation, something the Constitution does allow when a president is corrupt and abusing his power.

Trump's Twitter rants this week included accusations that the impeachment is really an attempt at a coup by the Democrats who will strip people of their 1st and 2nd amendment rights as well as the right to vote.

This is nonsense and Trump knows it.

Trump is the only one who would strip people of their constitutionally protected rights if he was given the chance. And for those who want him to be a dictator like his friends in Russia and North Korea, here's some important information. There would no longer be a Constitution or Bill of Rights to protect the people from the federal government. As there are no dictatorships with armed citizens what would this mean? No 2ndAmendment, no right to bear arms.

Trump would take your guns.

It is interesting to read the Federalist and Anti-Federalist arguments about ratifying the Constitution and put it in context of what is going on today. Imagine what would have happened if the Federalists had won the argument. How long would the United States have lasted without any guarantee of individual rights?

In the age of Donald Trump, we are thankful the Anti-Federalists pushed for the Bill of Rights, particularly freedom of the press, freedom of speech and freedom of peaceful assembly.

These rights are the only thing keeping Trump from wielding absolute power over the American people.

A Pleasant Surprise

By Steve Hamelman

November 4, 2019

As with all presidents, Donald Trump has a knack for drawing like-minded ideologues into his orbit. The difference between him and previous presidents is that Trump's choices tend to combine rigid opinions (e.g., anti-immigrant, anti-climate advocacy, anti-tax laws that might actually help everyday people, including his own base) with unpleasant personalities, at least as seen in their public roles.

For Democrats wishing to understand the political psychology of this type of hack, it's a0 good idea to spend some time, once in a while, in the other camp, where clues abound.

There's no better way to do this than to dip into their major publications.

The Washington Examiner is as good a place as any for the curious Democrat to visit.

Clawing through the reporting, the pop-ups, and the op-eds, not to mention the barrage of visual dissonances reeking in all online tabloids in our post-print epoch, one may come upon a pleasant surprise.

Exception to the Rule

This one, for example.

On 30 October, Mark Weinberg, former insider in the Reagan administration, drilled into Trump's newish press secretary (Stephanie Grisham, appointed 1 July 2019) for saying, according to Weinberg, "things that are appalling and below the dignity of her office."

Weinberg directed his disgust at two things in particular: (1) Grisham's parroting of Trump's recent description of his political foes as "human scum" and (2) her smearing of General John Kelly, whom she claimed "was totally unequipped to handle the genius of our great president."

In his comparison of Grisham with Trump's earlier press secretaries, Weinberg piles on his disgust: "she refuses to take questions from the White House press corps at a daily briefing. Instead, she doles out unchallenged answers to questions from reliably friendly outlets such as Fox News."

Weinberg brings his reprimand of Grisham to a fine point by calling her a "coward."

This is another way of saying that Grisham is too intimidated by non-partisan reporters to venture into dialogue with them, choosing to keep herself within the protective radius of her boss eavesdropping in the wings.

In other words, it's getting worse by the hour in the White House.

The (once) free press continues to take a beating from third-rate incompetents, who increase their foreclosure on open debate.

Grisham's party-line palaver ("genius," "great"!) would be amusing if she hadn't said it with a straight face, and if she didn't wield such power over the First Amendment.

But it was straight, and she wields exactly that.

Taking What We Can Get

It's normal to hear Democrats reprove stooges like Grisham, who comes out looking pretty bad even in the non-biased Wikipedia biography of her life. But to hear a dyed-in-wool Republican dress her down for nastiness and stupidity is delightful for two reasons.

First, Weinberg's disapproval, printed in the conservative Washington Examiner no less, makes it impossible for Republicans siding with her and the "genius" president to write the criticism off as another instance of sourpuss Democratic nitpicking.

Second, it means common sense and decency are not totally absent in the Republican Party. That means there's hope for the country. The United States may yet pull out of this downward spiral.

Weinberg's reproach of Grisham doesn't give Democrats the satisfaction that impeachment would give, but it is something to relish, the more so because it appears in an unlikely place—indeed, a strange place for Democrat drop-ins who can't fathom the loyalty of lackeys like Stephanie Grisham.

Lest we Democrats, whether in power or not, are tempted, in this season of vitriol and division, to seek reprisal for the disrespect shown by the other side, let us remember never to allow a Democrat version of Stephanie Grisham to be the voice of any branch, line, or sub-group of the Democratic Party.

Alarming Federal Debt, Little Action

By Stacy Fitzgerald

November 6, 2019

The American taxpayer is getting buried by President Trump's massive federal deficit. And the Republican Party is doing nothing about it.

In the shell game of Trump scandals currently underway, few politicians have publicly addressed the fact that for the first time in history, the U.S. debt has surpassed $23 Billion.

Moreover, increasing deficits have added to the debt at a remarkable rate since the Trump presidency began in 2017.

Alarmingly, the debt is expected to continue to grow in the coming years. How is it possible that the party of fiscal responsibility is at the helm of the federal government during this remarkably spendthrift period and why has today's Republican Party seemingly abandoned its historically debt-averse ways?

The Road to Ruin

It all started with the 2017 GOP tax law, which is estimated to cost $1.9 trillion over a decade. Add to that bipartisan defense and domestic spending bills that increased outlays each year and a clearer picture of the financial predicament we find ourselves in is easy to understand: lower corporate and individual taxes juxtaposed with higher spending will always will always lead to deficits that over time, which now have accumulated at astronomical levels.

At a time when our elected officials should be addressing the big problems that face our country, like healthcare, housing affordability, the environment and the national debt, much of the nation remains transfixed with the never-ending circus that is the Trump presidency as Washington literally ignores the enormity of the issues we face as a nation.

To be fair, the current impeachment inquiry is warranted and should be completed, but the reality is that even before the whistleblower complaint that led to the inquiry being launched, little had been accomplished on any of the priority issues that present the most difficult challenges for our nation.

Unfortunately, this is unlikely to change in the coming years, especially with regard to the fiscal policy of the government – at least without a change in administration.

When "Business as Usual" is Treacherous

The ticking time bomb that is the national debt crisis cannot be ignored. Addressing the debt cannot be done without more tax revenue and reduced government spending. While there are many potential methods to address the debt, the most promising include some politically polarizing options that make immediate debt-reduction unlikely.

Forbes Magazine cites several ways the U.S. can get out of debt. One way to increase the tax revenue base is opening the borders to allow workers from all over the world, which would accelerate the creation of businesses that pay taxes. Yet, this is a policy that Republicans would determine to be untenable for the base, which is largely anti-immigrant.

Another way to increase the tax revenue is abolishing $1 trillion in tax breaks for individuals and corporations. Again, this proposal would likely be doomed with a Republican controlled government.

Raising the Social Security Retirement age to 70 could increase the amount of time Americans pay income taxes into the Social Security System, but it's likely to be unpopular with Americans affiliated with all political parties.

Acting May Take Years

So how and when do we address this encroaching debt burden?

At this point, it's anyone's guess. With Trump looking to win re-election by any means necessary and Congress embroiled in the impeachment inquiry, the national debt will continue to take a back seat to that process, which could either end before the Iowa caucuses in February or last through the general election in November.

Either way, the ghost of Christmas future, the resulting impact of kicking the debt can down the road, may be slow or no economic growth, higher interest rates and increasing likelihood of a more alarming fiscal crisis.

None of those options would bode well for the nation, or for generations to come.

◆◆◆

The Uncounted Casualties of War

November 11, 2019

By C J Waldron

This past weekend we honored those who made the "ultimate sacrifice." Over the years, so many have died in defense of our country or our country's values. Yet, there are other casualties that have no memorials.

Veterans are committing suicide at epidemic rates. Soldiers come home missing limbs, only to find adequate medical care lacking. And then there are those who suffer from wounds we cannot see. Soldiers suffering from PTSD are often overlooked. These are the uncounted casualties of war.

The suicide rate among veterans is 1.5 times that of average Americans, with the largest increase in those under 35 years of age. On average, twenty veterans a day are taking their own lives, yet funds that have been made available for suicide prevention has been largely unspent, with only $57,000 of the $6 million allocated being used for a social media presence. Despite these alarming numbers, these veterans are not considered casualties.

Then there are the wounded. Those who come home missing body parts due to being in highly dangerous areas of the world are not counted as casualties that are remembered with honor on Memorial Day. Yes, they get their recognition in November, but why are they any less honorable than those who died in battle? They survived horrific injuries and endured unimaginable pain and suffering, and have continually issues with depression as they adjust to life outside the military that many hoped would be a lifelong career.

Then there those with unseen injuries. Call it Soldier's Heart, shell shock or the more clinical Post Traumatic Stress Disorder, the result is the same. These soldiers fight a daily battle that goes unseen to others. These veterans are more likely to commit suicide because they are unable to adjust to the world around them.

What can we do to help? Lifeline for Vets offers support and mental health assistance. If you know a vet who is struggling, they can call 888-777-4443 to connect with a mental health professional. Consider making a donation, yourself.

Wag the Dog

November 12, 2019

By C J Waldron

Watching the stock market bounce up and down on a daily basis, I can only imagine the childish glee Donald Trump appears to be getting with each Tweet about his self-initiated trade war with China. On an almost daily basis, he Tweets first about a possible trade deal, causing the stock market to rise, or a snag in the process, causing the stock market to fall.

While Trump laughs at the power of his words, and their ability to cause such wild shifts in the markets, Americans are left feeling uneasy, and in some cases, downright panicky as they watch their potential retirement vanish with each Tweet.

This game of wag the dog has been the hallmark of how this administration has operated. Using deflection, self-created controversies, conspiracy theories and out and out lies, Trump has controlled the news cycle since moment he descended the escalator, which is why the impeachment process is such a threat.

Trump doesn't fear being impeached as much as he fears being irrelevant. With each news cycle now focused on impeachment, Trump is seeing his relevance fading. More and more, the news is about impeachment testimony and less about him, even though he is central to the hearings.

This is why he is playing wag the dog both with the stock market and his daily rants against the impeachment process. By continually commenting, blasting those testifying as "never-Trumpers", he is trying to shift the narrative from the damning testimony to what he and his base see as his self-described "genius".

Of course, this tactic isn't just used BY Trump, it is also used AGAINST him. Foreign leaders have quickly learned that a little shallow flattery goes a long way. The dictatorial leaders of Russia, North Korea, Turkey and Saudi Arabia have easily manipulated Trump using this means while the leaders of France, Germany and the United Kingdom, along with other memos NATO and the United Nations, have run afoul of Trump by not offering him lavish praise, and in one case, out and out laughed in his face at his outlandish claims.

Each is a case of the tail wagging the dog to achieve their means. But like the dog chasing its tail, do we actually get anywhere? And given the recent mission to capture the ISIS leader, isn't it a coincidence that the hero was indeed a K-9?

Stacking the Judiciary Deck With Jokers

November 14, 2019
By C J Waldron
Federal judges who are friendly to Trump are being appointed at a record pace. The sad thing is, many of these judges have been deemed unqualified by the American Bar Association.

The number of open Federal judgeships can be traced back to one man: #MoscowMitch McConnell. Since Federal judges are approved by the Senate, McConnell has used his powerful position as Senate Majority Leader to first block those appointed by President Obama, thereby leaving these positions open, and rapidly approving Trump appointees, regardless of their qualifications .

So, what makes someone unqualified? Pretty much the same as any job; namely, lack of experience. Yet they are still being nominated, and appointed to lifetime positions simply because they share similar views with the Conservative majority. Yes, I said lifetime, which is leading Trump to choose younger members of the bench, thereby ensuring a right-wing judiciary for years to come.

Labeling potential Federal judges as "not qualified "has led Republicans in the Senate to accuse the ABA of a having a Liberal bias. They are ignoring the lack of judicial experience in these nominees in favor of stacking the deck in hopes of overturning such controversial decisions such as Roe v Wade, thereby achieving a long-held Conservative dream of taking away a woman's right to choose.

The evidence of this was obvious in appointment of Lawrence J. C. VanDyke, whose "not qualified" status led to a tear-eyed appearance before Congress. The ABA stated, after they had conducted sixty interviews, that his treatment of LGBTQ litigants while describing him as "arrogant, lazy, an ideologue, and lacking in the knowledge of day-to-day practice including procedural rules."

Considering this scathing review, and that of several other nominees, Republicans have threatened to abandon using ABA guidelines for judicial nominees.

While the impact of these lifetime appointments may not be immediately apparent, by putting pro-business judges in such positions there will be long-lasting consequences.

Environmental protections put in place by President Obama to combat the dangers of Global Warming have been erased by Executive Orders from the current administration. Fortunately, the current judiciary has ruled many of these efforts to be Unconstitutional, allowing many of these protections to remain in place.

With the future make-up of the Federal courts, these protections are in jeopardy. It is future generations who will pay the price of these short-sighted actions.

With yet another school shooting, the appointment of pro-NRA judges threatens the lives of innocent children as efforts to limit certain firearms and expand background checks fall to the wayside of right wing decisions.

As an educator with over thirty years of experience, it has been only in the latter stages of my career that I have been required to attend active shooter training, which is marketed under the unassuming name, Safe Schools.

How is allowing the proliferation of firearms in any way "safe"?

And finally, one more judicial appointment has become available. Donald Trump's sister, a Federal judge herself, retired as she faced an ethics investigation regarding her taxes. I can only wonder what the qualifications of her replacement will be.

It is without a doubt that the current push for right wing judges, many of whom have been deemed "not qualified" represents an extreme danger to future generations. And at this point, the damage cannot be undone.

The Trump Mystique: The Economy

January 10, 2020

By C J Waldron

Prior to his election, Donald Trump called the economic numbers under President Obama fake. Once he assumed office, he did a quick about-face, declaring they were no longer fake. And thus, we were off and running as the twists and turns of the economic numbers flowed at a dizzying pace.

The economy is indeed doing well, but many argue that this is in spite of and not because of Donald Trump. Business leaders love his deregulation policies, but these policies were enacted to counter the issues of predatory lending that led to the Great Recession, as well as to address climate change. So, perhaps these are the actual "fake" numbers.

When you take a closer look at what Trump has done for the economy, you will see that it is teetering on the brink of a recession. Much like the Dot.com bubble of the 1980s or the housing crisis that led to the Great Recession, the key indicators of this soaring stock market are pointing to its inevitable fall.

First, there is the budget deficit, which is predicted to top $1 trillion for the first time in our history. This is due, in part, to Trump's so-called "tax reform" and his self-created trade war with China. Both of these have resulted in a skyrocketing budget deficit as the rosy economic growth Trump predicted has failed to materialize at a pace he claimed would offset his "tax cuts".

As many of us discovered when filing our 2018 tax returns, the slight boost in our paychecks was offset by tax penalties and limited deductions. This required many to have more money withheld from their paychecks in order to avoid these penalties in 2019.

The trade war with China had Trump providing farmers with a bailout to offset the lost revenue from the trade war, adding even more to the deficit. While many Republicans are quick to point out that President Obama bailed out the auto industry, this money was paid back, with interest. No such payback is seen forthcoming from farmers, so this is merely a political ploy to garner votes.

As for other aspects of the trade war, despite Trump's insistence that China is paying the costs of increased tariffs, history has shown that the cost is ultimately paid by the consumer. Even so, there have been over

1,100 applications for exemptions, which begs the question, what items are being influenced by these tariffs?

Trump has used the trade war to cause wild shifts in the stock market. A Tweet about progress in the trade war has led to the market soaring, while news of stalling trade talks has seen it plummet. Such wild fluctuations have created a sense of panic amongst those who see their retirement plans evaporating with this volatile market.

Trump supporters claim he is a successful businessman, as evidenced by his name on so many properties. They believe he actually built these structures, when in fact, he simply bought the rights to the building, similar to a sports franchise selling the naming rights to their stadium. So, while the Trump name may be on many things, his actual ownership is an illusion.

His multiple bankruptcies, failed business ventures and multiple fraud investigations are ignored by his supporters as being "mean-spirited attacks". Yet, he refuses to release his tax returns, as he promised to do multiple times, to show his true financial status.

Like his business ventures, the Trump economy threatens to fall like a house of cards. False promises, ballooning deficits and out-and-out fraud will cost future generations dearly.

What Makes a Leader?

March 18, 2020

By C J Waldron

The health and economic crises that has befallen our nation demands strong, honest, forthright and wise leadership if lives are to be saved and if we are to avoid a financial catastrophe not seen since the Great Depression. So, the question becomes: What makes a leader?

A leader inspires us, not belittles others.

A leader takes responsibility rather than blaming others when things go wrong

A leader takes into account all points of view and does not refuse to listen out of spite.

A leader shares credit for positive results and does not demand thanks for "fixing" a crisis they created.

A leader accepts blame for things they did wrong and takes measures to correct them instead of lying about the situation and deflecting the issue to others, even if it's not true.

A leader doesn't demand thanks for doing what they were elected to do, but quietly does these things without fanfare.

A leader does not demand personal loyalty over country.

Think about it. There have been many great leaders of this country.

Leaders who said, "Ask not what your country can do for you. Ask what you can do for your country." Or, "The only thing we have to fear is fear itself". Or, one who described America as "a thousand points of light".

A leader does not call the media "fake news" or "the enemy of the people" when they don't agree with him. A leader does not pledge to "Make America Great" by dividing the country and including only his supporters.

During this period of crisis, America needs a leader. We need someone who leads by example, who takes responsibility, who unites us as a people. Whose word we can trust.

This is why the next election is to vitally important to preserve the values America was founded upon. We cannot survive another four years of "us versus them", xenophobia, racist attacks and vindictiveness that stems from the White House.

The world needs to stop laughing at us and instead we need to retake our place as a world leader. And we need a leader who can accomplish that through diplomacy and cooperation instead of trying to bully other nations to do our bidding.

America was already great. We need a leader who recognizes this; that we are a nation of immigrants and white does not make right. We need to embrace ALL of America and attempt to understand our differences.

America was founded upon the ideal that anyone can succeed. It was supposed to be the Land of Opportunity. We need to return to those core values where human life was more valuable than "the right to bear arms".

We need a leader who will make all this possible.

Will America Ever be Great Again?

May 8, 2020
By CJ Waldron
You've seen the images. The MAGA hat wearing zealots who claim they want to "Make America Great". Their idea of greatness is a sad distortion of reality. They long for an America where white makes right. They hug

their guns and pretend to love the flag. They're fiercely intolerant of anyone who is not like them and are so filled with hate and anger they cannot broach any disagreement with their rigid dogma.

They are the Proud Boys, neo-Nazis, white supremacists and religious bigots. They hold rallies on government property, proudly displaying their "Second Amendment rights," including guns, while denying First Amendment rights to others. They shout "White Power!" as they hold MAGA signs and swastikas.

During this time of a health crisis they shun masks and social distancing, claiming it infringes on their individual rights even as they threaten to spread disease to others.

Then, there is the religious right; a group so blissfully ignorant they believe any illness is a sign their god supports whatever they hate. They shout "God Hates Fags!", claim to be able to "cure" homosexuality and called the AIDS epidemic "God's Curse on Homosexuals".

They claim to support the teachings of Jesus, but hate foreigners, the poor, other religions and people of color. Instead, they cherry-pick Bible verses to support their bigoted narrative.

They deny a woman's right to choose in healthcare matters, but then later deny them assistance after a child is born.

Here's a clue to those people: It's not your right to force your beliefs on others like you have for centuries!

America: Changed Forever?

America has been indeed lost its way. Once the leader in world matters, we are being shunned by other countries who have taken the lead in matters of the environment, economics, diplomacy and healthcare.

It's ironic that it took an American Hitler to make Germany the Leader of the Free World.

Thinking back to the 70s sitcom, "All in the Family", which was a satire on right wing policies, I'm reminded of the words of the theme song, "Those Were the Days", where Archie Bunker harkened back to the days when Herbert Hoover, the president at the start of the Great Depression, was in charge.

While most laughed at the outlandish caricature of right-wing figures in the Archie Bunker character, we are now being surrounded by Trump-era Archie Bunkers.

No matter who will succeed this deplorable administration, it will be a long time, if ever, that we will be trusted on the world stage.

Has America been changed forever? We can no longer pretend to be the Land of Opportunity. We have abandoned being "The Land of the Free", as our National Anthem promises. When a government official changes the wording inscribed on the Statue of Liberty to support xenophobic policies, we no longer hold the moral high ground.

When a leader compares himself to Abraham Lincoln yet declares he has "absolute power", what's to stop him when the Congressional mandate of being a check on Executive overreach is abandoned? There are no words.

Hubris and nepotism have replaced patriotism and honor.

America had its time in the sun, however brief. Our greatness was lost in a distortion of the voting process.

Putin has his revenge.

America, and Hillary Clinton, saw the downfall of the Soviet Union. Now, he has forever altered America. And all it took was the empowerment of a group of incompetent individuals and handing them the keys to power.

Will America EVER be great again? Not as long as Donald Trump occupies the White House.

But What About Trump?

Make no mistake, Trump has a definite path to victory in November. For this to happen, it will require a complete character overhaul. It's a stretch. Hell, it's an impossibility, but it could happen – if he follows an unlikely path.

No matter what he does, he will have his base. His base is only about 35 percent of the American people. So, to win he must broaden his reach. He can endure this transformation with a nod and a wink to his followers; convince them that he's in it to win it, and once that happens it will be back to business as usual.

So, he needs to get off Twitter. His tweets, while meat for his base, are not helping him. They give those of us with a working brain a window into his disturbed mind. He dares to speak, or tweet, the things others keep inside their heads. He has no social filter.

Withdrawal is never easy. Often addicts replace one addiction with another. Perhaps he could take up painting or some other less destructive hobby. And make no mistake, Trump has several addictive habits, whether it be Diet Coke, junk food, pretty women, sexual depravity or megalomania.

Getting off Twitter and not commenting on everything that gets under his thin skin would go a long way towards repairing -- or at least hiding -- his obvious character flaws.

On top of that, he must admit his mistakes, become humble and acknowledge those flaws. Self-reflection is difficult for any of us, but for Trump to become contrite would permit people to see him in a different light. Indeed, it would humanize him.

Hey Waldron: What are you smoking?

Also, he must embrace both Democrats and the media. Getting them on his side, instead of demonizing them, would make him the great unifier he always portrayed himself as being. Invite Nancy Pelosi and Chuck Schumer over for lunch. It would be a great photo op.

Then, if all of that was not enough, Trump must acknowledge CNN and the New York Times as having legitimate points and state that, while he may disagree with some of their reports, he respects their rights under the First Amendment.

I'm sure by this point you are either laughing so hard you can't breathe, or you're looking for a receptacle in which you can upchuck. Sorry.

We all know the saying "A leopard can't change his spots". Trump is a leopard.

And so, we must kick him to the curb in November.

The Plague of Trump; Listen to the Aztecs

May 14, 2020

By Bob Gatty

Long ago, on a distant day, the American people, beset by misinformation, prejudice, sexism and hate, elected a new leader for their land.

He was a tall man, one with a shock of "blonde" hair, a growing girth, and an attitude that he, and only he, could save our nation from disaster.

His name was Donald John Trump, a self-proclaimed billionaire businessman and reality television star, who promised to "Make America Great Again."

In the three-plus years that have followed that fateful day in November 2016, our nation has been beset by a growing plague, one that can only be laid at the feet of Mr. Trump, he who is so famous that he can grab women by the crotch whenever he wants and they will rejoice, smile and say thank you.

Today, it is known as "the Plague from Trump."

Unlike the "the Plague from China," which Mr. Trump has labeled the coronavirus that has so far felled nearly 85,000 people in our nation, "the Plague from Trump" is much more severe than even that.

For he has turned many of our people one against the other so that even wearing a mask to fend off the deadly virus has become a political statement, and where a black man cannot jog on the street in his own neighborhood without being gunned down by white supremacist vigilantes.

Simmering racism has been set free by Donald John Trump.

"Now, we can say just about whatever we want," one South Carolina redneck said the day after Trump's election as he cheered Hillary Clinton's defeat. It was a sign of things to come.

There is no need to recount the vicious and racist acts that have occurred since that day, as The Trump Plague has been visited upon us. There is no need to recount the lies, the distortions, the pandering to the powerful, and the pandering by the once powerful to him.

It is enough to say this is what we confront today, even as our people are now without jobs, in food lines, begging for credit forgiveness, and fearful of succumbing to the virulent virus known as Covid 19.

But while we worry about venturing forth for long-needed haircuts, groceries, and delayed doctors and dental appointments, even strolls around the block, this American leader spends his time sending vicious tweets belittling and denigrating perceived foes and accusing them of imagined crimes, boasting of false achievements that would be life-saving if true, and trying to shift blame for his own deadly transgressions.

Listen to the Aztecs

Today, He-who-would-be-King, Donald John Trump, would be wise to heed the advice given to Aztec kings (source: Zocolopublicsquare.org):

Sickness will arrive during your time. How will it be when the city becomes, is made, a place of desolation? Just how will it be when everything lies in darkness, despair? You will also go rushing to your death right then and there. In an instant, you will be over.

Facing a plague, it was vital that the king respond with grace. They warned:

Do not be a fool. Do not rush your words, do not interrupt or confuse people. Instead find, grasp, arrive at the truth. Make no one weep. Cause no sadness. Injure no one. Do not show rage or frighten folks. Do not create a scandal or speak with vanity. Do not ridicule. For vain words and mockery are no longer your office. Never, of your own will, make yourself less, diminished. Bring no scorn upon the nation, its leadership, the government.

Retract your teeth and claws. Gladden your people. Unite them, humor them, please them. Make your nation happy. Help each find their proper place. That way you'll be esteemed, renowned. And when our Lord extinguishes you, the old ones will weep and sigh.

If a king did not follow this advice, if his rule caused more suffering than it abated, then the people prayed to Tezcatlipoca for any number of consequences, including his death:

May he be made an example of. Let him receive some reprimand, whatever you choose. Perhaps punishment. Disease. Perhaps you'll let your honor and glory fall to another of your friends, those who weep in sorrow now. For they do exist. They live. You have no want of friends. They are sighing before you, humble. Choose one of them.

Perhaps he [the bad ruler] will experience what the common folk do: suffering, anguish, lack of food and clothing. And perhaps you will give him the greatest punishments: paralysis, blindness, rotting infection.

Or will he instead soon depart this world? Will you bring about his death? Will he get to know our future home, the place with no exits, no smoke holes? Maybe he will meet the Lord of Death, Mictlanteuctli, mother and father of us all.

Clearly, the Aztecs took the responsibility of leadership seriously. King Donald would do well to heed their warning, for they knew that "a king's principal duty in times of contagion was deploying his subjects to 'their proper place' so that the kingdom could function."

◆ ◆ ◆

American Nero

May 20, 2020
By CJ Waldron
We've all heard the story of how "Nero fiddled while Rome burned". The implication was that Roman Emperor Nero stood idly by while his capital city was being consumed by flames. It has long stood as a model of incompetence when referring to those in charge.

The fact is, it is simply untrue. Nero wasn't even in Rome when the Great Fire took place, and the fiddle had yet to be invented. It was an early form of political propaganda aimed at destroying the reputation of an unpopular leader.

With no records to dispute the account, the story spread (excuse the pun) like wildfire. So, opponents were free to spread whatever unsubstantiated rumors they wanted to without fear of contradiction because there was no way to dispute the voracity of their statements.

As a result, Nero has been relegated, however unfairly, to the level of a pariah. He stands as an example of what can happen when a weak leader is in charge during a crisis.

In Donald Trump, we have an American Nero. The difference, however, is we have the facts to back up his incompetence during this current pandemic. We have his own words, via his numerous press briefings and his countless Twitter rants, as a record of his administration's inept handling of the worst health crisis in a hundred years.

Trump always will have his defenders; his die-hard "base" that stands by him, no matter what. They waver between "he tells it like it is" to "that's not what he meant", depending on his latest statements, even if those statements contradict something he said earlier.

This gives Trump the illusion that he's actually "doing a great job" even as the death toll rises.

If Nero were around today, I'm certain his strategy would have been far different. Rather than explain the origins of the fire, he'd simply blame it on Caesar.

Similarly, Trump is trying to lay the blame for our current crisis on President Obama: "Obama left us nothing" to replenish supplies after the H1N1 crisis (Trump had three years to re-stock the shelves); Obama didn't leave us with a plan (he did), and finally, "no one saw this coming" (Obama

<u>warned</u> of this years ago). Trump is attempting to lay responsibility elsewhere, while saying he <u>"take(s) no responsibility"</u> for the current crisis.

Failing in that, Nero would shift his strategy by claiming Caesar has been undermining him for years, in an effort to deflect from the fire.

Trump is employing a similar strategy in perpetuating his <u>"Obamagate"</u> conspiracy theory which conveniently arose at a time when the <u>economy</u>, once seen as a means of catapulting Trump to a second term, suffers its worst performance since the Great Depression.

Douglas McArthur was called the <u>"American Caesar"</u> because, like Caesar, many saw him using his military career to promote his political aspirations.

In Donald Trump we have an American Nero. In a time of crisis, instead of leading, he is fiddling away with his Twitter thumbs, while America goes up in flames.

That included mobilizing those with medical knowledge, the doctor-healers, the very people upon whom we rely upon today as we face all of the uncertainty caused by the coronavirus and "the plague of Trump."

Voter Fraud Trump Style

May 21, 2020

By Bob Gatty

President Trump hates the idea that several states are allowing people to vote by mail because of the coronavirus pandemic, claiming that it will lead to massive voter fraud.

That's interesting from a politician who was fraudulently elected in 2016 because of Russian-induced voter fraud.

Yesterday, he threatened to hold up unspecified federal funding to Michigan "if they want to go down this Voter Fraud path!"

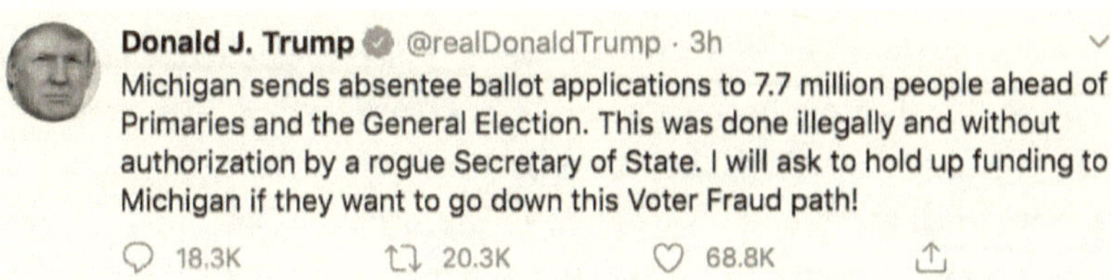

Of course, Michigan's governor is "that woman," Gretchan Whitmer, who

Trump has repeatedly insulted because of her tough stand on behalf of her state for coronavirus assistance. But remarkably, there are Republican states, including South Carolina, that have authorized mail-in voting in one form or another. Haven't heard a peep about them, though.

Then, he made a similar threat to Nevada.

Later he backed off the claim that Michigan's secretary of state had acted illegally, but not from his claim that both states are taking steps that will encourage voter fraud.

In a fact-checking piece this evening, Amber Phillips of The Washington Post's "The Fix," pointed out that Trump last month warned Republicans to "fight very hard when it comes to state wide mail-in voting."

That warning also came in a tweet, in which he said Democrats are "clamoring" for voting by mail. "Tremendous potential for voter fraud, and for whatever reason, doesn't work out well for Republicans."

Yea, it doesn't work out well for Republicans because the more people who actually vote, the better chance Democrats have of being elected.

Trump knows that, doesn't like it, but it's called democracy: he or she who gets the most votes wins.

Phillips researched some of Trump's main arguments against mail-in voting and found them wanting.

First, she said, there is no evidence of widespread fraud, either in regular voting or mail voting, according to election experts in the five states that do all-mail elections -- Colorado, Hawaii, Oregon, Washington and Utah. Those states have established requirements to prevent fraud.

Moreover, Phillips said she found no evidence mail-in voting helps Democrats win more, despite the logic that I just mentioned above, and despite Trump's contention.

Wrote Phillips, Several studies I detail here have found the following: Voting by mail does help voters who don't normally participate in most elections increase their participation, and it can help people participate in more down-ballot races.

But no study has found that it gives a noticeable benefit to either party. One study called the benefit "neutral." It's worth noting that Utah is a state that regularly votes Republican with all-mail elections.

So, to all the Trumpers who are always saying "What about Hillary?" or "What about Obama?", I say to Trump and his supporters, "What about Utah?"

Trump's argument, in fact, is a fraud. He is simply afraid that by making it as easy as possible for people to vote, even in a life-threatening pandemic, he and the Republicans who support him will be toast.

Struggling for Words?

June 4, 2020

By Bob Gatty

Sen. Lisa Murkowski (R-Alaska) says she is "struggling" to find the right words about Donald Trump's presidency. Is this an indication that at least some Republicans are experiencing pangs of conscience, having had enough of this would be dictator who is willing to use military force against our own citizens?

Murkowski's remarks were reported today after former defense secretary Jim Mattis said in a statement published by the Atlantic that Trump is trying to deliberately divide Americans.

"I have watched this week's unfolding events, angry and appalled," Mattis wrote. "The words 'Equal Justice Under Law' are carved in the pediment of the United States Supreme Court. This is precisely what protesters are rightly demanding. It is a wholesome and unifying demand—one that all of us should be able to get behind. We must not be distracted by a small number of lawbreakers. The protests are defined by tens of thousands of people of conscience who are insisting that we live up to our values—our values as people and our values as a nation." He goes on, "We must reject and hold accountable those in office who would make a mockery of our Constitution."

If Murkowski is having difficulty finding the right words, Mattis, a retired Marine general with the call sign, "chaos," is not.

"Donald Trump is the first president in my lifetime who does not try to unite the American people—does not even pretend to try. Instead, he tries to divide us," Mattis continued. "We are witnessing the consequences of three years of this deliberate effort. We are witnessing the consequences of three years without mature leadership. We can unite without him, drawing on the strengths inherent in our civil society. This will not be easy, as the past few days have shown, but we owe it to our fellow citizens; to past generations that bled to defend our promise; and to our children."

Trump, of course, responded via Twitter by saying "The only thing Barack Obama & I have in common is that we both had the honor of firing Jim Mattis, the world's most overrated General. I asked for his letter of resignation & felt great about it."

Well, not so fast.

President Trump's former chief of staff, John F. Kelly, also a retired Marine Corps general, defended Mattis, who resigned in 2018 in disagreement with Trump's decision to pull U.S. forces out of Syria. Kelly said Mattis was not fired by Trump.

"The president did not fire him. He did not ask for his resignation," Kelly said in an interview with The Washington Post. "The president has clearly forgotten how it actually happened or is confused. The president tweeted a very positive tweet about Jim until he started to see on Fox News their interpretation of his letter. Then he got nasty. Jim Mattis is an honorable man."

But apparently, Gen. Mattis' words are having an impact.

Said Murkowski, "When I saw Gen. Mattis' comments yesterday I felt like perhaps we are getting to a point where we can be more honest with the concerns that we might hold internally and have the courage of our own convictions to speak up. And so, I'm working as one individual to form the right words, knowing that these words really matter so I appreciate General Mattis' comments."

Saying that she is "struggling" over whether she can still support Trump, Murkowski said she has "struggled with it for a long time."

"I think right now, as we are all struggling to find ways to express the words that need to be expressed appropriately, questions about who I'm going to vote for or not going to vote for, I think, are distracting at the moment. I know people might think that's a dodge, but I think there are important conversations that we need to have as an American people among ourselves about where we are right now," she said.

Murkowski, who had called Trump's actions "shameful" during the Senate's impeachment trial, but voted to acquit, was joined by the only Republican senator to vote to convict, Sen. Mitt Romney (R-UT), in supporting Mattis. Romney called him "an American patriot" and "an individual whose judgment I respect," and said the former defense secretary's statement was "stunning and powerful."

But then, there were the lapdog Republicans who still hold the Trump party line, like <u>Sen. Lindsey Graham</u> of South Carolina, who is in a <u>tough race for reelection</u> against Democrat Jaime Harrison, and who appears to have just <u>colored his hair to look suspiciously like Trump's</u>.

"I admire his service to the nation," Graham told Fox News. "But the one thing I would tell General Mattis is that you don't quite understand that from the time President Trump wakes up until he goes to bed there's an effort to destroy his presidency."

That effort, Sen. Graham, is well deserved. His presidency needs to be destroyed

November 3. Remember that date.

3

THE CONTINUING SIN OF RACISM

Donald Trump's presidency has been fraught with acts of blatant racism, acts that have sewn discord and division among the American people. In act after act, he has preyed on latent emotions and brought them to the surface. As this is written, the latest example — the killing of a black man, George Floyd, by a white Minneapolis, MN police officer has triggered massive demonstrations against police brutality and other forms of racial discrimination and a subsequent movement for police reform. The question is how long will it last? What will come of it?

A Brand, a Baller and the Backlash

By Stacy Fitzgerald
September 5, 2018
In choosing Colin Kaepernick as one of the faces of its 30th Anniversary advertising campaign and signing him to a multi-million-dollar endorsement deal that includes apparel and footwear, Nike managed to spur a heated backlash against the brand.

Images of people setting fire to Nike gear and calling for a boycott of its products flooded social media and created such marketing buzz for Nike, that one estimate puts the value of the free publicity at more than $40 million.

In less than 24 hours, the Nike brand managed to elevate a former football player, now activist to near icon status despite the backlash, which is sure to be ineffective, just like similar protests against corporations that that have made political statements through their marketing and social justice activities.

When Brands Take a Stand

Nike is one of the most identifiable and popular brands in America and its popularity has always been driven by young people, who are the trend setters and taste makers of our time. So, a bunch of middle aged angry white men setting aflame five-year-old kicks is likely to do little to damage the brand's reputation, since this group isn't a core demographic for the company.

Moreover, anyone who thinks that Nike made a massive PR blunder in signing Kaepernick to an endorsement deal doesn't get marketing at all.

Brands are keenly aware that taking a stand on often divisive political issues will result in commentary from both supporters of their position and detractors. The supporters in this case are people who agree with Kaepernick, who was the first professional football player to take a knee in protest of racial injustice in America.

Kaepernick's protest became a hot button issue when opponents of it, including President Trump, blasted the move as unpatriotic and disrespectful to our troops, which Kaepernick and those who support him have repeatedly denied.

In our world of divisive political issues, few have been more public and more contentious than Kaepernick's non-violent political protest and Nike knows this. By signing Kaepernick to and endorsement deal, Nike is making a bold political statement consistent with the values of its primary base of customers: young people, including Millennials, who are among the most politically and socially conscious Americans in our time.

It was not an impulsive move, but a calculated marketing strategy by a brand that signed an endorsement deal with a former football player made much more famous due in part to being one of the targets of the president's angry, divisive and vitriolic tweets. Being a target of Trump has actually elevated Kaepernick's status from unemployed football player and social activist to icon and Nike knows this. It's a brilliant marketing strategy.

The Backlash

As you can expect with the announcement of Nike's deal with Kaepernick, those who see Kaep's protest as unpatriotic were vocal and visible in the 24 hours following the announcement of the deal. They cut swooshes off of their socks, spurred the hashtag #boycottNike and lit fire to their sneakers (some of them while wearing them).

While these antics resulted in five seconds of fame for some of the protesters in now viral videos with third-degree burns, they will do little to permanently sully the reputation of Nike's brand.

In fact, other brands have not only survived, but thrived after taking positions on controversial political issues. Dick's Sporting Goods was the subject of angry protests by gun enthusiasts when it announced that it would no longer sell guns in its stores following the Parkland shooting.

Pro-gun activists painted the company as cowardly and accused it of abandoning its core customer base. The controversy was not only short-lived, but the company managed to turn the announcement into a sales boost fueled by supporters of gun control legislation.

When brands take a stand on political issues, they realize there will be supporters and detractors. The supporters will become loyalists and the detractors will be vocal initially, but silent eventually.

You better believe that Nike ran the numbers, assessed the risk and determined that in the end, they'll gain much more from making a statement than remaining neutral. It's a bold political statement, but also a calculated marketing strategy that will ultimately, increase its street cred and stock.

Oh, and by the way, it was the right thing to do.

◆◆◆

Is There No Safe Place for Black People in America?

By Stacy Fitzgerald

September 13, 2018

If there's one place in the world that should be a safe place of refuge, comfort and safety for everyone, it's your home. But that was not the case a little more than a week ago for a young black man in Dallas, TX.

The Fourth Amendment to the U.S. Constitution says this:

"The right of the people to be secure (i.e. safe, protected or sheltered) in their persons, houses, papers and effects against unreasonable search and seizures, shall not be violated."

But the most egregious of violations was committed in Dallas by police officer Amber Guyger, ending the life of Botham Jean, a 26-year-old black man.

Jean was alone in his home when Guyger, who has said she believed she was entering her own apartment, walked through Jean's open apartment door and shot and killed him, believing him to be a burglar.

This traumatic news leads many blacks, already traumatized at the frightening number of police killings of unarmed black people, to the horrific realization that they aren't even safe in their own homes from the threat being killed by the police.

Questions Surround Officer's Account

Almost immediately questions began to swirl about Guyger's recounting of the circumstances that led to Jean's killing, which The National Review, a leading conservative magazine and website, has called "the worst police shooting yet."

To be believable, Guyger must have had an unimaginable level of obliviousness to her surrounds to miss all the clues that she wasn't entering her own apartment: she was on the wrong floor of the building in front of an apartment with a red door mat, which she did not own.

She also opened a door she said was ajar and entered a room she said was dark. Who leaves a door open and the lights off in their home? Why didn't she turn on the lights?

She then issued verbal commands that she said Jean ignored, then fired her weapon twice striking Jean once. Then, she turned on the lights, realized she wasn't in her apartment and called 9-1-1.

At least one resident of the apartment claims she heard knocking on a door and then "Let me in, let me in." Then she heard two gunshots and a voice saying. "Oh my God. Why did you do that?"

This directly disputes Guyger's account.

Given the circumstances of the events leading to Jean's death, Guyger was arrested and charged with manslaughter, a crime defined as "recklessly" causing the death of a person. She wasn't charged with murder though, which is simply defined in Texas as "knowingly or intentionally causing the death of an individual."

Texas is a "stand your ground state," and juries are typically sympathetic to law enforcement officers, giving leeway to those using deadly force in perceived situations of danger when in pursuit or making criminal arrests.

But because Guyger was not making an arrest or in any kind of perceived eminent threat, there is little evidence that she had cause to use deadly force, according to this Washington Post article.

What if the Victim Were White?

Even if you believe Guyer's account of the events, you must admit her actions belied appropriate police training. Details and clues are important. Yet she seemingly missed so many details that would have prevented this tragic death.

Jean was an innocent man in his own space, minding his own business. He was home. He was safe. He wasn't suspected of a crime and had no reason to believe that the police would enter his home, even with the door ajar, and kill him.

If the officer in this case was a black man and the victim was a white man in his own home, would the charge be different? Would the public support a murder charge for illegal entry into a private home and killing the occupant?

If you believe in the Constitutional rights of all Americans, then you must acknowledge that Botham Jean's rights were violated. He had the right to be secure and safe in his home. Amber Guyger callously violated his rights and tragically ended his life.

Tragically, given the history of near zero accountability in incidents of police killing of unarmed black people, there's little reason to believe justice will be served in this case. The police officer should be charged with murder.

Regardless of the race of the citizen, every American has the right to be safe in their own home. Allowing police to be let off with a slap on the wrist for taking a life of an innocent citizen in their own home without cause should never be tolerated.

And if it is, the U.S. Constitution isn't worth the paper it's written on.

The President is a Bully; Black Women His Favorite Targets

November 13, 2018

By Stacy Fitzgerald

Though it shouldn't be so, most Americans are now accustomed to the president of the United States having frequent, uncontrolled juvenile meltdowns via Twitter. But his nasty comments last week about three Black female journalists graphically illustrates what a bully he is and that Black women are his favorite targets.

We're familiar with the rage that he bellows regularly at congressional Democrats, world leaders, perceived enemies and the press, which Trump consistently labels "the enemy of the people."

So perhaps we shouldn't have been surprised last week at the vehement verbal assaults Trump leveled at members of the media, particularly Black women reporters April D. Ryan, of American Urban Radio, Abby Phillip of CNN and Yamiche Alcindor of PBS.

Nonetheless, the mean spirited, petty and noxious comments from Trump may have caught many off guard. Though they shouldn't have, because what many Black women know for sure is that the president of the United States is a bully and Black woman are his favorite target.

Who's Caping for Him?

It's no secret that Black women aren't caping for Trump. What's "caping?" Urban Dictionary defines "caping" as blindly defending someone, no matter how wrong they are.

No, Black women aren't doing that. We know this president's wrongs and the narcissist in Trump likely knows how much or how little support he has among this demographic in America.

Black women who support Trump will be as tough to find as a hamburger at a vegetarian convention. In fact, 94 percent of Black women voted for Hillary Clinton. Trump's weak support, particularly among Black women is well documented, but so is his history of racist statements and actions in the past (see his position on the Central Park Five, lawsuits for racial discrimination in the '70s and comments about African and poor developing countries, which he's referred to as "shithole" countries).

Even against this backdrop of mutual side eye, there should still be some civility – a basic level of respect, particularly when it comes to public interactions and statements from the President of the United States.

But, Trump's remarks about Black women have been vicious, vile and threatening. He referred to former White House staffer Omarasa Manigault Newman as a dog, called Congresswoman Frederica Wilson a "wacky" liar and has repeatedly issued veiled threats against Congresswoman Maxine Waters, one of his most vocal critics.

So perhaps we shouldn't have been shocked that he chose to publicly berate and demoralize three Black women reporters last week.

He called Ryan a "loser." He insisted that Alcindor's question about whether his self-identification as a nationalist would embolden white nationalists was racist. He berated Phillip by saying "'what a stupid question, I watch you and you ask a lot of stupid questions."

In those moments, we witnessed the president of the United States do what he's done consistently in public: berate, demean and belittle Black women. Given this consistent history of disrespect against them, it's no wonder Black women aren't caping for him and it's no doubt that the president is aware of this.

But that doesn't give him justification to attack Black women publicly, berate or demean them or anyone else. It's offensive, juvenile and below the dignity of the office.

All We're Asking is For A Little Respect
It's perhaps ironic that in this year of Trump's widespread disrespect and berating of Black women that the good Lord saw fit to call home the Queen of Soul Aretha Franklin. It was the Queen herself who blessed us with her not iconic anthem, "Respect," and thus delivering the most fitting line to address what Black women want from Trump:

"All I'm [We're] asking is for a little respect."

When Justice is Bought, It's Unequal

By Stacy Fitzgerald

March 10, 2019

When former Trump Campaign manager and convicted felon, Paul Manafort was sentenced last week to just 47 months in prison for tax evasion and bank fraud, there was shock and outrage that the recommended 19 to 24 year sentence requested by Special Prosecutor Robert Muller's team was ignored in favor of a sentence just shy of four years.

Despite the seriousness of Manafort's crimes and the post-conviction obstruction charges, the man was lauded by Judge T.S. Ellis as a man who had lived a mostly "blameless life." It's hard not to see the inequity in Manafort's sentencing and treatment compared with that of the typical black or poor defendant.

At least one Congresswoman agrees that the American criminal justice system is rife with disparities based on race and/or economic status. Rep. Alexandria Ocasio Cortez, tweeted: "Paul Manafort getting such little jail time for such serious crimes lays out for the world how it's almost impossible for rich people to go to jail for the same amount of time as someone who is lower income."

She's right.

Others also have spoken out against the inherent inequity. Scott Hechinger, a senior staff attorney at Brooklyn Public Defender noted how many of his clients, mostly minorities, received much harsher sentences for far less serious crimes. He tweeted: "For context on Manafort's 47 months in prison, my client yesterday was offered 36-72 months in prison for stealing $100 worth of quarters from a residential laundry room."

He went on to add that a Black woman in Texas who voted in the 2016 election without knowing that she was eligible because she was on probation received a 5-year prison sentence.

Said Democratic presidential candidate Sen. Kamala Harris (D-CA), "The criminal justice system as evidenced by that judgement is broken in America. Manafort gets off with a 47-month sentence while a young black man in Mississippi who had weed run his car got a sentence of 12 years."

A former prosecutor, Harris said she always said that "people who commit white collar crimes should bring their toothbrush and be prepared to spend as much time in prison as anybody else. Everyone needs to be treated equally."

As the senator noted while campaigning in South Carolina Friday, the American criminal justice system is rife with examples of stiff sentences handed down to poor, black and brown people versus the lenient punishment doled out to wealthy whites.

For example:

- Brock Turner, who is white, received 6 months in jail for raping a woman because the judge felt like a harsher sentence would ruin his life.

- Brian Banks, who is black and was also a promising athlete in 2002 when he was convicted of raping a white woman, spent more than 6 years in prison before the woman recanted the story and he was released from jail.

Now consider this: Much of white America believes that Colin Kaepernick, who mounted a peaceful protest by kneeling during the national anthem to protest both police brutality and inequities in the American criminal justice system has no right whatsoever to protest. In their view, kneeling is unpatriotic, and he should just shut up and play ball, particularly since he was at one time, paid very well to play football.

As a privileged athlete, the kind of crimes and sentences that Kaepernick is protesting wouldn't likely affect him, opponents' reason, so he should ignore it. But Kaepernick wasn't satisfied to turn a blind eye to unequal treatment of black people at the hands of law enforcement and the American criminal justice system.

I for one am glad he stood up.

Every day, we witness the justice system work for white, wealthy men and women and against black and poor people. It happens in arrests and sentencing and if we remain quiet about it, it is sure to continue. No defendant, no matter how rich or privileged, should escape full punishment for committing serious crimes while black and poor people have the book thrown at them for committing minor infractions.

What's Good for the Clerk is Good for the Congressman

By Stacy Fitzgerald

March 18, 2019

This past Friday, in yet another public episode of racists behaving badly, an East Haven Connecticut woman lost her job because of a racist rant in a grocery store. It was appalling, vile, disgusting and violent and the punishment, definitely fit the crime.

But when it comes to addressing similar acts of racist behavior and violence from our lawmakers, America has a largely "hands off" approach. But, If a Connecticut school employee can lose her job for violent, racist rants and comments, then why can't a Congressman -- like Rep. Steve King (R-IA)?

Racist Attack Condemned

The viral video of the woman, identified as Corinne Terrone, sparked immediate condemnation and social media outrage for its vile acts, including spitting on a black man and woman in a Shop Rite supermarket and calling them the N-word, all in front of her children.

The incident apparently happened in the early afternoon on Friday and the video spread rapidly. Roughly six hours after the incident, Terrone's employer, the Hamden Public School System, issued this statement:

"Someone who will use that sort of language in any setting, whether in public or private, is not someone we want anywhere near our children. The employee is separated from service and we hope that her children will receive the support they need after witnessing such a traumatic event."

The statement was swift and definitive in condemning the school clerk's behavior. Terrone is said to have resigned effective immediately once contacted by the school system and the mayor of Hamden, Curt B. Leng, who released the following statement:

"What I saw was vile and shocking. While I am disgusted and disheartened seeing such hateful behavior, wildly unacceptable anywhere, I am thankful for the swift, effective actions taken by our school system to address this head on and make clear that hate and violence will not be tolerated."

So, the action against this hate-filled clerk was swift and certain and she lost her job. But it's not the same standard when it comes to Congressman King.

A History of Racist, Violent Comments

The Iowa Congressman on Saturday posted a meme (now deleted) of a mock civil war between the "blue" states and the "red" states with the following comment. "Folks keep talking about another civil war. One side has about 8 trillion bullets, while the other side doesn't know which bathroom to use."

It was the latest in a very long history of inappropriate public comments that include racism, xenophobia and violence. In fact, the Congressman in January, was stripped of his committee assignments after questioning why white supremacy was considered offensive.

Frankly, it's surprising that any action was taken by House Republicans to rebuke King, given their propensity to ignore such remarks. And it was long overdue, but it wasn't enough. Steve King, like Corrine Terrone, should also be stripped of his job.

At a time when we as Americans have accepted, and some even embraced, tribalism, racism and political divisiveness, we don't need elected leaders who revel in spreading racist, xenophobic and violence-inciting messages. King's abhorrent behavior has no place in the Capitol and frankly the people of Iowa and America deserves better and should demand that he resign from Congress immediately.

Steve King ultimately answers to the people of Iowa. In a perfect world, though, his "boss," the people of Iowa, would be swift to condemn him and vote him out of his job. They'll have that chance in 2020. Let's hope he faces a similar rebuke to that faced by Terrone.

Race Relations in Trump's America

By Stacy Fitzgerald

April 15, 2019

Today across all of major league baseball every player on every team in every game is wearing No. 42 on their uniforms in honor of baseball great Jackie Robinson, the first black player ever to play in the big leagues.

Robinson broke the baseball color line when the Brooklyn Dodgers started him at first base on April 15, 1947, heralding the end of racial segregation in professional baseball that had relegated black players to the Negro leagues since the 1880s. Robinson overcame unspeakable racial bias during his career, but he let his baseball skills speak for themselves.

As a result, he was inducted into the Baseball Hall of Fame in 1962 and today hundreds of African American and other people of color benefit from his courage and are having productive and lucrative MLB careers.

But despite the advances indicated by the recognition of "Jackie Robinson Day" in MLB, racial bias flourishes in America and a new report from Pew Research Center shows 40 percent of Americans believe the country has not made enough progress toward racial equality. Moreover, most Americans feel that President Trump has made race relations worse, rather than better.

Well, Duh.

While it's true that Trump didn't create racism in America, he certainly stokes it regularly and seemingly enthusiastically. We see this time and time again in his campaign rallies, tweets and public remarks about people of color, particularly immigrants.

We're all familiar with the comments, most of which are so obviously offensive and uncouth that they should never be repeated. Some would argue that the president is one individual and can't solely be responsible for declining race relations in America.

However, the president of the United States, much like a corporate CEO, sets the tone and tenor for our national discourse in America. If his language is consistently insulting, offensive and racially divisive, that only gives license to those within America who quietly harbor racist views and who actively promote white nationalism and reject equality.

In fact, Pew's research shows that two-thirds of Americans say it's become more common for people to express racist views since Trump became president. Frankly, it is evident in everyday life.

It's almost unfathomable that the tenure of America's first black president was immediately followed by the election of Trump, who will likely have the most racially divisive presidency in modern history. Yet, here we are.

Whereas Obama's tenure was to represent a "post-racial America," where blacks and other minorities would be judged on the content of their character rather than the color of their skin and be given equal opportunity to advance in America, Trump's rhetoric before, during and after his arrival in the Oval Office demonstrates that he has little interest in advancing anyone who isn't white or wealthy.

Thus, white supremacists protesting in Charlottesville are "some very fine people," while black reporters and politicians are labeled "low-IQ, losers who ask 'stupid' questions."

Comments on the former display a level of esteem, while remarks about the latter serve only to perpetuate a history of racist tropes used to denigrate blacks.

So, I ask, is it any wonder that race relations aren't improving? Is it any wonder, that, according to Pew's research, blacks are particularly gloomy about the country's racial progress?

Pew's study showed that more than eight-in-ten black adults say the legacy of slavery affects the position of black people in America today, including 59% who say it affects it a great deal. About eight-in-ten blacks (78%) say the country hasn't gone far enough when it comes to giving black people equal rights with whites, and fully half say it's unlikely that the country will eventually achieve racial equality.

Moreover, 56% of all adults say being black hurts people's ability to get ahead at least a little, and 51% say the same about being Hispanic. In contrast, 59% say being white helps people's ability to get ahead. Views about the impact of being Asian or Native American are more mixed.

According to Pew, Democrats and those who lean Democratic are more likely than Republicans and Republican leaners to say it has become more common and more acceptable for people to express racist and racially insensitive views since Trump was elected president.

Among Democrats, 84% say this is now more common and 64% say it's more acceptable; fewer than half of Republicans say it has become more common (42%) and just 22% say it has become more acceptable for people to express these types of views.

Until we get to a place where the President of the United States stops his racist dog whistling, we're not likely to go very far toward equality in America. Were he to change his actions, that alone would not solve the problem, but it would definitely be a solid step in the right direction.

Clearly, there is still a long way to go.

A Black Beauty Queen Trifecta -- and the Fallout

By Stacy Fitzgerald
May 6, 2019
For the first time in American history, the reigning queens of the Miss America, Miss USA and Miss Teen USA are black women, leading some to protest, claiming it's a sign that "political correctness" has corrupted the process and led to black women having an unfair advantage in the contests.

I call BS.

It took 63 years for the first Black Miss America, Vanessa Williams, to be crowned in 1984 and 38 years for the first Black Miss USA, Carole Anne-Marie Gist, to be crowned. Yet, it took only eight years for the first Black to win the Miss Teen USA title.

Decades of exclusionism, bias and racism prevented black women from even competing in the Miss America Pageant (established in 1921) and the Miss USA Pageant (founded in 1952).

These were important periods in America history when segregation and the civil rights movement were critical to removing barriers that that prevented blacks from vying in most competitions, including beauty pageants. When those barriers were broken for the first two pageants, it set the stage so that by the time the Miss Teen USA Pageant was established in 1983 -- some 62 years after the Miss America Pageant was founded and the Civil Rights movement began -- it took just eight years to crown a Black Miss Teen USA.

Times changed. Attitudes changed. Pageants became more diverse and judges were less inclined to let the taint of racial bias influence the outcome of the competitions. Thus, Black women broke history on the strength of their ability to compete effectively with White women for these titles.

Yet, the more things change, the more they stay the same.

Three Queens, One Common Refrain

Following the announcement on May 3 that for the first time all three winners of these elite contests are black women, hundreds of media outlets reported on this historic achievement.

Black women hailed this as a hard-fought achievement decided in favor of worthy competitors who just happened to be black. But many White commentators on social media claimed it was political correctness run amok, as they claim it has with recent, historic wins for Black actors and actresses at the Oscars, American film's most prestigious awards. Suddenly, these competitions were handing out awards to undeserving Blacks rather than white people who deserved to win.

It's hard to take this patently false and unfair criticism seriously, mostly because these same people had zero criticism when most of the competitors and 97% of the winners of these contests were white women. The assumption then is that these women deserved to win, but black women somehow don't.

Forget the fact that most of the judges in these competitions are white and that the competitors have to meet the same minimum criteria of academic excellence, outstanding character and a history of winning in previous competitions. In the minds of these critics, none of this matters – blacks were just handed these titles in the name of political correctness.

BS.

These same critics never questioned the merit of the hundreds of white competitors; yet deign to demand proof that the black competitors "deserve" to win. How hypocritical and racist is that? What these pageants demonstrate is that you can't win a contest when you're shut out. However, once the barrier is broken, black women, like women of other ethnicities, will see that as an aspiration and work hard to achieve such a title.

Given the opportunity, black women can and will contribute their mathematical genius to help America win important achievements in space (like Katherine Johnson in Hidden Figures), become the first black and most educated first lady in American History (like Michelle Obama) and all in the same year, hold the titles of all three signature beauty pageants in America, like Cheslie Kryst, a lawyer from North Carolina, who won Miss USA; Kaleigh Garris, a high school senior from Connecticut who won Miss teen USA and Nia Franklin, a composer and reigning Miss America.

When will America accept that blacks who work hard to excel have earned the right to that same recognition that it never questions when the winner is white?

Rigging the Census for White Republicans

By Stacy Fitzgerald
July 1, 2019
Just a few weeks before the Supreme Court is expected to rule on whether the Trump Administration can add a citizenship question to the 2020 Census, evidence has been found to show that the question was designed to give an electoral benefit to White Republicans, as opponents had argued from the start.

The source of the evidence: the files of a now deceased Republican operative that reveal just that. Notably, the operative's estranged daughter shared hard drive files with Common Cause for a gerrymandering lawsuit it is pursuing in North Carolina.

Opponents of the citizenship question have long argued that it will suppress participation in the Census for households with noncitizens, leading to an undercount of immigrants and communities of color. The administration argued that it sought the addition of the question to better enforce part of the Voting Rights Act.

When prominent Republican strategist Thomas Hofeller died last August, his hard drive files indicate that he played a significant role in orchestrating the addition of the question to the Decennial Census to create, in his words, a "structural electoral advantage for Republicans and non-Hispanic whites." Moreover, the files reveal that the Trump Administration purposely obscured Hofeller's participation in court proceedings challenging the addition of the question.

Why the Question Matters

Results of the Decennial Census are used to determine how many seats each state receives in the House of Representatives and to distribute federal funds to local communities. Any effort to discourage minority participation in the Census would ultimately benefit White Republicans, giving them a stronghold on the electoral vote and underfunding local communities where those dollars are especially needed.

Through gerrymandering, voter suppression and now this attempt to suppress minority participation in the Census, Republicans have shown consistently that they will stop at nothing to maintain and strengthen their political advantage in an America that is expected to have a majority minority population by 2045. It's all a part of a calculated effort to strengthen the GOP's political power while weakening that of minority communities, which typically support Democratic candidates.

Power Concedes Nothing Without Struggle

If stacking the deck were a competitive sport, Republicans would surely take the gold based upon their history of underhanded and blatantly illegal tactics.

The late Republican Strategist Hofeller concluded that "adding a citizenship question to the 2020 Census would clearly be a disadvantage to Democrats" and benefit White Republicans in redistricting. Hofeller then pushed the idea with the Trump Administration in 2017, according to the Washington Post. The evidence of Hofeller's involvement contradicts the sworn testimony of Trump administration officials, including Commerce Secretary Wilbur Ross, whose agency is responsible for the Census.

At this writing, it's not known whether the new revelations detailing Hofeller's involvement will impact the Supreme Court's ruling, but lawyers for the plaintiffs challenging the addition of the question wrote U.S. District Judge Jesse Furman about the issue. Furman was one of the federal judges who ruled against the addition of the citizenship question to the Census earlier this year.

As we await the outcome, we've been granted another reminder that power concedes nothing without struggle. It's the duty of every American citizen to support a truly representative democracy and to fight against these dirty, underhanded tactics to disenfranchise voters and rig the electoral system in favor of one political party.

Toddler Takes a Doll; Cops Draw Their Guns

By Stacy Fitzgerald
July 1, 2019

A now viral video of Phoenix Police threats against an engaged African American couple whose four-year-old daughter took a doll from a dollar store is causing outrage at the treatment of black citizens at the hands of law enforcement.

While conflicting details of the incident are coming from the couple and the police, the video prompted Phoenix Mayor Kate Gallego to issue a statement of apology to the couple, stating that she was "sick" at the inappropriate and unprofessional actions of the officers who pulled the couple over with guns drawn and shouted expletives following a call from an employee at a local Family Dollar store about a stolen doll.

In late May, an employee of a local Family Dollar store called the Phoenix police to report a possible shoplifting case. Following receipt of the description of the vehicle, police identified the car carrying Ames, Harper and their four-year-old and one-year-old daughters. The cops followed it without sirens into the parking lot of a nearby apartment complex, where the couple was to have dropped off their kids at the babysitter.

The police approached the vehicle with guns drawn.

One of the two officers shouted expletives telling Mr. Ames to get his hands up. That officer can be heard saying that he's going to "put a cap" in Mr. Ames's head. As he exited the car, the officer pressed him against the pavement, handcuffed him then pushed him against the police vehicle.

The second officer pointed his firearm toward the car as the couple's four-year-old daughter climbed out from the back seat, followed by Ms. Harper, who was carrying the one-year-old.

As he ordered Ms. Harper to put the child down, she released her daughter and the officer grabbed her arm, handcuffed her and began to question the couple over the doll and a package of underwear that also was reportedly stolen.

The couple allegedly acknowledged that they realized their four-year-old had taken the doll, only after they got back to the car and were eventually released by the officers without charges being filed. However, the damage had been done and the incident was filmed by two bystanders.

An Excessive Response, A Prompt Lawsuit

Following the release of that video, the Phoenix Police Chief apologized to the couple, announced that its Professional Standards Bureau was reviewing the incident and that the officers had been placed on leave while the investigation proceeds.

Meanwhile, the couple has filed a $10 million lawsuit citing the violation of their civil rights.

This is only the latest in a disturbing increase in excessive police encounters with unarmed black citizens. All too often, unarmed blacks are subject to harassment, intimidation, excessive force and even shot at the hands of police officers over relatively minor offenses.

Thankfully, that didn't happen in this case, but why was such force used in response to a toddler taking a doll valued at less than $10 from a retail store? Would the police response have been the same if a white child had taken the doll?

Police Officers Must Do Better

Most parents can recall an incident where they discovered their own child had left a store with an item that they didn't notice and, therefore, hadn't paid for. It can happen quickly and easily when fast-moving toddlers are afoot.

It's innocent and easy enough to fix, which is why the overzealous and egregiously violent and profane response from the officers is so riling. A stolen doll should not compel the same response as an armed bank robbery, and police must do better in checking their racial bias, practicing sound judgement and treating every citizen equally when presented with such calls.

No one should have to fear for their life over a child's toy.

The Arbiters of Race

By Stacy Fitzgerald
July 1, 2019
Who gets to decide Kamala Harris's Race?

Following what many characterized as an impressive debate performance last week, Sen. Kamala Harris came under attack this weekend on Twitter by critics who refute her claim of being a Black American.

Harris, who was born in Oakland, CA to a Jamaican father and an Indian mother, is no doubt a natural born American citizen, but critics argued, she is not black. If this line of attack seems familiar, it is.

It's like the "birther" claims leveled at President Barack Obama before and after becoming a U.S. president. In each case, the attacks are wrong and rooted in racist ideology that shouldn't be tolerated in America.
Seeking to Divide and Delegitimize
We've seen this kind of attack on bi-racial and multiracial candidates before. Often, they're a deliberate, thinly disguised attempt from White Evangelicals on the right to delegitimize and divide. Obama wasn't black because he was born to a white mother (despite having a Black father).

This weekend, the attack was amplified by Donald Trump, Jr., who retweeted and then deleted a tweet attempting to stir this pot.

Harris isn't Black (or American), because she was born to an Indian mother and a Jamaican father (although, again, she was born in the United States – a natural citizen). But when it comes to race and ethnicity, who gets to be the ultimate arbiter?

What Makes One Black?

America historically has defined any person with any known Black African ancestry as Black. In fact, in the Jim Crow South it became known as the "one-drop" rule, meaning that a single drop of "black blood" make's a person Black.

By virtue of the fact that her father is a Jamaican of African Ancestry, Harris meets the standard definition of Black in America. Moreover, Harris herself identifies as a Black American, not as an Indian American nor as a Jamaican American.

Generally, being a person of part African descent born in America makes you a Black American. Except, of course when there is a reason for the opposition to dispute your race, like a hotly contested political campaign. In that case, it's almost obligatory for the right to question the "legitimacy" of the Black candidate for any reason, be it race, nationality or citizenship or even religion.

If you can't attack a Black person's qualification, the next best option is to attack their heritage, as was done with Obama.
An All Too Familiar Tactic Met with Sharp Push Back
White Americans can't have it both ways.

If their historical definition of Black, means a person who has any African ancestry, then Kamala Harris meets that threshold. You can't then subsequently argue that she isn't Black or "black enough" because she has an Indian mother and a Jamaican father —especially when that Jamaican father is of African ancestry. Having lighter skin does not negate her African lineage either.

How is it that Harris can have African ancestry, self-identify as Black and yet still have her racial identity questioned

Such attacks on Harris' race are another way that predominantly white, right wing operatives particularly seek to divide and delegitimize qualified candidates of color, pointing to their biracial or multiracial background or "otherness" as a sign of their supposed inferiority.

Thankfully, Democratic politicians, including former Vice President Joe Biden, whom Harris called out last week on his anti-busing stance decades ago, rallied to Harris's defense, sharply criticizing the birther claims for what they are: racist attempts to smear Harris and her racial identity.

It's predictable that these attacks will continue. Let's just hope that we also see a continued groundswell of opposition against the racism that fuels them in the first place.

Black Women Voters: Fired Up, Ready to Go

By Stacy Fitzgerald

October 9, 2019

In the run up to the 2020 presidential election there's an exceptionally engaged, inspired and active political voting bloc that most experts predict will be a central force in 2020: black women voters. We are fired up and ready to go.

So, politicians, pollsters and others had better start paying attention.

Highly Engaged, Much at Stake

Experts peg the percentage of eligible black women voters who cast ballots in the 2018 mid-term elections at 55 percent – a full six percentage points higher than other voters and just slightly lower than the all-time high of 58 percent participation for all voters in 2008, according to FairVote.org.

While voter participation in the mid-terms is typically lower, black female voter participation was exceptionally high, in fact rivaling the show black women delivered in the 2008 presidential election. While history would suggest a decline in participation, black women are the most politically engaged voting bloc and will likely be a major force in the 2020 presidential election.

That should have Republicans candidates in particular on guard, since historically, black women voters vote overwhelmingly for Democrats (95 percent of black women voted for Clinton in the 2016 presidential election). That said, Democratic candidates also need to get the memo: they must verbalize their political positions and articulate ideas on policy issues that are critically important to us.

Action, Activism and Audacity

One might ask why black women are so politically engaged even ahead of the next presidential election.

In short, it's because the issues that are so critical to securing better futures for ourselves and our families aren't being addressed. And that inaction has spawned a new level of action, activism and audacity among the black female voting bloc and prompted many black women to run for political office themselves.

Bolstered by the presence of Sen. Kamala Harris as a presidential candidate and the high-profile black female congresswomen who mounted successful campaigns for office, including Reps. Ayanna Pressley (D-MA) and Ilhan Omar (D-MN), we're energized and ready to make a political impact when it comes to addressing the issues most important to us: education, social justice, income inequality and health care disparities for women of color.

Addressing the Issues at Hand

Despite the progress black women have made collectively over the past few decades in education, non-white school districts today get $23 billion less in funding annually when compared to school districts in predominately white neighborhoods, a statistic that directly impacts our children's' futures.

Moreover, black men and boys face a 1 in 1,000 chance of being killed by the police, while white men and boys face odds of 39 in 100,000.

Income inequality has staggering impact on black women, leading to the establishment of Black Women's Equal Pay Day, marked this year on August 22 and designated to call attention to the fact that black women earn just $0.61 per $1.00 paid to white non-Hispanic men. Why August 22? That is the approximate day that black women must work into the new year to make what a non-Hispanic white man earned at the end of the previous year.

Relative to healthcare, black women again face alarming disparities in maternal health care and are four times more likely to face pregnancy-related death than white women, an unconscionable and unacceptable statistic among developed nations.

These and other issues are driving a new level of activism and political engagement among black women and that's why experts predict we will continue to be a force headed into the 2020 presidential election. And politicians in both parties must speak to the issues that directly and disproportionately impact us if they are to earn our votes.

Black Deaths, Blue Lives & White Indifference

By Stacy Fitzgerald

October 13, 2019

No person should have to die in their own home minding their own business at the hands of the police, yet for the second time this year in Texas, an unarmed black person has been killed in their own home, minding their own business, by a white police officer.

This time, it was 28-year-old Atatiana Jefferson of Fort Worth. Her neighbor called the police for a welfare check in the early morning hours of Saturday, October 12 when he noticed that her front door was open.

According to Fort Worth police, officers arrived and also found the door open and the lights on but did not see anyone inside. One officer went to the back yard and saw a figure through a window and "perceived a threat," called out "put your hands up, show me your hands," then fired a shot less than a second later. In less than a second, Atatiana Jefferson was lying dead in her own home.

That is frightening, maddening and alarming. I'm tired. I'm angry and I'm scared.

Transparency and Relevant Information

Fort Worth police released heavily edited body cam footage of the incident it said in an effort to provide "transparency and relevant information." But by virtue of the fact that it was edited in the first place, the video is far less transparent than it could be, since the editing process alone would exclude information.

That is unacceptable and every single second of that film is relevant to determining why an unarmed black woman was perceived as such a threat in her own home that she was shot dead in less than one second.

At this stage, there's no indication that the officers present ever identified themselves and Atatiana Jefferson certainly had no opportunity to identify herself in such a short period of time, nor was she asked to. She was commanded only to put her hands up and then was shot less than a second later.

It's ironic that a neighbor called the police to assure her welfare and instead, they caused her death in her own home. When has that ever happened before? Why has it happened for the second time to a black person at home in Texas?

Is There Any Hope?

To be a black person in America is to live daily with the knowledge that your skin color will be automatically perceived as a threat to many white people, and it seems, particularly police officers. In fact, getting shot by the police is the leading cause of death for black men and boys in America and they are 2.5 times more likely to be killed in an encounter with police than are white men and boys. This is not hyperbole, but a fact.

At the same time, the last several years have seen an alarming rise in the death of unarmed black people during police encounters. This second Texas police killing of an unarmed black person in their home is the trauma-inducing, fear-evoking nightmare scenario that is feeding the post-traumatic stress disorder of the African American community as a whole.

It's not paranoia, but reality that there's no place safe in this country for black people if they are not safe in their own home. Minding their own business.

Respect Blue Lives, Yes. But when will Blue Lives respect black people? How long will white people remain indifferent to the killing of unarmed black people, especially in their homes?

There's no single societal problem that is more damaging psychologically to blacks than racial injustice at the hands of police.

It has destroyed all semblance of trust between law enforcement and the community, is increasingly triggering trauma in black Americans and engenders a belief in blacks that nothing will change, especially because white Americans remain indifferent.

There's no outrage among white America. There's no justice.

Is there any hope?

Making Lending Discrimination Great Again

By Stacy Fitzgerald
February 6, 2020
Barely a week after the celebration of Dr. Martin Luther King's birthday, the Trump Administration announced it intends to reverse the Obama administration's rules that target racial discrimination in home lending.

The administration also is targeting a federal law that supports the desegregation of American neighborhoods, according to published reports. These moves could undo decades of progress for people of color in home ownership and undercut a 50-year-old law, the Fair Housing Act.

While the Trump administration frequently touts developments that have benefitted minorities, such as criminal justice reform and job creation, this inextricable move toward discriminatory housing lending and practices is overtly racist and bizarre. It should not go unnoticed that Housing and Urban Development (HUD) Secretary Ben Carson, Trump's sole African American cabinet member, had no comment on the proposals, which have been excoriated by civil rights and housing experts as "reckless and wrong."

Reversing Decades of Progress
HUD Secretary Ben Carson has been a vocal critic of federal desegregation of neighborhoods, referring to it as a "failed socialist experiment." He has also stated that requirements that banks collect data to better track patterns of neighborhood development and segregation to obtain federal housing funds have "suffocated investment in some of the poorest, most distressed neighborhoods that needed the investment the most."

His argument is that data collection, something that banks routinely do anyway, is hampering investment in minority neighborhoods.

Carson's cognitive dissonance is profoundly bewildering on these issues. As a black man, advocating for policies that will reverse decades of progress for African Americans in housing is deeply disturbing and beyond spiteful.

Homeownership is the key to building wealth in America. Since the passage of the Fair Housing Act to fight lending discrimination some 50 years ago, policies like redlining have declined significantly, helping to boost the African-American Homeownership rate to 44 percent as of the fourth quarter of 2019 – the highest level on record since 2012, according to the U.S. Census Bureau's Housing and Vacancy Report.

Yet despite the progress in African American home ownership, racial disparity in mortgage lending persists, according to a study by Northwestern University, which found that black homebuyers are more often denied mortgage applications and pay high loan costs than white buyers, even with similar incomes and credit.

Perhaps Prevention of Wealth is the Goal

It's hard to view the administration's intent to roll back regulations that prohibit discrimination as anything but a carefully calculated move to prevent black wealth accumulation. With documented evidence that black homebuyers continue to be rejected for mortgage loans more frequently than white buyers, why would any measure that would ultimately give license to banks to increase discriminatory practices make sense otherwise?

For an administration that constantly claims progress that supposedly benefit black Americans, like criminal justice reform and job creation, an open attempt to increase lending discrimination is in direct opposition to progress the administration claims to seek for African Americans. It's regression on a large scale. It's spiteful, racist and wrong.

It's upsetting the administration's only African American cabinet member, Ben Carson, is a proponent of policies that would damage all Blacks, including ostensibly, members of his family.

These are indeed strange, unsettling and dark days for all Americans, but especially for people of color.

Deadly Exercise: Jogging While Black

May 12, 2020

By Stacy Fitzgerald

Add yet another non-criminal offense to the list of things that black men can be killed for in America: jogging.

Though it happened in February, video surfaced just this week of the killing of Ahmaud Arbery a 25-year-old black man who was jogging a few miles from his neighborhood in Brunswick, Georgia on February 23.

More than two months after the killing, Georgia officials finally arrested and charged the killers, Gregory McMichael and his son Travis.

Apparently, authorities were shamed into action by the national outrage sparked by the video, shot by a bystander who didn't know Arbery or the men who killed him.

"I will be looking into how the Ahmaud Arbery case was handled from the outset," Georgia Attorney General Chris Carr said in a statement to The Washington Post, reported May 9, "The family, the community, and the state of Georgia deserve answers. We need to know exactly what happened, and we will be working tirelessly with the Georgia Bureau of Investigation, the Brunswick community and others to find those answers."

Glynn County commissioner Peter Murphy said he also plans to call for an investigation into the prosecutors and police agencies that investigated Arbery's shooting over the past two months, The Post reported.

Short and shocking, the video appears to show Arbery running at a jogger's pace as he approaches a pickup truck parked in the street. There are two white men -- one outside in the street with a shotgun and the other standing in the truck's flatbed. Armed with the shotgun is 34-year-old Travis McMichael and in the flatbed is his father, 64-year-old Gregory McMichael.

As Arbery approaches the truck, he jogs around it and just as he clears the truck he is confronted by Travis McMichael and they wrestle with the shotgun. Shots are fired and Arbery tries to run away but is clearly wounded and his knees buckle as he collapses to the ground. This is where the video ends.

The McMichaels' Story
Travis and Gregory McMichael admitted they chased down Arbery believing he was responsible for a spate of neighborhood burglaries and they intended to make a citizen's arrest, permitted under Georgia law.

They did not call the police. When the younger McMichael confronted Arbery, a struggle ensued and Arbery was shot and killed. Travis McMichaels said Ahmaud Arbery attacked him and he defended himself. He also told investigators that he rolled Ahmaud Arbery's body over to view it after he had fallen.

Travis' father, Gregory McMichael, is a former investigator for the local District Attorney's (DA) office. When the video was presented to the local DA of the shooting, he punted the case to another local jurisdiction because he considered it a conflict of interest. That jurisdiction also transferred the case to a third jurisdiction for Grand Jury consideration.

Initially, it was expected the case would not be considered until mid-June due to the COVID-19 pandemic. However, the announcement by a Georgia prosecutor that the case would be presented to a grand jury for consideration of murder charges against the two men came Tuesday. That was the day the video surfaced, sparking outrage and reigniting America's debate about whether black lives matter. Two days later, the two men were arrested.

Ahmaud Aubrey Was Unarmed

Unarmed., Aubrey was jogging just a few miles from his home and the McMichaels didn't call the police to confront the person they thought was a suspect. They simply took matters into their own hands, went out armed and killed a black man on suspicion that he might have been a burglar.

If this story sounds familiar, it's because it happens all too often in America. An unarmed black man is killed by a white person because he is perceived as a threat. No weapon. Making no threat. And in this case, no evidence of any stolen items from the alleged burglaries. Nothing. Just the assailant's perception that the black man was a threat.

Rights Stolen from Black Men

What's agonizing and infuriating in this case and so many others is that unarmed black men are killed by white men because they are perceived as being a threat, whether they know the killer or not. Often, the killer's sole defense is that they felt threatened. Even if there is no weapon.

Ahmaud Arbery likely felt threatened. Who wouldn't be if accosted by an unknown assailant brandishing a shotgun? He struggled to save his life with the only weapon he had, his hands. He was shot and killed. For what reason? He was black.

Are Armed Whites Less Threatening Than Unarmed Blacks? Juxtapose this case with the current protests regarding stay at home orders. It's ironic that today, protests resulting from those orders are revealing a stark racial contrast in treatment of citizens in America.

As mass demonstrations at state capitals by white, armed protesters standing before law enforcement officers are televised, black Americans are noting the difference. The protesters are demanding their freedom to move about and that businesses be opened during the pandemic. Despite being armed, they stand in the face of law enforcement officers often with their teeth bared and their weapons visible, screaming for their "freedom".

These armed, angry protesters always walk away unharmed. They may be peacefully protesting, but the mere presence of weapons poses a threat to others and to law enforcement.

Conversely, an unarmed black man out for a jog near his neighborhood and minding his own businesses winds up dead because he was merely suspected of having committed some past crime, chased down like an animal by vigilantes, shot and killed.

There's no clearer demonstration than this that black men – black people in America – armed or unarmed – don't have the same rights and privileges as white people -- despite the Constitution's assertion that all men are created equal. But equality doesn't extend to black people. Especially black men.

So, blacks are left to scream in rage at funerals for unarmed black men killed unjustly every year by white assailants.

When will it end?

Cries for racial justice may go unanswered, but we black Americans will never stop demanding it -- for Ahmaud Arbery and every other black man killed unjustly.

Today, Friday May 8 would have been Ahmaud Arbery's 26th birthday. Supporters of Arbery are asking that people jog 2.23 miles, representing the date of his death to mark the occasion.

Running in Your Shoes

May 15, 2020
By Bob Gatty

I am a 77-year-old white man, and unlike many of my friends, I need not be afraid to jog down the street for fear some hate-filled redneck will take a shot at me -- unless I'm wearing one of my anti-Trump T-shirts, that is.

While I won't like it if a blue flashing light pulls up behind me with siren burping a couple of times, I don't need to be afraid that a racist cop will immediately consider me a threat as he walks towards my car, resting his hand on the unstrapped gun at his side. Because I am not black.

I've never had to confront concerns like that, and it's hard for me to fathom running in the shoes of those who face that every day, and who must prepare their kids--especially little black boys--on how to respond in such circumstances.

I've never been a black man walking down the street with a friend, only to see a white woman walking towards me cross the street because she is afraid.

The other evening, a young black man, Jaime Harrison, who has a good chance to unseat Trump's pal Sen. Lindsey Graham (R-SC), appeared on an online forum in which I participated that was sponsored by the Horry County, SC, Democratic Party and the Young Democrats of Horry County.

He told a story about how, when he was in his early 20s and had just purchased a new car after graduating from Yale University, he was pulled over by a white trooper because his car had struck something in the road and it apparently flipped up and smacked into the patrol car following him.

The incident ended peacefully, although Harrison was repeatedly grilled regarding what he might have in his vehicle, where he was going, etc. But he felt like the cop was attempting to intimidate, even threaten him, simply because he is black.

Living While Black

Harrison pointed out that while his incident ended without difficulty, many, many other similar incidents, mostly unreported, all across the nation, do not. And, of course, the killing of the young black jogger, Ahmaud Arbery, in Georgia by two white vigilantes is a tragic example of a black man losing his life because of the color of his skin.

But while living while black has been Harrison's life experience, he insists that he requires himself to be positive, to look for good, to not be bitter. Otherwise, he says, it would simply be too depressing.

How he does that, I do not know.

But those life experiences, combined with a childhood of poverty and then remarkable educational and professional success, are what he intends to take to the Senate should he succeed in his uphill battle to defeat Trump's kiss-up pal, Sen. Graham.

During the online candidates' forum, Harrison called on people of all races to join together to overcome bigotry.

A Call for Unity

"We all have to stand up," he said. "If you are a good person in this country and you see things that are not right, it is incumbent that you stand up and say enough is enough. As a black person, I should not have to carry all of that weight. Not in America. We shouldn't have to do it. It's not fair for us to do that because we already carry the weight of being black each and every day."

That, alone, was a powerful statement. Then, he added:

"It's time for us to unify as a people and say enough is enough. We have to stop this. We have to stop the target on black men. We have to stop the target on black women. We have to start treating each other the way we want people to treat us, because right now I can tell you that people in the African American community are not being treated (fairly)."

This is a man I admire.

Overcoming abject poverty to graduate from Yale University and Georgetown Law School, Harrison returned to Orangeburg, SC, to teach at his old high school, then served as a top aide to legendary South Carolina Rep. James Clyburn, where he was able to help shepherd key legislation through Congress, including the last federal minimum wage increase.

Now, he wants to bring to the Senate that background, combined with the experience of growing up in a family that had to choose between paying the electric bill and putting food on the table. He wants to be a voice for all people, not just the wealthy and the well-connected.

"How many people in the Senate do you think were ever on food stamps?" he asked.

No doubt, the answer is zero. But they need that perspective in the Senate, they surely do.

I don't think I could ever run in Jaime Harrison's shoes and end up the way he has. I just don't.

But I can tell you this. We need more people in our leadership positions like him today, people whose priorities are helping bring safety and prosperity to everyone regardless of ethnicity or social standing, not just a chosen few. People who have experienced the lows, as well as the highs; who have turned challenges into opportunities, and who are ready to use that experience, that perspective, for the good of all mankind.

Minneapolis Burning: Cry of the Unheard

May 30, 2020

By Stacy Fitzgerald

While a global pandemic can shut down sporting events, concerts, public and private schools and other group gatherings, apparently, even a pandemic can't stop some police officers from murdering unarmed black men.

George Floyd was detained and arrested on Monday night by police on suspicion of passing a counterfeit bill. He was unarmed and four police officers responded to the incident, captured by a teenage girl on video (above) that by now, much of the world has seen. The detainment of this unarmed black man led to murder.

In fact, the United Nations on May 29 called for a halt to police killings of unarmed black men. How precipitous our fall. Just 11 years after U.S. President Barack Obama won the Nobel Peace prize, for "extraordinary efforts to strengthen international diplomacy and cooperation between people," the United Nations, an international body, calls for massive reform in U.S. police practices because of the continued killing of unarmed black men in America.

Outrage at the barbaric killing of George Floyd by Minneapolis Police Officer Derek Chauvin (and the three other officers present at the scene) has led to riots, looting, arrests and arson attacks in the city of Minneapolis. The protests spread to a dozen cities nationwide. It was the Reverend Martin Luther King himself who said "a riot is the language of the unheard."

Can You Hear Us Now?

We can collectively condemn the rioters, the arsons and the looting that has taken place and, frankly, many of us will. But simply condemning these acts ignores this basic truth: those things are all symptomatic of the anger, frustration and pain that most black Americans feel in the wake of yet another police killing of an unarmed black man: will it ever end?

Black Americans have mounted and supported peaceful protests, like Colin Kaepernick's kneeling during the National Anthem. We have signed petitions and formed organizations like Black Lives Matter.

We've even run for Congress hoping to be part of the solution, rather than sitting on the sidelines, like Rep. Ayanna Pressley (D-MA), the only child of a single mother and a father who was in and out of the criminal justice system. We've engaged in ways that are visible, peaceful, meaningful and yes, violent.

But it seems little gets the attention of the American Public at large (the white American public) unless there's an economic impact.

Trump's Gasoline on the Flames

President Trump on Friday tweeted (in part) "when the looting starts, the shooting starts," a phrase that was used historically by Miami's Police Chief Walter Headley, and by presidential candidate and segregationist George Wallace in 1967 and 1968, respectively, in response to civil unrest by blacks demanding civil rights. Inevitably, when protests lead to riots and looting, the "crack down" that ensues is all the more forceful because property and economic loss are at the forefront of the law enforcement response.

But what about black human lives?

If we are indeed in the land of the free and the home of the brave, and if we are all as the Constitution declares "created equal" and endowed with the unalienable rights of life, liberty and the pursuit of happiness, why then is it that 155 years after the Emancipation Proclamation was signed, ending slavery, does it still feel like black Americans remain in bondage? Denied basic dignity, human rights, ignored when pleading for air to breathe during an arrest, and asphyxiated to death in broad daylight on a public street before witnesses and as three other police officers look on.

Black Americans have the right to be outraged by that. All Americans have the right to be outraged. The "good white people" of America also must be enraged. But are they? You know, the ones who are the first to say "but I'm not racist." What are they doing? Are they speaking up? Are they speaking out?

If an animal were treated the way the police treated George Floyd, there would likely have been immediate outcry and demands for a swift arrest.

Instead, it took four days for Officer Derek Chauvin to be arrested for the murder of George Floyd. We can assume that after the arrest, at some point, there will be a public trial and a verdict.

But we likely already know the outcome: A slap on the wrist, if that, or a complete exoneration for what is undeniably an execution. Not guilty will likely be the verdict. We've seen this play out before.

And that is why Minneapolis is burning.

Black Americans are sick and tired of being sick and tired. Tired of being exterminated and denied basic human rights.

Something has to change.

The #BunkerBoyBully & the Bible

June 2, 2020

By Bob Gatty

It now is abundantly clear that we have a President who is willing to hurt, terrify, perhaps even kill his country's own people to feed his own ego and satisfy his political ends. That was proven beyond a shadow of a doubt with yesterday's #BiblePhotoOp by the #BunkerBoyBully.

Determined to prove his toughness after his security people hustled him to a basement bunker at the White House Sunday because of protestors outside the heavily guarded White House fence, Trump decided to take a little stroll to the historic St. John's Episcopal Church across the street.

And, for good measure, he would hold up a Bible to prove to his religious-right faithful what a devout, God-fearing Christian he really is.

Only one problem with that plan, though. There were several hundred demonstrators in the way, protesting the white cop killing of black George Floyd in Minneapolis.

But true to Trump, his lapdog attorney general, William P. Barr, ordered the authorities to do whatever it would take to get rid of those people. So, they fired flash-bang shells, tear gas and rubber bullets into the crowd, to clear a path for his highness to proceed.

Little did he care that he was attacking Americans, the people he has sworn to protect. No. It was all about Trump. It was all about proving he is in charge, and not a weak sissy like those governors whom he challenged to get tough with the demonstrators, and to use force, if needed.

"Get tough Democrat Mayors and Governors...The World is watching and laughing at you and Sleepy Joe," tweeted Trump. And then, in a phone call, he belittled them even more.

Also in play for Trump, no doubt, was his falling poll numbers against former Vice President Joe Biden, who currently has a 10-point lead over the exalted one.

The headlines had to drive him crazy.

The Hill: Trump lags in polls as crises press

USA Today: Biden lead over Trump jumps 8 points in ABC News/Washington Post poll

So, besides verbally attacking and ridiculing Biden on Twitter, he had to demonstrate to his blindly loyal base that he's the tough guy in town. And so, he had his National Guard put on gas masks and fire rubber bullets at protestors, release tear gas, and set off flash-bang shells in the midst of the crowd.

His action was condemned by the Right Rev. Mariann Budde, bishop of the Episcopal Diocese of Washington, who said she learned of the president's visit by watching it on the news.

"I am outraged," she said. "I am the bishop of the Episcopal Diocese of Washington and was not given even a courtesy call that they would be clearing with tear gas so they could use one of our churches as a prop, holding a Bible, one that declares that God is love and when everything he has said and done is to inflame violence."

What did Trump really prove?

He proved that he is an insecure, despicable coward whose only interest is himself and his own self-preservation.

But his bullying actions are resulting in another poll that no doubt will anger him even further.

A new Morning Consult poll conducted Sunday and Monday revealed that Biden leads Trump 47 percent to 30 percent on addressing racial inequalities and 44 percent to 32 percent on police reform.

In the poll, 32 percent gave Trump positive marks on how he's addressed the demonstrations, and 57 percent supported those demonstrations, compared with 28 percent who back coronavirus-related protests to open the country.

Meanwhile, Trump has been tweeting, "November 3," to remind voters of the day he will be seeking re-election.

As if we needed to be reminded that is the day we can get rid of this tyrant for good.

◆ ◆ ◆

Struggling for Words

June 4, 2020
By Bob Gatty

Sen. Lisa Murkowski (R-Alaska) says she is "struggling" to find the right words about Donald Trump's presidency. Is this an indication that at least some Republicans are experiencing pangs of conscience, having had enough of this would be dictator who is willing to use military force against our own citizens?

Murkowski's remarks were reported today after former defense secretary Jim Mattis said in a statement published by the Atlantic that Trump is trying to deliberately divide Americans.

"I have watched this week's unfolding events, angry and appalled," Mattis wrote. "The words 'Equal Justice Under Law' are carved in the pediment of the United States Supreme Court. This is precisely what protesters are rightly demanding. It is a wholesome and unifying demand—one that all of us should be able to get behind. We must not be distracted by a small number of lawbreakers. The protests are defined by tens of thousands of people of conscience who are insisting that we live up to our values—our values as people and our values as a nation." He goes on, "We must reject and hold accountable those in office who would make a mockery of our Constitution."

If Murkowski is having difficulty finding the right words, Mattis, a retired Marine general with the call sign, "chaos," is not.

"Donald Trump is the first president in my lifetime who does not try to unite the American people—does not even pretend to try. Instead, he tries to divide us," Mattis continued. "We are witnessing the consequences of three years of this deliberate effort. We are witnessing the consequences of three years without mature leadership. We can unite without him, drawing on the strengths inherent in our civil society. This will not be easy, as the past few days have shown, but we owe it to our fellow citizens; to past generations that bled to defend our promise; and to our children."

Trump, of course, responded via Twitter by saying "The only thing Barack Obama & I have in common is that we both had the honor of firing Jim Mattis, the world's most overrated General. I asked for his letter of resignation, & felt great about it."

Well, not so fast.

President Trump's former chief of staff, John F. Kelly, also a retired Marine Corps general, defended Mattis, who resigned in 2018 in disagreement with Trump's decision to pull U.S. forces out of Syria. Kelly said Mattis was not fired by Trump.

"The president did not fire him. He did not ask for his resignation," Kelly said in an interview with The Washington Post. "The president has clearly forgotten how it actually happened or is confused. The president tweeted a very positive tweet about Jim until he started to see on Fox News their interpretation of his letter. Then he got nasty. Jim Mattis is an honorable man."

But apparently, Gen. Mattis' words are having an impact.

Said Murkowski, "When I saw Gen. Mattis' comments yesterday I felt like perhaps we are getting to a point where we can be more honest with the concerns that we might hold internally and have the courage of our own convictions to speak up. And so, I'm working as one individual to form the right words, knowing that these words really matter so I appreciate General Mattis' comments."

Saying that she is "struggling" over whether she can still support Trump, Murkowski said she has "struggled with it for a long time."

"I think right now, as we are all struggling to find ways to express the words that need to be expressed appropriately, questions about who I'm going to vote for or not going to vote for, I think, are distracting at the moment. I know people might think that's a dodge, but I think there are important conversations that we need to have as an American people among ourselves about where we are right now," she said.

Murkowski, who had called Trump's actions "shameful" during the Senate's impeachment trial, but voted to acquit, was joined by the only Republican senator to vote to convict, Sen. Mitt Romney (R-UT), in supporting Mattis. Romney called him "an American patriot" and "an individual whose judgment I respect," and said the former defense secretary's statement was "stunning and powerful."

But then, there were the lapdog Republicans who still hold the Trump party line, like Sen. Lindsey Graham of South Carolina, who is in a tough race for reelection against Democrat Jaime Harrison, and who appears to have just colored his hair to look suspiciously like Trump's.

"I admire his service to the nation," Graham told Fox News. "But the one thing I would tell General Mattis is that you don't quite understand that from the time President Trump wakes up until he goes to bed there's an effort to destroy his presidency."

That effort, Sen. Graham, is well deserved. His presidency needs to be destroyed.

November 3. Remember that date.

Why is Lynching NOT a Federal Crime?

June 5, 2020

By Stacy Fitzgerald'

It's 2020 and your country, America, is in the throes of civil unrest after witnessing the police kill yet another unarmed black man, asphyxiating him on camera in a video that has resulted in global condemnation.

At the same time, you're a U.S. Senator, charged with advancing legislation for your country that should be uncontentious: an anti-lynching bill, one that makes this heinous act a federal crime.

If you're Kamala Harris (D-CA) or Cory Booker (D-NJ) you work tirelessly to secure the signatures needed to make the bill a law. But if you're Rand Paul (R-KY), you twice try to offer non-relevant amendments to the House-passed legislation trying to kill it, adding insult to grievous injury.

Rand Paul argues that his most recent attempt at amendment is needed because as the proposed legislation currently stands, "any bodily, including a cut, an abrasion, or a bruise, physical pain, illness or other injury to the body" could be called lynching.

This is the latest of similar stall tactics he's pulled to prevent this bill from passing. This goes without saying, but it's unnecessary in an anti-lynching bill to add an amendment that paper cuts, stepping on someone's toes or a slap to the face aren't lynching, but this is Rand Paul's argument.

Thus, defines the malcontent of Rand Paul.

His entire argument is predicated on the fact that this anti-lynching legislation as written could result in convicting a person who had committed a lesser offense of the crime of lynching. In my lifetime, I'm not aware of one person who was charged with lynching who'd actually thrown a punch in a bar fight or on a playground.

That's why his argument is nonsensical and insulting. It's also a clear stall tactic. But, the time for stalling over this issue is over.

The Emmett Till Anti-Lynching Act

The Emmett Till Anti-Lynching Act was introduced by Rep. Bobby Rush (D-IL) in January of 2019. Let's set aside for the moment that the U.S. has tried and failed for 120 years to pass federal anti-lynching legislation and cut to the chase: the brutal and barbaric practice of hanging black bodies until their death in the U.S. is well-known, well-documented and indisputably the most horrendous of racial intimidation acts.

And yet…401 years after the arrival of the first enslaved Africans to America, there is no law punishing lynching as a federal crime, which would automatically mean a much harsher sentence. One hundred and fifty-five years after the abolition of slavery there is no federal law, and 66 years after the death of Emmett Till, there is no federal law.

Passing a federal anti-lynching law is not just long overdue but would come at what is the most significant period of racial unrest and tension in the United States since the Civil Rights era. A time of unrest brought about following the killing of an unarmed black by a white police officer, who for eight minutes, blocked the airway of that man with his knee across his throat, cutting off his air.

It is a manner of death similar to lynching, the forced blocking of the airway cutting off breath. And yet, neither of the officers charged with the crime were charged with lynching. Because as gruesome, heinous and barbaric as that act it was, it wasn't lynching.

I don't think anyone other than Rand Paul would be confused by that. Though, I'd argue that Rand Paul isn't confused at all. He just doesn't want the bill to become a law.

While we will never know all the reasons why Rand Paul is single-handedly holding up anti-lynching legislation at a time when the country most needs clear, definitive action at the federal level making lynching (and other hate acts) a federal crime, we do know that adult temper tantrums are antithetical to fully functioning government. But this tantrum isn't just juvenile, but also reckless and callous.

Bruises aren't lynching. Minor cuts aren't lynching. An anti-lynching bill needn't spell this out. As a medical doctor, Rand Paul knows this, but he simply doesn't care. It's just a stalling tactic to delay legislation that he simply doesn't want to pass.

And that's the real crime.

Trump: Despicable You

June 6, 2020
By Bob Gatty
Donald Trump, you are despicable. How dare you say George Floyd, whose killing by a white police officer has left a six year-old girl fatherless, is having a "great day" in the hereafter because the unemployment rate announced Friday was "only" 13.3 percent?

And, if you bothered to look, the unemployment rate among blacks is 16.8 percent, the highest in a decade.

How dare you presume to believe that Floyd, the victim of brutal knee-to-the-neck asphyxiation by a white police officer now charged with murder, "is looking down right now and saying, 'There's a great thing that's happening for our country?'"

Are you crazy?

George Floyd is dead, and he should not be dead. And his little girl should still have her daddy.

But Floyd's death may have finally awakened white America to understand that things are not OK for our black brothers and sisters. I hope so. He was just the latest black person to be killed simply because of the color of his skin.

The police murder of this young black father has prompted demonstrations worldwide and perhaps even a serious reexamination of policing in our country. That is good. But we need to go further, every one of us, and closely examine our own views and actions regarding race; the way we act, the way we think. The way we look out for our fellow human beings -- or not.

That is the big picture. But right now, we have this despicable president in the White House.

So, I say again to Trump, what gives you the right to say everything is fine? It is not.

How is it fine that your egomaniacal Bible toting photo op resulted in peaceful demonstrators -- American citizens -- being teargassed and shot with rubber bullets so you could have a nice safe stroll to St. John's Episcopal Church for your photo op?

How is it fine that our nation, since your presidency began, has been ripped apart by your vicious and deliberate acts of racism and sexism? How is that fine?

How is it fine that black Americans, especially black men, must fear for their lives every time they see the flashing light from a police vehicle signaling them to pull over? Or that they are automatically a criminal suspect? How is that fine?

The gall of you to tout those unemployment numbers and brag about the recovering stock market and say that's a "tremendous tribute to equality." You don't know the first thing about equality, nor do you care.

And then, you bragged in your favorite third person when patting yourself on the back, "Nobody's ever done for the black community what President Trump has done."

What a crock. How disgusting. How despicable.

And, oh, by the way, those unemployment numbers that you bragged about? They weren't even real. A major error resulted in the rate being listed at 13.3 percent, when it should have been three points higher.

So, stop your bragging. Stop presuming to speak for the dead, especially someone whose death your own racist actions may well have encouraged.

Just shut up, despicable you.

November 3.

Crossing the Thin Blue Line

June 8, 2020

By C J Waldron

We've all seen them. Flags with a blue line meant to show support for law enforcement. But what happens when the line is crossed? What happens when members of law enforcement break the law?

As protests continue around the nation, there are still instances of law enforcement crossing that blue line; most notably when protestors were forcibly pushed back and gassed so Donald Trump could have his photo op, that was crossing the blue line.

When police from Buffalo, NY were videoed shoving a 75 year-old man to the ground, then walking past as he lay bleeding, that crossed the blue line. Two officers have been charged with assault, yet members of his unit resigned en masse in support of the charged officers.

When Atlanta police officers used a taser to subdue and drag someone out of their car because officers thought one of them was armed, that crossed the blue line. The victim later said he refused police orders to get out of his car because he feared for his life.

Even as the nation mourns the death of George Floyd, there are still numerous examples of members of law enforcement using excessive force, particularly on minorities. Videos of people being beaten, of injuries caused by "non-lethal weapons" and even a black reporter being arrested as he was reporting live, are all the stark reality that many minorities face when confronted by law enforcement -- whether they have done anything wrong or not.

When Colin Kaepernick took a knee to protest this treatment, he was vilified, and even blackballed by the NFL. Donald Trump referred to Kaepernick and those who supported him as "that son of a bitch...", using the racism of the thin blue line to push his own disgusting beliefs.

Trump targeted Kaepernick on Twitter, pushing the divisive position that kneeling was disrespecting the flag rather than an honest protest of police brutality. This position was, until recently, supported by the NFL, as owners feared they too could be singled out for supporting the players.

And yet, Trump did not issue a single tweet about Derek Chauvin, the former Minneapolis police officer charged now with Second Degree murder in relation to the death of George Floyd.

Similarly, NFL commissioner Roger Goodell finally admitted he was wrong in not supporting players, but he avoided mentioning Kaepernick in his admission. So, while he acknowledged past wrongs, he fails to correct the one major issue, which is why Kaepernick took a knee in the first place.

There are still many issues that need to be addressed in confronting the thin blue line. While this does not represent the entire make-up of the law enforcement community -- in fact, many have been taking a knee along with the protestors -- it is a large enough portion that can infect the total make-up of a police department.

Unfortunately, the lead comes from the top and until there is administration, and a Congress, that supports systematic reform of the police force, there will be more wrongful deaths…and more protests.

Fortunately, Democrats in the House of Representatives today released new legislation, the Justice in Policing Act of 2020, which would ban chokeholds, establish a national database to track police misconduct and prohibit certain no-knock warrants, among other steps. The bill was drafted by members of the Congressional Black Caucus. How will House Republicans and those who control the Senate respond?

Law and Disorder

Meanwhile, Trump has declared himself the president of "law and order." He said during the 2016 campaign, when, at the same time, he was telling his supporters to "knock the crap" out of protestors who were heckling his campaign speech. He also encouraged police not to "be so nice" to suspects who were under arrest, suggesting they should be shoved forcefully into a police car, rather than guided so as not to injure themselves.

And he said it, during a phone call to governors, when he stated they should dominate those protesting the death, at the hands of law enforcement, of George Floyd. He repeated it as, in a further display of his "law and order" attitude, his Attorney General ordered peaceful protestors to be forcibly pushed back so Trump could have a photo op after it was reported that he'd been taken to the White House underground bunker as protestors chanted outside the White House.

Make no mistake, Trump's version of "law and order" has nothing to do with what is good for the country. Like everything else, it's what benefits Trump and, by extension, his base. It's all about appealing to a select group that he hopes will help him maintain his hold on power.

And Yet…

- He refuses to release his tax returns so we can have an accurate picture of his financial holdings.
- He claims mail-in ballots would result in widespread voter fraud, despite zero evidence and the fact he and members of his cabinet have used mail in ballots for years.
- He refuses to acknowledge Congressionally mandated oversight to investigate potentially illegal activities by himself and members of his administration.
- He refuses to divest himself of his business holdings, or put them in a blind trust, but instead violates the Emoluments

Clause if the Constitution by using his multiple properties and charging taxpayers exorbitant prices for this.

- He claims **done" more** for African-Americans despite having rampant unemployment, the Coronavirus death rate being three times as high as that for white Americans and refusing to acknowledge systematic racism among law enforcement .
- He threatened to violate the Insurrection Act and the Posse Comitatus Act by ordering 10,000 US troops deployed on the streets of America in reaction to peaceful protests.

The bottom line is there is no "law and order" in this administration. Instead there is blatant hypocrisy. His claims of being for "law and order" are more akin to an episode of The Three Stooges…except no one is laughing as he repeatedly crosses that thin blue line.

Defund the Police? Not So Fast

June 9, 2020
By C J Waldron

Many of those taking part in the nationwide protests in response to the murder of George Floyd are calling for local officials to defund the police. They see law enforcement as the enemy. They view police as the cause of so many evils that have fallen largely on minorities.

Is this the solution or is it a knee-jerk reaction to a long-standing problem?

Police brutality, particularly against minorities, is nothing new. Singer Marvin Gaye released the protest anthem "What's Going On" in 1971. Racial profiling, Stop and Frisk and redlining have been used for years to target and restrict minority populations.

During the recent protests, when my area was under a curfew, I had a conversation with an African American co-worker. I commented that I was concerned about possibly driving home after the curfew had been enacted. I further added, I wasn't as concerned with myself, and elderly white male, as I was for my African American colleagues. Seeing what happened to a college student in Atlanta, I expressed my concern, to which my co-worker merely shrugged and muttered the non-sequitur, "It is what it is".

While I will never fully comprehend the fear a person of color must feel when approached by a member of law enforcement, I can empathize with the emotional turmoil and yes, resentment, they must be experiencing.

Yet, defunding the police is not the answer. Police serve a vital role in our communities. Their motto, "To Protect and Serve" is one most officers abide by. Without police bringing people to justice, and indeed, serving as a deterrent to wrongdoing, there would be chaos because there would be no one to stop criminals from terrorizing their neighborhoods.

Predictably, lawmakers are seeing this as a polarizing issue. Democrats, while supporting protestors, feel defunding the police is going too far. Many Republicans, led by Donald Trump, are pushing for stricter actions against those who violate curfews that many cities imposed in response to sometimes violent actions by certain protestors.

And while Trump seeks to blame left wing agitators, other evidence points to right wing extremists who seek to create an atmosphere of violence to paint otherwise peaceful protests in a bad light.

Stuck in the middle are members of law enforcement, who are tasked with the duty of enforcing curfews while maintaining public order. Yet, even in the midst of this, there are members of law enforcement, despite being under the watchful eye of multiple cell phone cameras, who have beaten, abused and even assaulted protestors.

But is the answer to defund the police? That would be akin to getting rid of a mole by cutting off your arm.

Instead, Democrats are proposing reform measures that would address the systematic racism that Republicans deny exists, despite overwhelming evidence to the contrary.

Included in this proposal are ending the use of chokeholds to detain a suspect, making lynching a federal crime, creating a national police misconduct registry to prevent police from going from one city or state where their previous acts can be overlooked, mandating racial bias training, requiring officers to have the "duty to intervene" when another officer is viewed as overreacting to a suspect, and limiting the use of military grade weapons by members of local and state law enforcement.

Of course, Republicans have declared this plan dead on arrival in the Senate as Trump claims to champion "law and order" even as his attorney general used tear gas and rubber bullets to push back peaceful protestors so he could have his Bible toting photo op.

The Democratic approach is a measured response to our current crisis. While not a perfect solution, it aims at addressing many of the wrongs Colin Kaepernick sought to address when he took to one knee to draw attention to police brutality.

There needs to be reform in law enforcement. Replacing or defunding existing institutions without a viable alternative is not the answer.

◆◆◆

Hear No Evil, See No Evil

June 10, 2020

By Bob Gatty

President Trump tweeted that it must have been a setup, a hoax when a 75-year-old protester was knocked to the ground by Buffalo police and left with his head bleeding, a claim that sent many of the nation's leading Republicans ducking for cover.

It was just another example of the "Hear No Evil, See No Evil" party that the GOP has become under Trump's presidency, which surely must have been a hoax. It simply couldn't be real, could it?

Well, it is real, just like the death of George Floyd at the hands of a white Minneapolis police officer is real. Just like the tears of his brother, Philonise, were real when he testified today before the House Judiciary Committee and urged lawmakers to "make the necessary changes to make law enforcement the solution and not the problem."

House and Senate Democrats, in the wake of nationwide protests in the wake of Floyd's murder, have unveiled sweeping police reform legislation, and Senate Republicans have a broad outline for their own proposal in an effort led by Sen. Tim Scott, R-SC, the only African American Republican in the Senate and one of only two in the entire Congress.

GOP Senators Silent

Nevertheless, when asked to react to Trump's suggestion that Martin Gugino, who police knocked to the sidewalk in Buffalo, was part of a "set up," several Republican senators dodged the questions or went silent, CNN reported.

Senate Majority Leader Mitch McConnell, who faces a stiff challenge for reelection for his Kentucky Senate seat, refused to say whether Trump's tweet was appropriate. Sen. Kelly Loeffler (R-GA) hustled onto an elevator without responding. Sen. Dan Sullivan of Alaska said he hadn't seen the tweet and that he didn't want to comment as he was heading to a meeting.

"Voters can evaluate that," Republican Sen. Lamar Alexander of Tennessee said, adding: "I'm not going to give a running commentary on the President's tweets."

Sen. Marco Rubio of Florida claimed he didn't see Trump's tweet, but that he didn't know anything about the man who was pushed. "I have no information about that man or who he is," said Rubio.

Why are they ducking for cover? Is it because they don't care about the action that resulted in the man's injury? Or is it because they are simply afraid of crossing Trump?

A Republican strategist quoted anonymously by The Washington Post put it like this: "It's all about operating outside of the tumult of the moment with him but leaving yourself in a position for him to rally for you this fall. Look — no one can afford at this point to get on the wrong side of Trump. But you can kind of play it cool and don't have to comment on everything he does."

So, it's a fine line that GOP candidates must walk. They can't afford to criticize Trump for fear of retribution, but they're afraid his actions and comments will bog down their own chances for reelection and jeopardize the GOP's three seat Senate majority.

A CNN survey released Monday showing Trump at a 14 percentage point deficit to Biden thoroughly angered Trump, who wrote on Twitter that the CNN survey and others were "FAKE based on the incredible enthusiasm we are receiving." He added, "Despite 3 ½ years of phony Witch Hunts, we are winning, and will close it out on November 3rd!"

But that survey compares to a May 25-28 Washington Post-ABC News poll that showed Biden leading Trump 53 percent to 43 percent, a margin of 10 points among registered voters nationally. The two candidates had been in a virtual dead heat two months earlier. So, a lot of ground has been lost since then.

Trump points out that those same polls showed him losing to Hillary Clinton in 2016, and he proved them wrong. He'll do it again, he predicts.

We'll see.

November 3.

The People's House? Not Now

June 14, 2020
by CJ Waldron

Donald Trump has destroyed yet another legacy of President Obama. By erecting barriers, refusing public access and walling himself off from those he is supposed to serve, Trump has completely reversed the People's House image President Obama sought to create.

The White House has a long and storied history. Built by both freed and enslaved African Americans, along with immigrants, it has stood for over the past two centuries as a symbol of American freedom and patriotism. In times of trouble, people would look to the White House for guidance and solace. In times of national tragedy or mourning, the flag atop the White House was lowered to half-staff.

Now, people see the White House, surrounded by barriers, a chain link fence and guarded by armed members of the National Guard who shine bright lights at peaceful protestors to deny them access to the very place every American has the right to visit.

Erected in 1800, burned in 1814 and again in 1929, coincidentally during the onset of the Great Depression, the White House has always been open to the public, even though various sections were closed off as renovations were made.

Receiving a gift of a big block of cheese, Andrew Jackson invited Americans into the White House to partake in this bounty. First Lady Jacqueline Kennedy gave a famous televised tour of the White House, welcoming America into the People's House, many for the first time.

Over the years, the White House has been a popular tourist destination for both Americans and foreign visitors alike. And while only certain sections of the White House are accessible on the official tour, it has always been available to the public, except during times of national emergency, such as World War II and 9/11.

Tours of the White House have always been free but require a three-month advance notice before tickets are given for admission.

In 2009, President Obama named the White House the People's House, culminating in the opening of a new White House Visitor's Center in 2014. The goal was to make the White House as accessible to as many people as possible.

White House tours have been cancelled since March 11th, due to concerns over the coronavirus, despite Trump's claim the pandemic is a Democratic hoax. Now, it has been transformed into an armed fortress in response to protests over the death of George Floyd.

And while it has not moved, the address for the White House has unofficially been renamed 1600 Black Lives Matter Plaza as the mayor of Washington, D. C. had the words "Black Lives Matter" painted on the street leading to the residence.

Will tours resume? No one knows. One thing is for certain. By turning the White House into his personal bunker, Trump has erased another Obama legacy.

It is the People's House no more.

Exploiting the Fear of Black Men

June 17, 2020

by Stacy Fitzgerald

Yesterday, President Trump, flanked by police officers from across the country, signed an executive order aimed primarily at encouraging police departments nationwide to undergo more training and stop using chokeholds as a means of subduing people.

It was an obligatory, though inadequate attempt to address the use of excessive force by police on unarmed citizens in black communities. In ways that were both obvious and infuriating, Trump's executive order/response was just the latest in an attempt to convey concern and commitment to addressing a problem he only exacerbates: fear of black men.

Sight and Symbolism

There were obvious similarities between the slave-patrolling sheriffs of the pre-war South and those law enforcement officers present for the signing of the executive order.

As the gathering of mostly white men, one even clad in a cowboy hat, stood clapping in support of a toothless executive order that does nothing to address a glaring racial disparity in how police approach and apprehend unarmed black people, it was apparent that the "us versus them" mentality that fuels unchecked and unpunished brutality in communities of color will likely continue as it is fueled by Trump himself.

The president has yet to publicly address the disproportionate deaths of unarmed black men at the hands of law enforcement, the lack of punishment for officers who are disciplined or charged for killing black citizens or the reason why nationwide and global protests have erupted: racism. Instead, he's tweeted messages that seek to create fissures in the multiracial, multi-ethnic coalition of protesters by feeding into underlying racial fears of black men.

The Boogey Man is Black

In a tweet this week, Trump asked if anyone thought suburban moms would be eager to defund the police.

Not one to waste an opportunity to reinforce stereotypes, his tweet implies that only white women (suburban women) are concerned about law enforcement while simultaneously stoking fear about the prospect of eliminating the police altogether. After all, if that happens, who will protect suburban (white) moms and their families from the boogey men (black men)?

To be clear, defunding the police does not mean disbanding them.

Most people advocating cuts in police funding want to re-direct money to other services – social services, education/training and mental health, for example – rather than pour massive funds into police departments, especially in black neighborhoods.

Supporting ever-growing police budgets while simultaneously reducing funding for social programs, mental health, training and education not only provides more resources in support of some officers who abuse their powers, but also does nothing to reduce the underlying causes of criminal activity: chronic unemployment, drug use, mental health and lack of education.

Thus, defunding may be an option to reduce abuse and fix the societal ills of black communities.

His Bet on Black Fear

Trump knows that reinforcing racial stereotypes rooted in white fear of black men works to his advantage as the self-labeled "law and order" president. If he can give lip service to quelling the racial unrest and concern about police killings of unarmed black people while simultaneously embracing white supremacist law enforcement tactics and optics, then he's achieved his goal of upholding the status quo while playing the part of a concerned leader.

And if he can do it as the cameras click at a largely ceremonial, yet obviously racially loaded photo opportunity, all the better.

After all, Trump's end game is to stoke racial fear and use it as a tool to win re-election. That's his only end game here. And you can bet he'll continue to play on fear of black men to win at all costs.

4

THE GUNS OBSESSION

America's obsession with guns and protecting the Second Amendment of the U.S. Constitution has only grown stronger under the presidency of Donald J. Trump. Meanwhile, children must practice drills to protect themselves from shooters with automatic weapons in school, while the politicians do nothing but send thoughts and prayers to grieving families. This must end.

Las Vegas. Why?

October 3, 2017

By Bob Gatty

It is unfathomable to believe that a 64-year-old apparently well-off man could hole himself up in a hotel room, smash out a window, and open fire on a crowd of more than 20,000 concert goers below, slaughter at least 59 and injure hundreds more.

Why would such a man do such a horrible thing? How could anyone, for whatever reason, be so deranged, so evil, so much of a coward as to hide 35 stories up and rain bullets down upon innocent people?

Why?

I've been to that hotel many times on business, and so has my son, Mike, who is a national event photographer, and some of the people who work for him. I have other photographer and event planning friends who have been there as well, and even though I haven't been touched by this tragedy directly, it has wrenched my soul.

Somehow, maybe, it would be easier if, indeed, this was an act of terror by Isis or some other crazy terrorist group. I don't know. Thank God it was a white man with no past criminal record and not a Muslim, black or Hispanic, or Trump would be railing against them and making all kinds of threats.

How can it be that anyone can smuggle 10 suitcases, apparently most filled with guns and ammo, into a hotel room without anyone noticing?

Why do we allow ordinary people to purchase weapons so deadly, weapons that have no conceivable purpose than to kill other people? Trump said Tuesday morning, "We'll be talking about guns as time goes by." We'll see what that means, but don't hold your breath. The 2nd Amendment? It was written when guns were muskets and it took two minutes to load a single shot.

Meanwhile, among the Las Vegas victims is a young woman from Maryland who was shot in the eye, and who will lose her sight should she survive. At last report, she was in a coma. Why? All she wanted to do was have fun and hear some music.

With all of the tragedies that have befallen us in recent weeks, this has touched me the most. Hurricane Irma, which cost me a business trip to Chicago and during which son Mike was hospitalized in Tampa (a big scare, but all is well), and which caused so much horrific tragedy for so many people, did not affect me in this way. My heart goes out to the people of Puerto Rico and I'm angered at Trump's self-centered, self-important attitude, but hurricane are unavoidable acts of nature.

This horrible shooting was not unavoidable. It was a deliberate act by a crazy man who was armed to the teeth.

And we still don't know why.

Senate, Choose: Guns or Women's Safety

April 9, 2019
By Bob Gatty
Now it's up to the United States Senate to decide where their priorities are: supporting the National Rifle Association and the powerful lobbying organization's paranoia over any restriction on guns or helping to protect women from domestic abuse, violence and even death.

The House of Representatives last week made that choice when it passed a bill to reauthorize the Violence Against Women Act (VAWA) 263-158, with 33 Republicans joining all but one Democrat in passing it. They did so despite threats from the NRA, warning lawmakers their vote would be counted in the sacrosanct NRA voter profile and ratings that many trot out during their campaigns to show their support for the Second Amendment.

As a result, 157 Republicans voted against the bill.

Republicans opposed the bill for a number of reasons, including protections for transgender people in prisons and a provision that would prohibit those convicted of domestic abuse, assault or stalking from buying or owning a firearm. They claimed that would infringe upon Second Amendment rights.

Current law already prohibits spouses or former spouses convicted of abuse from purchasing firearms, but a new amendment would close the so-called "boyfriend loophole," adding unmarried partners to the language.

Guess if you get beat up by your boyfriend it's OK. How does it hurt any less than if it was your husband? Or how are you any less dead?

""The gun control lobby and anti-gun politicians are intentionally politicizing the Violence Against Women Act as a smokescreen to push their gun control agenda," NRA spokesperson Jennifer Baker told the Associated Press.

"I am deeply disappointed that some Republican Members of this House are using the NRA as cover to vote against this reauthorization, which has been overwhelmingly in a bipartisan fashion reauthorized over and over again," said House Majority Leader Steny Hoyer, D.-Md. "These are commonsense protections that prevent domestic abusers from obtaining the guns that have sadly been used so frequently to harm or kill their partners."

Republican lawmakers like Georgia's Rep. Doug Collins, ranking GOP member of the House Judiciary Committee, disagreed. Collins said he supports VAWA, but that Democrats "have sought at every turn to make this bill into a political weapon, rather than a critical resource for victims and tools to support law enforcement."

Dead in the Senate?

Congressional insiders speculate that the House bill's gun control provision means it is most likely dead in the Senate, which is controlled by Republicans. So, a bipartisan effort is underway to craft a version that can avoid the contentious debate over guns.

Sen. Joni Ernst (R-IA) and Sen. Dianne Feinstein, D-CA, are working on their own version that may stand a chance of passage in the upper chamber.

"I have had discussions with Ranking Member Feinstein of the importance of the Violence Against Women Act, and the need to get this vital piece of legislation reauthorized. This committee has an important responsibility to ensure reauthorizing legislation moves forward in the Senate, and both myself and Ranking Member Feinstein look forward to creating a bipartisan bill that will not only reauthorize but modernize VAWA in order to provide protections that best fit the needs of our victims and our communities," Ernst said in a recent Judiciary Committee business meeting,

At this writing, it is unknown just how the Senate bill will differ from the version passed by the House.

We'll see who wields the power in the Senate, right? Don't bet against the NRA.

Assault on Assault Weapons Gains Strength

April 18, 2018

By Bob Gatty

Increasing public opposition to the sale of assault-style weapons like the AR-15 to the general public is having a significant impact on major gun retailers, with many either flat-out stopping their sale or imposing stringent restrictions.

The latest indication of the power of the ongoing campaign against those weapons in the aftermath of the Parkland, FL school shooting came when Dick's Sporting Goods announced that it will actually destroy such weapons that it did not sell before imposing its ban following the school massacre.

Originally, the Pennsylvania-based retailer said it would ban the sale of assault-style rifles at its 35 Field & Stream stores and would stop selling firearms and ammunition to anyone younger than 21. Since then, numerous companies have responded to the public's growing demand for responsible gun control measures.

The New York Times reported that several retailers have joined Dick's in stopping the sale of firearms to those under 21, including Walmart, the nation's largest gun seller; L.L. Bean; and Kroger, which said it would restrict gun sales at its Fred Meyer stores.

Going even further, Walmart said it will stop its online sale of toys that look like assault-style rifles, and Kroger announced it would stop selling "assault-rifle themed periodicals."

In addition, The Times reported, Citigroup said it would restrict the sale of firearms by its business partners, demanding guns not be sold to people younger than 21 or those who have not passed background checks. (The restrictions apply to clients who, among other things, raise capital via Citigroup or offer Citigroup-backed credit cards.)

Moreover, Delta Air Lines, United Airlines, Hertz and Avis announced they would end discount programs for the National Rifle Association's five million members. Delta and United also instructed the N.R.A. to remove their information from its website.

So, while our representatives in Congress and the orange monarch in the White House refuse to ban the sale of AR-15 type weapons and impose other sensible restrictions, the court of public opinion is on its way to achieving that objective through the marketplace.

Republicans always say that they want to leave things up to the marketplace rather than imposing governmental restrictions, so they should be happy with the outcome in this case. But, probably not since so many of them are lapdogs for the N.R.A. and its financial largesse.

The Time for Responsible Gun Control is Now

April 29, 2019

By C J Waldron

You wouldn't expect a fireman to pour gasoline onto a blazing inferno. You wouldn't expect a doctor to give you medication that makes you feel worse. So, why do gun advocate believe that the answer to a mass shooting is more guns? Where is the logic in that?

How has the rest of the world dealt with this issue?

In Great Britain, on March 13, 1996, there was a shooting in Dunblane. Sixteen students and a teacher were killed before the gunman turned the gun on himself. Britain reacted by banning all handguns. There has not been a school shooting since.

In Australia, in Port Arthur, Tasmania, a gunman open fired on a crowded cafeteria, killing 35 and wounding 23 people. This was shortly after the Dunblane Massacre. Australia reacted by outlawing automatic, semi-automatic and pump action rifles. They also instituted a gun buyback program which saw 640,000 guns turned in. It was twenty years before there was a mass casualty shooting in Australia.

Most recently, there was a massacre in Christchurch, New Zealand. Fifty people died and twenty were seriously injured. The very next day, the New Zealand Prime Minister announced that she was introducing legislation to ban assault weapons.

Each of these countries took immediate action to address gun violence. The United States leads the world in mass casualty shootings when compared to the countries that have enacted sensible gun control laws. It is second only to Brazil in gun related deaths.

Despite this, with every mass casualty shooting, the reaction of Republicans is to say, "Now is not the time to talk about gun control." They offer useless "thoughts and prayers" as the next attack is being planned. Because they are controlled by the pro-gun lobby, namely the NRA, Republicans refuse to take action.

Democrats have control of the House, but Mitch McConnell refuses to allow any mention of gun control onto the Senate floor. Trump made the token gesture of banning bump stocks but bowed to NRA pressure right after promising stricter gun control laws following the Parkland shootings.

The only way we can have sensible gun control laws is to take back the White House and the Senate, and to take away the NRA's stranglehold on our government. It's time to take a stand for reasonable gun control laws.

Trump's Lies: Myrtle Beach Gun Shop Owner Right on Target

May 18, 2018

By Bob Gatty

The owner of the Myrtle Beach, SC 707 Gun Shop must be generating a lot of attention with his latest ad in the free advertising newspaper that's distributed free in pizza joints, cleaners and other stores frequented by locals and tourists alike around here.

Check out the image above and the NEWS WEATHER FORECAST, which features a caricature of President Trump and the text line:

"STORMY, with SCATTERED LIES, SLIGHT CHANCE OF TRUTH IN THE MORNING."

That's pretty ballsy, considering that Trump is popular among many locals here, and I would guess extremely popular among gun owners -- of which there are many.

But this guy's right on with his message, whatever his motivation.

Trump's Lies Catalogued

The Washington Post, in this May 1 article, catalogued 3,001 false or misleading statements by Trump since taking office in January 2016. The Post's Fact Checker says that's an average of 6.5 per day. So obviously, that Myrtle Beach gun shop owner is right on target.

As we all know if we've been listening, Trump loves to repeat his lies -- as if that makes them true. According to the Post, through May 1 he had repeated 113 false claims more than three times each and had falsely claimed that he passed the biggest tax cut in history 72 times, when, in fact, bigger tax cuts had been enacted seven times.

One claim that really irks me is when he has claimed repeatedly (41 times by May 1) that Democrats are to blame for not passing legislation to save the Deferred Action for Childhood Arrival (DACA) program, established by President Obama. In fact, Trump killed that program and then held it hostage trying to force Democrats into supporting funding for his wall. That was Trump's idea of a "good deal."

It just goes on and on to the point that most reasonable people don't really believe anything he says. How can you when you realize the simple truth is that Trump lies.

Of course, as this Politico Magazine article points out, lies by presidents are not unusual. Like Politico notes, Richard Nixon said he was "not a crook." Ronald Reagan said he wasn't aware of the Iran-Contra deal. Bill Clinton said he "did not have sex with that woman."

Then Politico adds, "But Donald Trump is in a different category. The sheer frequency, spontaneity and seeming irrelevance of his lies have no precedent. Nixon, Reagan and Clinton were protecting their reputations; Trump seems to lie for the pure joy of it. A whopping 70 percent of Trump's statements that PolitiFact checked during the campaign were false, while only 4 percent were completely true, and 11 percent mostly true. (Compare that to the politician Trump dubbed "crooked," Hillary Clinton: Just 26 percent of her statements were deemed false.)"

Repeatedly, Trump has denied "collusion" with the Russians to rig the 2016 presidential campaign. A "witch hunt," he has repeatedly claimed.

Well, the special counsel's investigation into that and related matters has now been underway for a full year. There have been indictments. White House staff and Trump associates have been interviewed and some may be squealing. It's clear from his Twitter feed that Trump is squirming.

I suspect that we'll see soon enough if Trump's denials about that constitute his biggest lie of them all -- or not.

SC Gov Hopeful Fires Gun in TV Ad

May 19, 2018
By Bob Gatty
Catherine Templeton, Republican candidate for governor of South Carolina, is shown in her latest TV ad firing a .38 revolver that she says her "granddaddy" gave her, in an obvious effort to pander to the Palmetto State's many gun toting voters -- and, of course, the National Rifle Association.

Templeton is a leading contender to unseat incumbent Gov. Henry McMaster, a good-ole boy type who ascended to the governorship when former Gov. Nikki Haley was appointed U.N. ambassador by President Trump. In his latest ad, McMaster extolls the state's virtues, and then in his best South Carolina drawl says, "We gonna keep it that way."

But a candidate for the highest office in the state actually firing a pistol in a campaign commercial? Obviously, her campaign team believes that plays well in SC, but what about now in the aftermath of the latest school shooting in Santa Fe, TX? Isn't it, at least, in poor taste?

In the ad, Templeton, who describes herself in other commercials as a "conservative buzzsaw," fires the .38 twice, purportedly at a snake shown in a separate image. She says her "granddaddy" gave her the gun to shoot snakes around her family's fishing trailer.

The ad talks about fixing corruption and wasteful government spending, a consistent target for Templeton in her campaign. She aims the gun toward the ground and fires two rounds.

"We can't shoot the snakes slithering around Columbia," says Templeton, "but we will end their poisonous big government ways."

Templeton's been taking some hits for her ad on social media, with many on Facebook saying it's misguided, particularly in the current environment with so many shootings by guns, especially in our schools.

But gun ownership is a powerful issue in South Carolina, a state that has seen its share of tragedy by guns -- including the deadly Charleston church mass shooting in 2015 and a shooting at Townville elementary school in 2016 that killed a first-grade student. Nearly six in 10 South Carolinians live in a home with a gun, according to reliable reports.

Efforts failed in this year's legislative session to tighten background checks, which proponents said would have presented the Charleston church massacre, even though polls show that 85 percent of state gun owners favor requiring such background checks.

And so, we have a candidate for the state's highest office who think it's just fine to go on TV and fire a pistol in a blatant effort to win votes.

Welcome to South Carolina.

Hate Has No Home Here

May 22, 2019

By Bob Gatty

Why is there so much hate and divisiveness in our country today? Why does it seem like we can't even have a civil discussion about just about anything without it dissolving into rancor and bitterness?

Why?

It seems like so much is tearing us apart these days.

Arguments over whether guns should be controlled as a way to stop the killing of innocent people.

Arguments over when life begins and whether a woman should have the right to choose what happens to her own body.

Arguments over immigrants and how they should be treated.

Arguments over whether President Trump is good or bad for our country.

Do athletes who refuse to stand for the National Anthem disrespect or flag and our country, or do they have a right to protest racial injustice?

Are we jeopardizing our planet by clearcutting forests to build houses, by insisting on single use plastics, by promoting the fossil fuel industry, by eliminating environmental protections to encourage business expansion and growth?

And then, of course, there are the racial divisions that continue to simmer, hidden prejudices that surface and are often whipped to a frenzy by those who seek to foment hate and discord.

I've just touched the surface here. But all of this came to mind as I walked along a narrow street in beautiful St. Augustine, FL, which we are visiting this week. I saw the sign in the photo above outside someone's home.

"Hate Has No Home Here."

Should not that be the way it is everywhere? Why is that thought so unusual that it requires a sign outside someone's home

Somehow this needs to change. Instead of political leaders who seek to take advantage of differences, of prejudices, of simmering suspicions to pit one group against another, we need leaders who will work every day to overcome those challenges, not benefit from them.

Somehow, some day that sign outside that home in St. Augustine, FL must become the watchword of our nation.

Hate has no home here.

The Consequences of Unfettered Gun Rights

May 23, 2019
By Bob Gatty

In 2008, the Supreme Court finally tackled the issue of gun rights. It was the United States vs. Heller, and the floodgates were opened.

In a challenge to a District of Columbia law, a DC police officer claimed he was unlawfully denied the right to keep a personal handgun in his home for the purpose of self-defense. The court ruled that such a law conflicted with the Second Amendment "right to bear arms".

The result has been to open the floodgates to a virtually unlimited arsenal of weaponry "for the purpose of home defense".

The case challenged the 1975 law that required firearms kept in the homes to be unloaded, locked and disassembled. Opponents argued that this made them useless for home defense, which they deemed was their intent in owning firearms. With the Heller decision, the Supreme Court re-asserted the rights of gun owners, not only in Washington, but throughout the entire nation.

In a 157-page decision, the court ruled that the Second Amendment categorically granted the absolute right of gun owners to their guns. It was a move hailed as "a God-given right" by the NRA and gun owners, while opponents, including retired Justice John Paul Stevens, said it was "the worst decision the court ever made".

What has happened since the Heller decision? This chart provided by the FBI illustrates the dramatic rise in active shooter incidents since Heller.

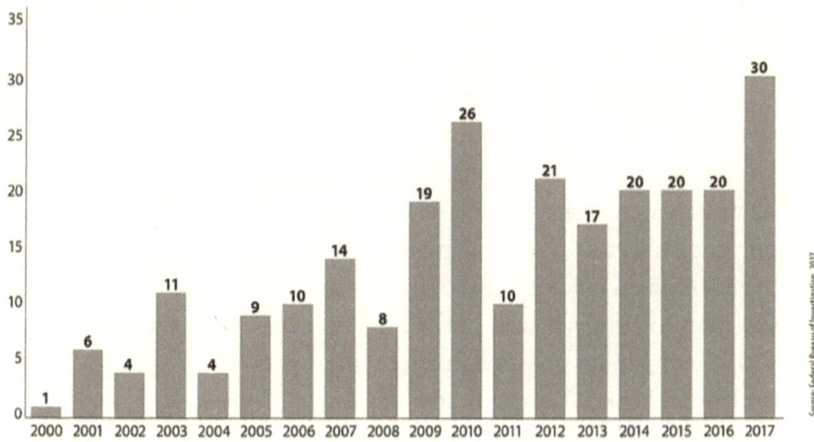

With conservatives in charge of the Supreme Court for the foreseeable future, the likelihood of this trend being reversed is little to none. The result will be more deaths and more carnage. The numbers speak for themselves.

Wear Orange Demonstration for Gun Violence Awareness

June 1, 2018

By Bob Gatty

Helping to lead the drive for gun violence awareness and advocating for sensible gun safety legislation, demonstrators in communities across the nation urged lawmakers to enact sensible gun laws to help prevent deaths caused by gun violence.

Volunteers, emblazoned in orange shirts, carried placards and signs on National Gun Violence Awareness Day. Demonstrators stood with Cleopatra Cowley-Pendleton and Nathaniel Pendleton, whose 15-year-old daughter was shot in Chicago in 2013. Her memory and recognition of countless others killed by gun violence were honored by those who wore orange.

Hadiya's friends chose orange because it stands for safety and means "don't shoot."

Here in Horry County, SC, demonstrators gathered in memory of gun suicides, school and other mass shootings and all deadly acts facilitated by weak legislation on guns, said county Democratic party chair Don Kohn, who was one of the demonstrators.

"We're speaking out because common sense gun regulations have been thwarted by the rich gun lobby despite the hard work of many South Carolina and Congressional legislators." Kohn called for banning the sale of bump stocks, silencers, assault-type weapons that have no sport or safety purpose, as well as removing guns from the hands of all domestic abusers.

Demonstrators here also urged stronger background checks to prevent gun sales to criminals who put our safety at risk. "Change the rule that allows gun sales to go through after a short period, even though a thorough background check has not been completed," Kohn said.

He also advocated closing the "Gun Show Loophole," which allows buyers to bypass a background check for gun show purchases and urged the South Carolina state legislature and all levels of law enforcement to "effectively address the torrent of illegal guns that plague our streets."

In addition, he called for education and training to prevent bullying and violence be provided at all educational levels and workplaces.

The local event here was just an example of the demonstrations that took place on National Gun Violence Awareness Day. Hopefully, these events will add to the public discourse that is occurring on gun violence and our lawmakers at both the national and state levels will take responsible action.

Kids Dying from Gun Violence: An American Epidemic

June 27, 2018
By Bob Gatty
According to the Brady Campaign, every day 46 children and teens are victims of gun violence. It's an American epidemic.

Every day, seven children and teens die -- four are murdered; three die from suicide. Forty children and teens are shot but survive.

- 31 are injured in an attack
- 1 survives a suicide attempt

- 8 are shot unintentionally

These are our children, whom we all claim to love, cherish and want to protect at all costs. Except if the cost means some sort of reasonable restriction, like keeping guns out of the hands of people with a history of mental illness or tightening up background checks or banning military-style weapons like the AR-15.

If that's the cost, it's too high.

My 16-year-old granddaughter, Karleigh Campman, is passionate about this issue and she's concerned about her future and that of her brother and sister and friends. I asked her what the pacifier in the illustration meant to her.

"The gun," she said, "is like a pacifier to a lot of people. It makes them feel secure, just like the pacifier does for a baby."

And then, she said, "It could have another meaning, too. A lot of kids are shot and killed by other kids accidentally. The pacifier could indicate that, too. People, if they are going to have a gun, need to keep it locked up and away from their kids."

If you are concerned about the fact that every day 318 people in America are shot and that 96 people die from gun violence each day, then you need to let the people who make the laws know of your concern.

It doesn't mean doing away with the Second Amendment. It doesn't mean that the feds are going to try to confiscate peoples' guns. It simply means that sensible gun laws and protections are needed to help end this epidemic that plagues our nation.

Thank you, Karleigh, for sharing this with Not Fake News.

The Shootings: Who is Responsible?

August 4, 2019

By C J Waldron

Over the past 24 hours two mass shootings have occurred with at least 20 dead in El Paso, TX and another nine in Dayton, OH, and what do we have from President Trump? The typical useless and lame expressions of "thoughts and prayers" expressed through Tweets that have undoubtedly been staffed out because they are written coherently.

After all, he's at his resort in New Jersey playing golf.

What's missing is the acceptance of responsibility, and that responsibility belongs to none other than @realDonaldTrump and the other racist members of his administration -- as well as the members of Congress, especially #MoscowMitch McConnell, the Senate majority leader, for refusing to stand up for what is right.

They are responsible because they demonize those along the southern border, calling them rapists and drug dealers. It's the same type of dehumanization that Hitler used to justify his treatment of the Jews during World War II, yet his base refuses to acknowledge this.

They are responsible when they call African nations "shit holes", furthering the hatred of people of color.

They are responsible when Trump tells sitting members of Congress to "go back" to where they came from. These women of color are being blamed for the ills of country and the attempt is to lay blame on their ethnicity or country of origin.

They are responsible when a civil rights icon is blasted for standing up to the multiple abuses of this administration. When you are only president for the part of the country that supports you, it's easy to use victim blaming to point out urban blight, even though your own son-in-law is complicit in this situation.

They are responsible when they refuse to enact sensible gun reform laws to prevent the deaths of dozens because they refuse to stand up to the terrorist NRA. Instead, they continue to spread the fearmongering lie that Democrats are "coming for your guns".

What will happen at his next rally? Will he condemn the violence, or will he continue to spread the hate and blame the media? My money is on the latter.

Make no mistake: EVERYONE WHO SUPPORTS THIS ADMINISTRATION MUST SHARE RESPONSIBILITY IN THESE DEATHS!

From Tears to Trash Talk

By Steve Hamelman

August 2, 2019

In Iowa this past weekend to address the recent spate of gun violence in the United States, Democratic presidential candidate Andrew Yang broke into tears while recounting the death of a child killed by a stray bullet.

That was impressive, for two reasons.

First, it was unrehearsed. Score one for Andrew Yang. Authenticity is in short supply on the national political stage.

Second, it showed that at least two of the Democratic Party's male candidates are not "afraid" to cry in public. (The other is Joe Biden, for whom tears arise when he reminisces about his late son Beau. He has also cried when bringing up the names of his first wife and daughter.)

Andrew Yang's compassion for the grieving mother probably touched as many Republicans as Democrats. I imagine Independents were moved, too. At the same time, it made Trump and his ICE-men seem like cold-hearted brutes.

Contrast the image of Yang in tears with the grinning Trump giving a thumbs-up as he held the baby who was orphaned in the Dayton shooting last week.

But within hours of this impressive display, Yang went after Trump directly. Saying he wanted to stay in "presidential form," Yang implied that American voters think favorably of candidates who maintain their physiques.

This theme gave him an opening—was it premediated? —for ridiculing Trump's physical condition. It would be "hysterical," Yang said, to watch Trump try to run a mile: "Oh my gosh, that would be so amazing for the American people."

Yang next mused, "What could that guy beat me at? Being a slob? He's an embarrassment."

This trash talk continued for another minute or so, Yang concluding that the only things Trump could beat him at would be an eating contest, keeping a hot air balloon on the ground, and playing golf."

Viewers and voters will have decided whether or not Yang, by virtue of the second interview, undid the good will achieved by his tearful speech the previous day. By mocking President Trump so scathingly, Mr. Yang may have shown that even the best-intentioned candidates cannot avoid the "new normal" of rhetorical disdain established by Trump.

What are we to make of a cultural climate in which the President excoriates whole cities (Baltimore) and Democratic hopefuls take ad hominem potshots at the President of the United States without the slightest hesitation?

Having no answer to this question, I can only hope the latter know what they are doing.

What Will You Do to Stop School Shootings?

August 6, 2019
By Bob Gatty
Today, a 10-year-old boy took a microphone, looked the United States Senator and presidential candidate straight in the eye and asked what he would do to stop shootings in schools that have cost so many lives and caused so much terror.

The boy's name is Elijah Lawson, and the candidate he was addressing was Sen. Cory Booker, who had come to the Bucksport Senior Center near Conway, SC, to address residents of South Carolina.

His question came after adults had asked Booker about his plans to fight high drug prices, improve healthcare, protect Social Security and other issues that are of particular concern to them.

But Elijah was focused on where he is, and what he must face when he goes to school where he's supposed to be safe, be able to learn, and maybe someday be standing before a crowd of people as a senator and presidential candidate.

But he won't be able to do any of that if he's shot dead as he hides under his desk from a deranged shooter at school.

After complementing Elijah for having the courage to articulate his question in front of the crowd and the media, Booker said he would "take the fight to the NRA," and that dealing with gun violence would be a top priority if he is elected.

"We are going to end this nightmare in this country so no child in America has to ask this question again," he promised young Elijah.

Booker briefly outlined the steps he would take as president, saying he would implement a federal gun licensing program, universal background checks, and ban assault weapons, high-capacity magazines, and bump stocks.

Booker's plan also calls for closing loopholes that allow domestic abusers and people on terrorist watch lists to obtain guns, regulate gun manufacturers and remove legal obstacles that prevent victims of gun violence from seeking justice.

"Were you happy with the senator's answer to your question," I asked Elijah later.

"It was amazing," he said. "Most presidential candidates wouldn't even answer that question."

Booker's appearance came just days after mass shootings in California, Texas and Ohio by hate filled gunmen wielding assault-style weapons capable of wiping out a crowd of people in seconds.

It followed accusations by many in his party that President Trump must share some of the blame for such shootings because of his racist and divisive remarks and tweets that seem to never end.

"We've had a dark few days in America," said Booker. But love, not more hatred is what is needed to bring the nation together and help it heal, he said.

"You can't lead the people if you don't love the people," he stressed. "You can't beat hatred with hatred."

Mass Shootings: It's Time to Stop Blaming Mental Illness

August 19, 2019
By C J Waldron

Whenever there is a mass casualty shooting, such as in El Paso or Dayton, Ohio people will invariably take sides. One side will demand stricter gun control laws while the other will offer "thoughts and prayers", claim "now is not the time" and scream about their Second Amendment rights.

For a brief time, the right will promise to "look at" gun control, but then shift to blaming mental illness.

Where did this mindset originate?

The answer lies in what has been considered the first mass casualty shooting, former Marine sharpshooter Charles Whitman murdered 14 people from his perch atop a clock tower at the University of Texas, in Austin. Prior to the shooting, Whitman had reported feelings of rage, confusion and having violent impulses. He was referred to a psychiatrist as a method of treatment.

Following the incident, in which he was killed by Texas law enforcement, an autopsy was performed. It revealed a pecan-sized tumor in his brain and cited it as the likely cause for his violence. Despite this, people latched on to his psychiatric history as a reason.

Thus, the image of the mentally deranged killer was born.

Sadly, this mantra has been largely supported by the NRA and so-called gun advocates who rely on this reasoning to support their ill-informed position. After the Parkland shootings Trump supported stronger gun control laws only to reverse his position after meeting with NRA members. He has done the same following the El Paso shootings, shifting the focus from gun control to mental illness.

The problem is, facts do not back this theory. On the contrary, studies have shown the opposite. Those with mental illness comprise only 16 percent of the overall prison population in America yet, due largely to their erratic behavior, are 3 times more likely to be arrested. This despite the fact 95-97% of all violent crimes are committed by those who are not deemed mentally ill.

Despite this, 48% of adult Americans associate mental illness with mass shootings; a stance the NRA is only too willing so perpetuate. They are hoisting a fraud upon America by pushing false information, or to use a saying often used by the right, Fake News.

It's long past time that we continue to blame mental illness. We need to remove the stigma so more people who need treatment get the help they need. And it's time we stopped using mental illness as an excuse for violence and put the blame where it belongs; on the NRA, the right and gun owners.

There are currently more guns than people in this country . So, if you still believe that the mentally ill and not gun ownership is the problem, perhaps it's time you were evaluated.

Bulletproof Back-to-School Backpacks

By Stacy Fitzgerald

September 8, 2019

As summer unofficially ends and kids head back to school post Labor Day consider this: among the many items on parents' back-to-school list are pens, pencils, highlighters, graphing calculators, paper – and for some, bulletproof backpacks.

And, here's a personal confession: I really, really wish I hadn't thought about the need to buy one for my kids.

There are companies that sell them online for $100 or more and there are plenty of parents actually buying them. I wish they didn't have to think that they were necessary.

In our crazy gun society, mental illness is always the excuse for mass shootings, including school shootings. But, there's no conclusive evidence that the U.S. has more mentally ill people than other countries, but we do have far more guns. In fact, there are 326 million people and 393 million guns in the United States. Yes, you read that right. There are nearly 70 million more guns than people in the United States.

It's not mental illness that's the problem. It's easy access to guns and lack of sensible gun control legislation.

A Department of Justice study of 2,655 homicides in 1988 drawn from a "representative sample" of 33 of the largest counties in the United States revealed that 4.3 percent of the assailants had a "history of mental illness."

Yet, mental illness is usually the default justification for mass shootings in America and our politicians, beholden to the powerful and well-funded gun lobby, are remiss to pass basic background check legislation that the majority of the U.S. population supports. Because "Second Amendment Rights" are more important than American lives -- than children's lives.

I can't say I'm completely surprised that seven years after Sandy Hook the massacre of 20 children still wasn't enough to prompt sensible gun control legislation. After all, like everyone else, I've witnessed the constant refrains of "thoughts and prayers" and "one lone mentally ill shooter" cycle through the news reports at regular, alarming intervals.

I've been alternately heartbroken and enraged that, still, no action has been taken to address the issue: the rampant and ridiculous fanaticism gun culture in America.

And the message is unmistakably clear: Your angry, irrational neighbor's right to own as many guns as he can buy has been and will always be more important than the safety of the public. Of your kids, of my kids, of all of us.

I wish I could make sense of it…. but right now, I'm just trying to make room in the budget for a couple of those backpacks.

Fear in a 'Safe' Place

September 12, 2019

By Bob Gatty

Two young teenage boys came home having been traumatized at school. That's what happens when kids are forced to participate in active shooter drills. It makes them think, "This is real. It could absolutely happen to me."

Those boys are the sons of Marcus Grainger and they are students at Myrtle Beach High School in South Carolina, where students were put through that active shooter drill.

"When they came home, they were really scared," said Grainger. "They know how often these shootings happen in schools. And when they have a drill, it makes it real, and it makes them afraid."

Grainger, who helped organize last year's March for Our Lives demonstration in Myrtle Beach, is campaigning to end such drills, which he says waste resources and unfairly stress out teachers as well as students.

Proponents of active shooter drills say they are needed to help prepare students and teachers in the event of an attack. But Grainger argues that the answer, instead, is to enact stronger laws to eliminate assault-style rifles and high capacity magazines, plus stronger background checks and other sensible gun laws.

"Schools should be a safe place for students and they shouldn't have to worry about people coming in and shooting up the school," he said. "We are now seeing more and more mass shootings happening because Congress won't do its job and pass common sense legislation. If you care about the safety ion students, you should be pushing for gun reform legislation."

Grainger put the blame for the gun crisis on the gun lobby and the politicians who take its cash and urged that such actions be exposed and made public. He challenged lawmakers and leaders of both political parties to make that happen.

When shooters show up at a school, Grainger said, the solution is not more guns, "At the end of the day, somebody is going to get killed," he said. "The only person who can do anything about it is the police. The answer is to get less guns in this country, not more."

Ironically, my conversation with Grainger occurred on the same day that it was reported in the news that nearly 150 corporate leaders from across America sent a letter to the U.S. Senate urging passage of effective gun legislation.

"Doing nothing about America's gun violence crisis is simply unacceptable and it is time to stand with the American public on gun safety," they said.

The question is this. Will Congress -- especially the Republican-controlled Senate where House-passed legislation awaits -- take meaningful action? Or will they wait around for President Trump, whose campaign received more than $11.4 million from the National Rifle Association, to give them permission to act?

◆ ◆ ◆

The Death Dance

September 13, 2019
By C J Waldron
After every mass shooting there is the predictable dance between the left and right. The left demands stricter gun laws while the right offers "thoughts and prayers". Both sides say they are seeking a solution, but they cannot agree on the issue.

For Democrats, the issue is guns; or at least the proliferation of assault weapons such as AK -47s and AR-15s, which are military grade weapons. They want meaningful gun control enacted before the next mass shooting.

For Republicans, the issue is mental health. They are certain that there must be some mental issue with someone who commits these atrocities, therefore their focus is on identifying those with mental illness and keeping guns out of their hands. (Of course, that way they don't cross swords with the National Rifle Association (NRA) which has contributed millions to their campaigns).

What if both sides are right? What if the obsessive need for such weaponry is in itself a form of mental illness?

According to the American Psychiatric Association one in five Americans experience some form of mental illness in their lifetime, with one in twenty-four being diagnosed with a serious mental illness. Could an obsession with guns be in itself a form of mental illness? Could their fixation on a specific section of the Second Amendment be another form and their belief that some government power is "coming for your guns"?

Each of these is an identifiable form of a specific mental illness.

Many mass shooters have hoarded many firearms. The Las Vegas shooter amassed huge amounts of firearms and ammunition, yet this raised no red flags from hotel personnel as he brought them to his room. Could he have been suffering from obsessive compulsive disorder in his need to have so many weapons?

Obsessive Compulsive Disorder (OCD) is defined as "a pattern of unreasonable thoughts or fears (obsessions) that lead you to do repetitive behaviors (compulsions)". The obsession with firearms and the compulsion to buy a seemingly endless supply certainly fits this definition.

Having an unhealthy fixation, such as those who focus only on a specific section of the Second Amendment is also a form of OCD, identified as a fixation disorder. Like religious zealots, who cherry-pick certain sections of their canon, those with fixation disorder use a limited interpretation of an issue to justify their overall stance.

In feeding the oft repeated claim that "_____ is coming for your guns", the National Rifle Association is targeting those with paranoid personality disorder. These individuals can also have elements of OCD and will latch on to conspiracy theories about government overreach in interfering with what they believe are their Constitutional rights. The NRA is only too happy to fuel this to further their pro-gun agenda.

If both sides agree, this could FINALLY be the breakthrough that will lead to meaningful gun control legislation. Identifying an obsessive need for firearms as a mental illness will satisfy the mental health advocates while keeping guns out of their hands would appease gun control proponents. That's really where the "red flag" legislation now before Congress comes in.

Could this be the solution we are seeking? It would at least be a start.

A New Year Without Fear

January1, 2020

By C J Waldron

It is an almost daily occurrence. Mass casualty shootings have, sadly, become the norm in our country. While a majority of Americans support stricter gun control measures, the pro-gun lobby, led by the NRA and their dead-from-the-neck-up Second Amendment distortionists have us living in fear that a trip to the mall or a simple fender bender might result in our death by gun violence, making us just another statistic in this horrific, uniquely American legacy.

The depth of this gun violence was epitomized by CNN anchor Brooke Baldwin who, when told by her producers that she was going to cover yet another mass casualty shooting, tearfully asked "Which one?". The resulting backlash from this, and her refusal to confront the late Elijah Cummins, has prompted those on the right to demand she be removed from the air. This is the world we live in.

As an educator with over thirty years in the classroom, I was shocked to discover that, in addition to my many other duties, I am now required to take annual active shooter training in the event I need to protect my students.

Are you kidding me?!

A shooting at a Texas church furthered the gun debate as the NRA hailed the parishioner who stopped the shooter as "a good guy with a gun who prevented even more people from dying", yet one has to wonder why armed guards are needed in a house of worship? Instead of addressing this issue, their response is "We need more guns".

The mind-numbing logic is astounding!

Meanwhile, South Carolina is considering legislation (H.3456) that would allow open carry of a firearm WITHOUT NEEDING A PERMIT. Supporters of this legislation claim it would be "a small step returning to the original vision of our founders, in which citizens had a duty to be armed rather than need permission to carry". They point to the original intent of having "all able-bodied men to have a working musket", using this archaic terminology, while ignoring the huge technological advances in firearms.

Using the states that ignore federal laws prohibiting marijuana possession and sale, the defenders of this bill want to ignore any potential federal legislation regarding gun control.

We need to have a new year without fear. We need sensible gun control laws. We need to defeat H.3456. We need to Take a Stand!

Buy a Truck, Get a Gun

February 9, 2020

By Chris Waldron

Yes, you read that correctly. A local car dealership is making this offer to anyone who buys a certain model of truck from their dealership. Sadly, this promotion isn't unique. I did a Google search and it came back with over 500,000 similar offers or related postings.

I was so shocked by this, that I posted a comment on my local neighborhood site, urging people to boycott this business. The responses I received were typical from the gun-loving right. I was called a "Liberal" (as if that was an insult), told to "go back to where I came from" (sound familiar?) and even received a death threat that I reported to the proper authorities.

The reactions were typical. Guns don't kill people. Cars and knives kill people too, why not outlaw them and, of course, the usual MAGA nonsense.

These are some of the response I received. (I didn't correct the spelling or grammatical errors.) I've also inserted my own comments in parentheses:

"Bad people with bad intentions or with mental issues kill people not the guns. Good people was carrying licenses save lives and protect themselves their family and other people. If there giving away guns whoever is receiving them have to go through rigorous background checks. So that all being said I believe in my first amendment and my second amendment carry arms. South Carolina will never ever take away your second amendment. And if that's what you're after you might as well move out of South Carolina and move to a sanctuary state like Virginia."

(Yes, let's blame mental health, and what was that about "Southern hospitality"?)

"Yankees liberals are some crazies!! Every household needs a gun."

"Every God Fearin, Tax Payin American citizen should own a gun!"

(Frightening)

"It's funny cars kill more people than guns but yet they keep on driving! But Dodge are horrible, I guess the Gun is to shoot the car later on! A little humor can't hurt- it's called bullet advertising! HA HA"

"I've been around guns my whole life. My father was a police officer. I never once saw any of our guns kill anyone. But then again, we trained them right, and kept them locked up and they never grew legs. I've never come across a gun that snuck out and killed anyone. People with knives kill people, drugs kill people, prescription drugs kill people, speeding drivers kill people, drunk drivers kill people. I could go on"

(Except cars, knives and prescription drugs don't have the express purpose of doing bodily harm.)

"Oh, my I guess no one realizes that most gun crimes are committed by people that didn't get their guns legally!

(Except the shooters in Las Vegas, Parkland, the Pulse night club and countless others purchased their weapons legally).

"Show me how a gun, can shoot without someone pulling the trigger!! You do know more people are stabbed to death, than shot every year, don't you?? I was at a Gun Show yesterday.. the place was filled with guns.. no incidents!! Amazing!! according to your "common sense", that shouldn't happen!! But it did, and ALWAYS does!!!"

(A gun show surrounded by people who agree with you? And they talk about Liberals needing their "Safe Space.)

I received over a hundred responses to my post in just a few hours. Most of them have been attacking me and calling Liberals "full of hate" while spewing their own hate-filled venom. I turned off notifications after I received a death threat, but I'm sure the same one-sided commentary is continuing.

If the answer to gun violence is more guns, why don't we put out a fire by making more fires? Why don't we cure a public health crisis like the current Corona virus by infecting everyone?

In my many years as an educator, I've lost many students, both current and former, to gun violence, so yes, this issue is VERY personal to me.

This madness needs to end!!

◆◆◆

Ban Assault Weapons. Join the Campaign

February 19, 2020
By Bob Gatty
On February 16, 2018, Robert Schentrup lost his sister, Carmen, when she was murdered at Marjory Stoneman Douglas High School in Parkland, FL -- shot four times by a gunman in her classroom who was armed with a weapon of war.

Today, Robert and his mom, April Schentrup, are working with the Brady Campaign in its effort to convince lawmakers across the country and in Washington, DC to support common-sense gun-safety legislation, including reinstating the federal ban on assault weapons.

They are urging Americans to sign the Brady Campaign petition calling on lawmakers to act, and urging those who want to see such carnage ended to contribute to that campaign. Since we at Not Fake News fully endorse this initiative, we are passing their message on to you.

Here's how Robert put it in the appeal email that I received the other day, talking about the shooting of his sister:

"It's hard to put words to the wrenching heartbreak that followed. I remember feeling an overwhelming emptiness ... part of me had been ripped away that I'll never get back. I could only break down and sob. Carmen is gone forever, and my family and I will never be the same – all because a weapon of war got into the hands of someone who should never have had one.

"No family in this country should ever have to endure the pain of losing a loved one in a horrific massacre like what happened in Parkland – and I'm working alongside Brady to make sure this never happens again.

"I'll be blunt: This isn't work I would necessarily have chosen. I was a college freshman when I lost Carmen. But all the work I do – traveling across the country to testify for lawmakers from Colorado to Pennsylvania to the U.S. Senate, working with Brady to launch their youth-led lobby collective in Florida, and writing op-eds to bring people together to take action – I'm doing it for Carmen. I'm doing it because I don't know how I'd carry on without trying to keep these shootings from happening again. I'm doing it because, truthfully, it's the only way I know how to cope.

"But in doing this work alongside Brady, something happened: I realized that we could take action into our own hands and fight for common-sense gun-safety legislation in Florida and across the country."

Those are the words of a young man who is grief stricken at the loss of his sister. Now, listen to his mother, Carmen's mom as narrated by Jackie Cristiano:

"Even though two years have passed, I still struggle to grasp it – like when people ask how many kids I have. I once tried "I have one in college, one here with me, and one in heaven" – but that didn't feel right, either. I'm still looking for a way to answer that question.

"Carmen was killed just a week before she turned 17. She dreamed of becoming a scientist and working to cure the neurodegenerative disease ALS, or Lou Gehrig's disease. It's excruciating to know that her murder could have been prevented – that I could still have Carmen here with me – if clear warning signs about the shooter hadn't fallen "through the cracks" and extreme risk laws had been in place.

"But that's not my reality. I have to fight every day to make sure I'm doing everything I can so no mother will ever go through what I've been through and lose their Carmen.

"Today, I'm asking you to stand with me to create that change by helping Brady. In honor of my daughter and lives taken from us two years ago, please, will you sign the petition to demand Congress prevent school shootings?

"Today, I'll hug my family close. But tomorrow, I'll be back out there fighting. "We need you in this fight."

Those were the words of Robert Schentrup and is mom, April. We hope you will listen to them. We hope you will care. Sign the Brady petition today.

Pass Violence Against Women Act

March 8, 2020
By Bob Gatty
While many Americans are celebrating International Women's Day today, Senate Majority Leader Mitch McConnell and the National Rifle Association (NRA) are putting women across the country in danger from guns in the hands of domestic abusers.

How are they doing this?

More than a year ago, McConnell chose to let the Violence Against Women Act (VAWA) expire rather than pass a measure to close the deadly "boyfriend loophole" – which allows convicted domestic abusers to purchase guns.

That matters because victims of domestic violence are five times more likely to be murdered if their abuser obtains a gun.

"Now, because of McConnell and NRA-financed politicians, women across the country don't have sufficient legal protection from domestic violence, and their abusers can still purchase firearms," said Renee Davidson of the Brady Campaign Against Gun Violence.

The organization, she said, "is fighting back to elect gun violence prevention champions to oust NRA puppets like Mitch McConnell and put women's lives ahead of gun lobby profits.

But if we're going to make real progress, we need you fighting with us."

Davidson said the Brady organization needs 20,000 supporters "to stand up for women" by signing a petition to demand Congress reauthorize the Violence Against Women Act.

"We need your help to make sure women aren't murdered by their abusers, and that means we need to reauthorize the Violence Against Women Act immediately and get guns out of abusers' hands," she said. "Thanks for doing what's right,"

Background

From the National Network to End Domestic Violence (NNEDV):

The VAWA creates and supports comprehensive, cost-effective responses to domestic violence, sexual assault, dating violence and stalking. Since its enactment, VAWA programs, administered by the U.S. Departments of Justice (DOJ) and Health and Human Services (HHS), have dramatically improved federal, tribal, state, and local responses to these crimes.

Through the original bill, which passed in 1994, VAWA created the first U.S. federal legislation acknowledging domestic violence and sexual assault as crimes and provided federal resources to encourage community-coordinated responses to combating violence. Up for renewal every five years, each VAWA reauthorization builds on existing protections and programs to better meet the needs of survivors.

Reauthorized in 2000 it created a much-needed legal assistance program for victims and included responses to dating violence and stalking. In 2005, VAWA created new, holistic responses programs to meet the emerging needs of survivors and communities, such as prevention, landmark housing protections for survivors, funding for rape crisis centers, and culturally- and linguistically specific services. VAWA 2013 enhanced access to safety and justice for Native American and LGBTQ survivors.

2019 Reauthorization

On March 7th, 2019, a bipartisan bill (H.R. 1585) to renew and improve VAWA was introduced in the U.S. House of Representatives by Rep. Karen Bass (D-CA) and Rep. Brian Fitzpatrick (R-PA) and was passed in the House of Representatives with bipartisan support. NNEDV urges the Senate to pass VAWA 2019 to ensure survivors have access to lifesaving protections and services.

The final VAWA 2019 reauthorization should reflect the provisions in H.R. 1585, which safeguard current protections to ensure all survivors have access to safety and justice. This includes ending impunity for non-Native perpetrators of violence against Native women and children; improving housing protections and providing safe housing options so that survivors do not have to choose between safety and homelessness; increasing investment in domestic and sexual violence prevention; promoting economic security for survivors; increasing avenues for justice; and supporting efforts to reduce domestic violence homicides.

While federal funding is still available for domestic violence programs, the lapse of the underlying law (VAWA) has meant uncertainty for providers around the country. Advocates across the country call on Congress to urgently reauthorize VAWA.

"The improvements proposed in VAWA 2019, especially those that will reach survivors who are most marginalized, are long overdue," said Monica McLaughlin, NNEDV Public Policy Director.

"Today, survivors and advocates share the urgency and impatience of those who first rallied to create a national response to end domestic and sexual violence. Our movement urges Congress to swiftly reauthorize and invest in VAWA."

5

THE BATTLE OVER HEALTHCARE

Obsessed by hatred of President Barack Obama, Donald Trump and his Republican allies in Congress have done everything possible to undo the Affordable Care Act (Obamacare). Meanwhile, Democratic presidential candidates debated Medicare-for-All. The Republican attack on women's abortion rights, both in Washington and in several GOP-led states, intensified, even as many states refused to expand Medicaid to help low-income Americans, and Republicans continued to seek reductions in programs designed to help children in low-income families.

Medicare for All? The Debate Begins

September 19, 2017

By Bob Gatty

The nation now has a new option to consider when it comes to covering the skyrocketing cost of health care: a new Medicare for All proposal introduced Wednesday, Sept. 13, by Sen. Bernie Sanders (I-VT).

Backed by at least 15 Democratic senators, the Sanders legislation would expand Medicare into a universal health insurance program, financing it through higher taxes.

"If we want to move away from a dysfunctional, wasteful, bureaucratic system into a rational health care system that guarantees coverage to everyone in a cost-effective way, the only way to do it is Medicare for All," said Sanders.

His plan would cover everything from emergency surgery to prescription drugs, mental health and eye care with no co-payments. Americans younger than 18 would obtain "universal Medicare cards," while those not currently eligible for Medicare would be phased in over four years. The new system would replace employer provided plans, with employers paying higher taxes but no longer having to provide coverage for their workers.

Private insurers would cover elective treatments in a system similar to Australia's, which President Trump once said is "much better" than what we have in the U.S. Providers would be reimbursed by the government, signing a yearly agreement with Medicare.

Republicans quickly dismissed Sanders' bill, with Sens. Lindsay Graham (SC), Bill Cassidy (LA), Dean Heller (NV) and Ron Johnson (WI) introducing another attempt to repeal the Affordable Care Act (ACA), replacing it with "a block grant given annually to states to help individuals pay for health care."

"If you want a single-payer health-care system, this is your worst nightmare," said Graham. "Bernie, this ends your dream of a single-payer health-care system for America."

While there is no chance the Republican-controlled Congress will pass Sanders' bill, the health care debate is sure to be front and center in the 2018 Congressional election campaign. Other Senate Democrats are proposing alternative plans for Medicare or Medicaid buy-ins, taking a more moderate approach.

It's clear the system is broken, and Congressional Republicans and Trump are doing everything possible to scuttle the ACA (Obamacare). Supporters of Sanders' plan cite a Kaiser Health News survey that says 57 percent of Americans support Medicare for All, a number that could change as the campaign debate moves forward.

The Seven Bad Words of the Trump Administration

December 16, 2017

By Bob Gatty

As if not uttering or writing them will make them cease to exist, officials at the Centers for Disease Control and Prevention (CDC) have been ordered by the Trump White House not to use seven words, including "fetus", "transgender" and "diversity" as they prepare documents for next year's budget.

According to The Washington Post, the instructions came during a meeting last Thursday. The four other forbidden words are "vulnerable", "evidence-based", "science-based" and "entitlement."

In some instances, CDC analysts were given suggested phrases to use in place of the forbidden words, but in other cases there were no suggestions, The Post reported. Instead of using "evidence-based" or "science-based," the recommended phrase is "CDC bases its recommendations on science in consideration with community standards and wishes."

Interviewed by The Post, a longtime CDC analyst who writes descriptions of the CDC's work for the budget, could not recall a previous time when words were banned from budget documents because they were considered controversial.

The reaction of people in the meeting was "incredulous," the analyst said. "It was very much, 'Are you serious? Are you kidding?' In my experience, we've never had any pushback from an ideological standpoint."

If, indeed, that is the policy, I would think it will be a bit difficult to enforce. Career CDC scientists and subject matter experts with integrity are not likely to give in easily to political pressure. Moreover, some of the agencies within the CDC have specific responsibilities dealing with some of those banned terms, so it will be difficult to write about them without using the words.

As The Post reported, the National Center for HIV/AIDS, Viral Hepatitis, STD, and TB Prevention is working on ways to prevent HIV among transgender people and reduce health disparities. How are they supposed to report on that work without using the forbidden term "transgender?"

The CDC's work on birth defects caused by the Zika virus includes research on the developing fetus. How are they supposed to report on that work without using the forbidden term "fetus?"

The thing is that federal agencies must submit their budget proposals to the Office of Management and Budget (OMB), which has authority about what is included, and which is a highly political arm of the White House. So, OMB non-scientists will probably be editing those documents to satisfy Trump or whoever else in the administration dreamed up this ridiculous edict.

Certainly, the attempt to ban those terms reflects the Trump administration's attitudes regarding all of the areas that they cover. It is an idiotic effort and simply demonstrates the utter stupidity of some of the Trump political hacks who are in charge.

More Health Care Lies

October 18, 2018
By Bob Gatty
President Trump would have you to believe that Democrats, if they control Congress, would gut Medicare and that only he and the Republicans can save it -- an absolute bold-faced lie.

He also tweeted that all Republicans support providing coverage for preexisting conditions -- another absolute bold-faced lie.

Let's look at the facts.

It is the Republicans, supported by Trump, who have repeatedly tried to privatize Medicare by giving everyone a voucher worth x-amount of money to pay for health care coverage in the private sector. When that money runs out, you would be up the creek without a paddle, so to speak.

That's been a favorite mantra of outgoing House Speaker Paul Ryan (R-WI), and fortunately it has not gained enough support even in the nutcase-right-wing controlled House of Representatives to pass. But one of these days, if they have the votes, that idea will be back, and future generations of seniors will be screwed.

Pre-existing condition coverage.

Where is that coverage guaranteed? The Affordable Care Act (ACA). Obamacare. That government program enacted when President Obama was in office that Republicans and Trump have railed against for years. And Sen. Majority Leader   Mitch McConnell (R-KY) is now saying that if Republicans retain control they will make yet another attempt to repeal the ACA.

Should they succeed, there goes coverage for pre-existing conditions. There goes Medicaid coverage for millions of the poor.

But what did Trump just tweet out today?

"All Republicans support people with pre-existing conditions, and if they don't, they will after I speak to them. I am in total support." And then he claimed that it is Democrats who "will destroy your Medicare, and I will keep it healthy and well."

I have one thing to say.

Trump, you are a lying sack of s--t.

Build-a-Wall vs Childhood Cancer

February 6, 2019

By Bob Gatty

So, what's more important? Building a wall that's supposed to stop illegal immigrants from crossing into the country but really won't, or using more money to fight dread diseases like childhood cancer?

Last night in his State of the Union address, President Trump once again demanded construction of his wall on the border with Mexico, for which he seeks a $5.7 billion down payment. In the same speech, he requested just $500 million over the next 10 years to combat childhood cancer.

That comparison, $5.7 billion for a wall to keep immigrant children and their parents out of the U.S. vs. $500 million to help find a cure for cancer in kids pretty much sums up the misplaced values of the Trump administration.

The repeated warnings of dire consequences if asylum seeking migrants are allowed into the U.S. continued unabated in his speech as did his claims of the effectiveness of walls on the border.

""The border city of El Paso, Tex., used to have extremely high rates of violent crime — one of the highest in the entire country, and considered one of our nation's most dangerous cities," he said. "Now, immediately upon its building, with a powerful barrier in place, El Paso is one of the safest cities in our country."

Problem is, that was a lie. Fact checkers at The New York Times explained:

"El Paso was never one of the most dangerous cities in the United States, and crime has been declining in cities across the country — not just El Paso — for reasons that have nothing to do with border fencing. In 2008, before border barriers had been completed in El Paso, the city had the second-lowest violent crime rate among more than 20 similarly sized cities. In 2010, after the fencing went up, it held that place."

It was just another of Trump's lies and exaggerations used to support the need for his obsession: "a big, beautiful wall," that would cost multiple billions more than the $5.7 billion currently being sought. In fact, a report by the conservative think tank, CATO Institute, said it "will likely cost about $59.8 billion to construct."

Now, for childhood cancer research

Trump called for a $500 million increase in funding for medical research on childhood cancer over a decade, a cause he said "all Americans can get behind." That would add about $50 million to the $462 million currently being spent by the National Institutes of Health -- a paltry 10 percent increase.

Trump plans to request the money in his upcoming federal budget, expected sometime this month. The NIH's National Cancer Institute estimates that 11,060 children will be diagnosed with cancer in 2019, and that 1,190 will die. Approximately one in 285 children in the U.S. will be diagnosed with cancer before their 20th birthday.

According to the American Childhood Cancer Organization (AACO), childhood cancer is statistically relatively rare. While survival rates for many types of childhood cancer have improved, for many children, cancer will shorten their lives. it remains the number one disease killer of children in the United States today.

Just think about that. How much more could be done to help save our children from the scourge of cancer if just part of that wall money could be used, instead, to combat that disease. And what if some of that wall money was used instead to search for cures to other dread diseases?

Just a thought.

Once again: what's more important? A wall or a cure for these children?

Trump's Priorities: Just Follow the Money

July 2, 2019

By Bob Gatty

President Trump's new budget unveiled Monday provides clearly demonstrates his priorities and highlights perhaps his biggest lie of them all. Just follow the money.

By slashing programs for health care, housing, the elderly, education, students, the environment, Trump's new budget seeks to cover the outrageous increase in the federal budget deficit caused by his tax cuts that mostly benefited the wealthy and the big corporations. At the same time, it seeks another $8.6 billion for his cherished border wall.

If the president had his way...
Trump's 10-year budget calls for more than $845 billion in reductions for Medicare, aiming to cut "waste, fraud and abuse" in the federal program that provides health insurance to older Americans. While it doesn't actually propose to cut benefits, it would slash payments to hospitals and health care providers who already are paid less than the going rate when they take care of Medicare patients.

What would that mean? Fewer doctors and fewer hospitals would accept Medicare patients, which would make it more difficult for them to obtain care.

His budget would turn Medicaid, which provides coverage for low income Americans, into a block grant program, with money going to states who would then decide what, or what not, to cover. What do you think would happen in those Republican-led states that already refused to participate in Medicaid expansion authorized by the Affordable Care Act? More people would be forced to go to hospital emergency rooms for care, placing even more burdens on hospitals that are already strapped for cash.

Social Security? Trump's budget calls for slashing Social Security spending by $26 billion, including whacking $10 billion from the Social Security Disability Insurance Program.

The big lie
In announcing his presidential bid in June 2015, Trump said he would "save Medicare, Medicaid and Social Security without cuts." He added that it was "not fair" to make cuts to a program that people had been paying into for many years, and that he would save it "by making us rich again" and cutting waste, fraud and abuse.

That sounded great to those who were becoming true believers. It's exactly what they wanted to hear. Trump would work his magic, and everything would be fine. But today, if they follow the money, they'll realize that was just one big con.

Some of his other budget proposals are not at all surprising. They would:

- Slash the Environmental Protection Agency by massive amounts. The nation's renewable energy program would be gutted. Who needs clean air and water anyway when we can have more fossil fuels contaminating the environment and exacerbating climate change? Oh, wait. That doesn't exist, so why do we need the EPA anyway?
- Cut education spending by 13 percent, undermining public education and failing to support teachers and students. The student loan forgiveness program would be ended.
- Cut funds by 16.4 percent for the Department of Housing and Urban Development, slashing support for public housing. The budget also eliminates many federal block grant programs that local communities depend on, including the Community Development Block Grant program, HOME Investment Partnerships, the Choice Neighborhoods Initiative, and the Self-Help Homeownership Opportunity program.
- Slash 22 percent from the Department of Transportation, It would cut funding for new transit projects by 39 percent and slash funding for Amtrak by 23 percent — even as it raises highway spending. Take that, California.

While Trump's budget was filled with lies and half-truths, there is light at the end of the tunnel. Democrats control the House of Representatives thanks to the November elections and Republicans, even if they wanted to, couldn't get it passed.

So, while his budget plan isn't important from a practical standpoint, it does demonstrate just where Trump's priorities lie. And that's not in supporting the needs of average, everyday Americans, including many of those who are still true believers. Instead, it's in playing the big dog with massive increases in defense and homeland security (read that "keep the Latinos out) and in financing his self-created budget sink hole.

It's also important because it gives Democrats an arsenal of weapons to use in the 2020 campaign.

Bring it on.

Politics & the Battle Over Your Healthcare

March 26, 2019

By Bob Gatty

A day after President Trump's Justice Department went to court to scuttle the entire Affordable Care Act, House Democrats announced a new plan to improve healthcare by strengthening the ACA.

The announcement from the Justice Department coincidentally followed Attorney General William P. Barr's four-page memo to Congress saying the Mueller investigation did not show Trump or his presidential campaign colluded with the Russians to rig the 2016 presidential election, but also did not exonerate Trump on possible obstruction of justice charges.

Does the timing indicate that Trump now feels emboldened, vindicated, and that his penchant for retribution means that any and all programs supported by Democrats are fair game regardless of how many people would be hurt? You decide.

The Democratic announced plan came after the Justice Department asked an appeals court to declare it unconstitutional, siding with a lower court ruling issued in December. The DOJ initially said only the law's protections for people with pre-existing conditions should be struck down.

So now, if the Trump administration has its way, even those protections would be lost. Too bad, dad, if your daughter had leukemia before you got your coverage. You're on your own.

That's despite Trump's claim Tuesday that the Republican party would be known as the party of healthcare.

""The Justice Department and the Trump administration decided not only to destroy protections for pre-existing conditions, but to tear down every last benefit and protection the ACA has," House Speaker Nancy Pelosi said at a press conference Tuesday. "The GOP will never stop trying to destroy health care."

Ironically, the announcement from the DOJ also followed a report by the Department of Health and Human Services saying that 11.4 million people selected a health plan through the ACA exchanges during the most recent open-enrollment period for coverage in 2019—the first year in which there is no penalty for not buying health insurance.

Across all states, enrollment slid by about 300,000 people, or 2.6 percent, from 2018. That decrease was driven by lower enrollment in the 39 states that use HeathCare.gov, the federally operated marketplace. Enrollment in the 12 states running their own exchanges ticked up by almost 1 percent.

The Democrats' bill would:

- Expand Obamacare's tax credits that help people pay for coverage to more middle-income families and individuals;
- Increase the size of those tax credits;
- Reduce premiums by helping insurance companies pay the claims of high-cost patients;
- Prevent insurance companies from selling non-Obamacare "junk plans" expanded by the Trump administration that are cheaper but cover fewer benefits.
- Block the administration from approving state requests to water down Obamacare's protections for people with pre-existing conditions and its 10 requirements for what insurance companies must cover, like maternity care and substance abuse treatment.

The Democratic legislation is expected to be brought to a vote in the House of Representatives later this year and assuredly will be a major component of the 2020 Congressional and Presidential campaigns.

Where is Trump's 'Great Healthcare'?

June 22, 2019

By Bob Gatty

When Donald Trump was seeking the presidency, he promised the American people would have "great healthcare." He won. The Republicans controlled Congress. But all they did was attempt to subject President Obama's Affordable Care Act to death by a thousand cuts.

Now, Trump is making the same promise again. In an interview yesterday with TIME Magazine -- during which he threatened a reporter with prison time if he published a photo of letter he showed him -- Trump bragged about scuttling the individual mandate, which required people to purchase health care coverage or pay a penalty. And then he said this:

"We got rid of, as I said, we got rid of the individual mandate, which was by far the most popular thing in Obamacare. We're managing Obamacare much better. But Obamacare is a very — it's very bad. And if we win, I will do healthcare. If we get the House. If we get back the House — you can't do it without the House.

"If we get the House, we get the Senate, we get the presidency, we will have a great health care plan, we will have tremendous healthcare. But we're doing a good job on that anyway. Doing a very good job."

So once again, a new promise: Re-elect me, put Republicans back in charge in Congress, and you'll have "a great health care plan." Really? You couldn't do it before, why should we think you can -- or will -- do it again?

What Trump and his Republican sycophants are doing is not even a very good job of disabling the ACA, even though that's what they are trying to accomplish. Yes, they've gotten rid of some regulatory burdens physicians have complained about for years, but they've really done nothing to improve the delivery of healthcare as it affects patients.

The mantra in his 2016 campaign was to "repeal and replace Obamacare," as it came to be called, but instead Trump could only manage to achieve repeal in the House of Representatives. He was thwarted in the Senate, largely because of opposition from his arch enemy, the dying Republican Sen. John McCain (R-AZ) and two other GOP senators.

There never was a viable plan ready to replace the ACA had it been repealed. Millions of Americans would have lost their healthcare coverage, causing a healthcare catastrophe of massive proportions.

Every step of the way, Trump and his GOP supplicants in Congress took whacks at what they derisively labeled Obamacare. They killed the individual mandate, striking at the heart of the program and was the most visible attack on the law. But there have been many, many more. Here's an analysis from the Center on Budget and Policy Priorities.

Much of it has been behind the scenes, not widely known or reported, but nonetheless, has been aimed at sabotaging the program now relied upon by millions of Americans. As of last year, eight years after passage of the ACA, the uninsured rate among U.S. adults ages 19 to 64 was 12.4 percent, statistically unchanged from 2016 — despite actions taken by the Trump administration and Congress to weaken the law.

However, because of the administration's determined efforts to undermine the law, many, many Americans are underinsured and do not have coverage that they really need. According to the Commonwealth Fund, 45 percent of U.S. adults ages 19 to 64 are inadequately insured — nearly the same as in 2010.

So today as we look towards the 2020 election and consider candidates to support, who do we believe? The president who brags and puffs up his chest about his phony accomplishments and makes false promises? Or candidates who actually are committed to improving our healthcare system and making it as affordable as possible for as many people as possible?

The choice really isn't that hard.

What Do Docs Think About Medicare for All?

July 10, 2019
By Bob Gatty

Medicare for All has become the battle cry for many of the 25 candidates for the Democratic presidential nomination as they declare that every American should have easy access to #affordablehealthcare and should not have to choose between going to the doctor and putting food on the table.

"Healthcare should be a right, not a privilege," they say.

But what about a huge segment of the population that would be dramatically affected by such a massive revamping of our healthcare system, the nation's doctors? What do they think about the idea?

Traditionally, organized medicine has opposed any sort of single-payer system. However, last month, the #AmericanMedicalAssociation's House of Delegates nearly voted to overturn that position. While the AMA doesn't represent every doctor in the land, it represents by far the majority, and so what its members say is significant.

When the votes were counted, 47 percent favored eliminating the AMA's official opposition to single payer, while 53 percent voted to maintain it.

That the vote was even that close was remarkable and represents a significant shift in opinion of AMA members whose livelihood depends upon a healthcare system that fairly and sufficiently reimburses them for their services.

The AMA supported enactment of the #AffordableCareAct, which has been ferociously attacked by the Trump administration and now faces a possible death sentence, depending on an expected ruling in federal court in a case brought by Republican-led states.

Healthcare coverage for some 20 million Americans who are covered by the ACA is at stake as it presumably would come to a halt should the court declare the ACA unconstitutional. It is just the latest instance, however, in which politics threatens Obamacare.

In fact, notes this editorial in Modern Healthcare, politics are at the root of the ACA's failures—"not its Rube Goldberg design." The Supreme Court allowed states to opt out of the Medicaid expansion, the editorial notes, "and when the GOP-controlled Congress eliminated the individual mandate, key to making rates on the exchanges affordable, it reduced sign-ups, raised premiums and stopped the expansion dead in its tracks."

More recently, the AMA joined the Partnership for America's Health Care Future, a group of hospitals, drug makers, and other industry groups that opposes and lobbies against Medicare-for-all. Instead, the organization supports former #VicePresidentJoeBiden, an opponent of the idea who prefers to strengthen the ACA, the legacy of his service with President Obama.

But the winds of change apparently are affecting the AMA just as they also may be affecting much of the electorate.

Bob Doherty, a senior vice president for government affairs and public policy at the #AmericanCollegeofPhysicians, tweeted that such a strong showing within the AMA for single-payer "would have been unimaginable in years past." As Doherty tweeted: "There is a lot more support for publicly financed coverage than ever before."

Some political opponents of Medicare for All have warned that hospitals would close if it is enacted because Medicare payment levels are well below private insurance rates. While Medicare for All would set prices at Medicare rates, they are higher than Medicaid rates. Medicaid and the Children's Health Insurance Program would be eliminated in #SenBernieSanders' legislation.

Moreover, doctors' administrative overhead, including paperwork, preauthorizations, limited formularies, narrow networks, and high deductible plans would be reduced or eliminated under the plan, some experts say, providing a major incentive for their support.

At any rate, if the healthcare provider community moves from opposing to supporting Medicare for All or a version thereof, that would be a significant boost for the idea as the presidential campaign heats up.

Addiction: A Personal Story

By Stacie Pearman

August 1, 2019

"What else can I do? Oh my God, it's going to be too late for me, I'm going to get sent right back to where I've used for 10 years."

These are the words of Susan, a 32- year-old, single mother who has struggled with addiction to heroin, fentanyl and crack cocaine, all stemming from prescription drug use. Now, for the first time in her life, she is seriously trying to find addiction treatment to save her own life and in turn, be able to raise the son who was taken away from her just months ago.

Susan resides in a Democratic state where she could qualify for Medicaid (the state took the Medicaid expansion provided under the Affordable Care Act (ACA)) and entered a rehabilitation facility. However, she and her treatment team know she must leave that state as it has been home to many of her drug-use triggers if she is to successfully remain clean.

Susan identified a rehabilitation facility in South Carolina where she could go as a single woman for addiction treatment and even bring her child with her for parenting skill support.

Perfect, right? Wrong.

Republican-controlled South Carolina refused to take the ACA's Medicaid expansion funding, so she will not qualify for Medicaid as a single adult fighting addiction. Had she not lost guardianship of her child, she MAY have qualified for Medicaid, but the requirements are many and they put into question whether she could obtain the help she desperately needs to save her own life.

"If I can't get out of this state and start over, I'll die," said Susan. She is desperate. Her life, and that of her little son, literally hangs in the balance.

There is much political noise about the opioid crisis in America. Voices from both side of the political aisle proclaim that something must be done. Then why, if we know most addicts need Medicaid to receive the addiction treatment they need, have 14 states refused to accept the federal money allowing them to expand Medicaid, thus denying potentially lifesaving treatment to addicts?

We know there are addicts who are holding down jobs, functioning as best as they can until their addiction drives them to joblessness and without medical coverage. Then, likely, they will seek out various forms of public assistance like food stamps or Temporary Assistance for Needy Families (TANF) to get by.

They will start using the hospital emergency room either to try and feed their addiction (pill seeking) or to get medical care for themselves and their families. They will reach out to charitable organizations for food, assistance with bills, maybe even for shelter once their addiction results in homelessness.

Children will be intertwined in an overburdened foster care system, resulting in a whole host of problems that could impact them into adulthood-potentially breeding another generation of struggling adults with addiction and mental health issues. Have you ever thought about the economics of not securing treatment for those willing to accept it?

This is a national crisis, but for Susan it is her life.

An election is coming, and we must secure local and national candidates who understand that their proclamation of wanting to address the opioid epidemic must include a plan to expand Medicaid.

Addicts are our friends, our family, and our neighbors. No one wakes up wanting to be an addict and it makes good economical and human sense to ensure that if someone is willing to save their own life through treatment, that they can do so.

There are 14 states in our country, Republican states, that said "No" to addicts through their cruel policy of denying the Medicaid expansion simply because they hate Obamacare. This is not a policy of life and compassion. This simply ensures that the crisis continues at an untold toll of human lives.

Doc Burnout and Your Healthcare

October 26, 2019
By Bob Gatty

A new report by the National Academy of Medicine (NAM) provides some alarming information that should concern every single person who goes to a doctor or a hospital in the United States of America.

A combination of cumbersome and sometimes seemingly idiotic rules and payment procedures, plus staff shortages, plus the pressure to enter the age of electronic medical records is nearly sending many of those dedicated professionals who care for us to the looney bin.

"Studies estimate that between 35 percent and 54 percent of U.S. nurses and physicians have substantial symptoms of burnout, and the range for medical students and residents is between 45 percent and 60 percent. There are indications that burnout is a problem among all clinical disciplines and across care settings," the report states.

"The high rates of burnout reported among U.S. clinicians and learners is a strong signal that the nation's health care system is failing to achieve its aims for system-wide improvement," the report added.

"Improving the U.S. health care system to achieve the goals of better care, improved population health, and lower costs depends in large part on a workforce that is functioning at its highest level. Positive, healthy work and learning environments facilitate and support the professional well-being that is so essential to the therapeutic alliance among clinicians, patients, and families and the delivery of high-quality care."

This should concern every single person who visits a health care facility, so that means every single one of us.

Say you are a clerk in a store. Your boss is a jerk. You are required to pull double shifts, fill in for workers who don't show up, and every day you deal with customers who can be downright rude and nasty. You go home exhausted and your spouse is upset; the kids are running around crazily, and the house is a mess.

"What's the use?" you think to yourself. "What am I doing? Why do I have to put up with this?" You go to bed exhausted, and it starts all over again the next day.

Well, that's not a happy scenario, but your work and your tiredness and your negative attitude is only affecting the store where you work, those pain-in-the-butt customers, your wife and your kids. That's not good, but you're not in danger of making a mistake that might make someone really sick or even kill them.

But that's the way it is for healthcare professionals. They are responsible for diagnosing and treating our illnesses. Sometimes what they do and how they respond is a matter of life and death.

But what if they are so tired on the job, feeling so rotten about their work environment, so discouraged about their worth and value that they misdiagnose you, prescribe the wrong medication, or, heaven forbid, operate on your left foot when it is the right one that's broken?

According to this study by the NAM, that's exactly how it is for between 35 and 54 percent of nurses and physicians and between 45 and 60 percent of medical students and residents. That is not a pretty picture.

In fact, get this, the <u>suicide rate among physicians</u> is TWICE that of the overall population. That's after all those years of medical school, the six-figure debt for education, the euphoria that once filled them when they first heard themselves called "Doctor" or "Nurse."

Here's more from that report:

Mounting system pressures have contributed to an imbalance in which the demands of the clinician's job are greater than the resources available to complete the job effectively. This job demand–job resource imbalance is intensified by the increasing push for performance improvement, technology that hinders rather than supports patient care, changing professional and societal expectations, and policies that are insufficiently aligned with professional values or the goal of better patient care. Adding to these health system pressures is an explosive increase in medical data and a growing demand for health care as the U.S. population ages and many disciplines experience workforce shortages. Overwhelming job demands and insufficient job resources cause physical, psychological, and emotional stress, including burnout — a workplace syndrome that is characterized by high emotional exhaustion, high depersonalization (i.e., cynicism), and a low sense of personal accomplishment from work.

Seems to me this is a problem that needs to be treated as the highest priority as our nation's healthcare system is reformed. It's fine to talk about "Medicare for All" or other aggressive ideas to provide affordable healthcare for more people.

But it won't do a hell of a lot of good if the people who are supposed to provide that care are so exhausted, overwhelmed and depressed that they can't do their work.

Red Tape, Healthcare Delays Frustrate Veterans

November 10, 2019
By Bob Gatty
All too often when our veterans who have served our country visit the Veterans Administration (VA) or other government agencies for help, red tape and bureaucratic requirements make it virtually impossible for them to obtain the timely assistance to which they are entitled.

Especially when it comes to applying for benefits, bureaucratic hassles often provide frustrating roadblocks that seem to prevent approvals for no apparent reason.

"Sometimes their claims get rejected, so they file an appeal, and then their appeals get rejected," said Ron Wilson, director of the Veterans Welcome Home and Resource Center in Little River, SC. "A lot of times they get so frustrated that they just give up. Then, they come to see us." Wilson served in Vietnam and was discharged from the Army as a Sergeant E-5 in 1972.

The Center is a 501c3 non-profit organization operated entirely by volunteers and financed by contributions. Its mission is to assist local honorably discharged veterans with job placement, filing claims with the VA, help with serious financial difficulties, and provide temporary shelter for those who need a safe place to stay.

It's ironic, said Keith Bacon, the chairman of the Center's Board of Directors, that "people on the (government agency's) staff are paid to serve our vets, but they send people to an organization run by non-paid volunteers to resolve their problems." Bacon served in Korea as an Army Captain.

Healthcare

Healthcare continues to be a major concern for many veterans, and those issues were a major part of a discussion among veterans participating in a group interview conducted at the Center, sponsored by the Horry County, SC, Democratic Party.

Susan Hayes Hatcher, a 20-year Air Force veteran who retired as a staff sergeant, discussed difficulties she experienced in coping with the Veterans Administration as she helped her ailing mother.

In July, she submitted paperwork for needed benefits, to which her mother as a widow of a veteran is entitled. In August, when she called to inquire as to the status, she was told she would not get an answer until July 2020. Then, in September she was told her answer would come in March.

"I said, 'I don't mean to be rude, but you know what, this is really ridiculous,'" she told the person at the VA. "This is a widow of a veteran. If you guys are taking this long on her paperwork, I think I need to submit my paperwork right now …so when my time comes due my paperwork will already be processed. I'm 60."

"When you enlist, they guarantee your health care," said Bacon. "So why isn't the federal government in general taking care of these issues? The VA should follow individual veterans until they don't need to be seen any more."

Wilson told her to bring the paperwork in and the Center would help.

"My experience with the VA has been that the care is excellent – when it's available," said Dr. Bruce Fischer, a U.S. Army veteran who was a helicopter pilot in Vietnam.

Dealing with a dermatology issue, Fischer said when he went for care, a technician photographed the area in question, and then it took over a month to get a specialty appointment more than two hours away in Charleston, SC, for the needed treatment. Then, when Fischer asked for them to deal with another related issue while he was there, he was told, no, we can only do one issue at a time – which, of course, was frustrating.

Other veterans participating in the discussion, including Don Kohn, a retired Air Force sergeant who also served in Vietnam, and Michael Pearman, an eight-year Army veteran, with deployments in Iraq and Kuwait and now a sergeant in the Army Reserves, said the care they received – and in Pearman's case, is currently receiving – has been fine.

Patty Hampton, who was a medic in the Air Force in which she served for eight years, said she feels "really thankful to have VA benefits due to being a disabled vet."

However, she told about the time she needed to go to the VA hospital and was "transported in a police wagon that would have carried people to jail." That, she said, was upsetting.

On another occasion, Hampton said, she was transported in an ambulance and kept receiving bills for the service for over a year because it took the VA so long to pay the ambulance company.

PTSD & Suicide

Nationwide, an average of 20 current and former military service members die by suicide each day. In South Carolina, veterans accounted for 16 percent of all suicides in 2017 when 120 veterans took their own lives. Still, according to the VA, only half of all veterans who need mental health services are receiving them.

Although retired and active military service members die by suicide at twice the rate of civilians, research shows that veterans who receive mental health care are much less likely to end their own lives than those who do not receive such care.

The big problem, according to Tracy Stecker, a psychologist at the Medical University of South Carolina's School of Nursing is stigma associated with seeking mental health services, which she said many male veterans, especially, consider a sign of weakness.

The veterans who participated in our interview agreed. Mental health issues, including PTSD, need to be made a priority at the VA, where necessary care is often lacking.

Dr. Fischer, as a retired clinical psychologist, is experienced in treating veterans with PTSD, an important contributing factor in many veterans' suicides -- but also has undergone treatment himself due to PTSD resulting from his service in Vietnam.

"It's different when you're on the receiving end," he said, explaining that he had been undergoing treatment at the VA, but then the therapist retired and still has not been replaced. "They currently don't have anybody who deals with PTSD," he said.

Harold "Buster" Hatcher, a decorated 20-year Army veteran who retired as a warrant officer with a Purple Heart, was shot three times in Vietnam and still suffers from PTSD. At one point in his life, he said, "I didn't understand what was happening to me. I was afraid that I would wake up at night and kill everybody in the house."

In fact, said Hatcher, he experienced dreams that he was back in combat in Vietnam, he gave his rifle to his oldest son and told him, "If I come out that door acting crazy, kill me."

His PTSD has lessened over the years, he said, adding that he attended group counseling sessions, which helped. "It's better now than it used to be," said Hatcher.

At the Center, veterans experiencing PTSD or possible suicide issues continue to seek help. "We know where to send them," said Wilson. "Until the U.S. stops having veterans, it will be a continuing process," he added.

Housing

For today's veterans, and for many current service personnel, housing is a key issue.

According to the Housing Assistance Council, veterans constitute 10.1 percent of South Carolina's population, for a total of just under 374,000, with 7.1 percent living in poverty. Roughly 13 percent of homes in the state are occupied by veterans, who own about 79.6 percent of those homes with a median value of $150,000.

But, the Council reports that more than 55,000 of those homes experience one or more problems involving quality, crowding or cost, adding that 22 percent "pay too much" for their housing.

However, it was reported in July that current military personnel in South Carolina who live in base housing experience rampant mold, exposed lead-based paint and many other issues in what is considered to be substandard housing. For some, it's causing them to leave the military.

That's a problem that Pearman said he and his family experienced when they lived at Fort Carson.

"If you're not an E6 or above or an officer, your housing is pretty bad," he said. "We had to set traps for rodents, and it was so cold that we had to wear layers in the house to keep warm. It's not very good housing – especially if you're an enlisted soldier."

Then, there is the problem of homelessness among veterans. According to the Housing Assistance Council, there are approximately 480 homeless vets in the Palmetto State, a problem that comes to the doors of the Veterans Welcome Home and Resource Center.

All of these concerns are the day-to-day experiences of today's veterans. It's incumbent upon our government to address them. No veteran should experience problems in obtaining healthcare. No veteran should live in substandard housing. And no veteran should be forced to sleep in a car, or worse.

Addressing all of that should be a huge priority for government at every level. It's fine to say "Thank you for your service" when you meet someone who served our country. But what really needs to be done is to encourage our politicians to address these problems on behalf of those who served and continue to serve our nation.

Anti-Abortion Politician Demands Docs Do the Impossible

By Stacy Fitzgerald

December 17, 2019

A Republican Ohio state representative, riding anti-abortion sentiment in his state, has proposed legislation requiring doctors to perform an impossible medical procedure, one that he had not even researched.

Rep. John Becker's bill would require doctors to re-implant ectopic pregnancies, which occurs when a fertilized egg implants somewhere outside the womb, such as in the fallopian tube. His idea is to reduce the number of abortions in Ohio.

Becker's uneducated, politically motivated attempt to demand doctors do the unproven and physiologically impossible is the latest example of rampant anti-intellectualism and the increasing effort of male politicians to policewomen's' bodies.

Citing Zero Evidence

Becker has admitted that he did no <u>research</u> to determine if an ectopic pregnancy could be implanted. A quick Google search would have informed him that obstetricians consider it "physiologically impossible" to re-implant an ectopic pregnancy, just as it is physiologically impossible for a genetically male person to give birth to a child.

Instead, Becker introduced legislation that demands medical professionals perform what is physiologically impossible, aided by anti-abortion activists who cited two studies – one in 1917 and one in 1980 that suggest, but don't prove, that there is the possibility of the procedure being successful.

But there is zero documented evidence that that such a procedure is possible or what side effects would be suffered by the mother. So, with zero evidence of success and unknown risks to the mother, Becker charged ahead and introduced a ridiculous and embarrassing piece of legislation in a blatant appeal to the religious right, and a misguided attempt to save pregnancies that can't be saved, according to most obstetricians.

As an increasing number of states move to <u>restrict</u> legal abortions in America, Becker's proposed legislation is just the latest attempt to stop abortion. The problem is that an ectopic pregnancy isn't an induced abortion; it's a natural one.

Becker's legislation is not only thoughtless, but potentially dangerous. Asking doctors to do the impossible with zero evidence of potential success while risking the health of the mother is cynical, dangerous and irresponsible.

Doctors estimate that 2 percent of pregnancies are ectopic pregnancies and worry that suggesting that such a pregnancy could be saved by an operation deemed physiologically impossible by obstetricians could give many women false hope and cause them to pursue unproven and dangerous strategies to save their pregnancy.

While it's doctors who swear by a code of ethics that includes the phrase "first do no harm," perhaps it's time for lawmakers to do the same.

Proposing legislation without the benefit of even the most basic research is irresponsible, misguided and politically reckless. But, then, these politicians don't seem to care.

Human Trafficking: An Evil Crime Against Humanity

By Steve Hamelman
January 11, 2020
This month, January, we are reminded of an evil crime against humanity that seems to take place in nearly every nation on earth: the trafficking of human beings for profit.

For by proclamation on December 31, 2019, President Trump declared January 2020 National Slavery and Human Trafficking Prevention Month (<u>NSHTPM</u>).
Easy to Define, Hard to Fathom

Wikipedia's definition of this atrocity merely hints at a crime of astonishing reach: "Human trafficking is the trade of humans for the purpose of forced labor, sexual slavery, or commercial sexual exploitation for the trafficker or others."

From Afghanistan and Albania to Zambia and Zimbabwe, no country is left untainted by human predators seeking to lure vulnerable or innocent people into their clutches.

Who's at risk? Impoverished young women in rural villages dreaming of a better life in the city, refugees, runaways, orphaned children, migrant workers, the homeless. . .

Criminal networks recruit, transport, sell, and coerce their prey into sexual, agricultural, and industrial bondage from which it is almost impossible to escape.

The conditions are unspeakable, the suffering beyond compare.

First Obama, Then Trump

The first observance of NSHTPM was announced in January 2010 by President Barack Obama. This act reinforced America's commitment to ending a problem tackled in 2000 with the Victims of Trafficking and Violence Protection Act.

President Trump has upheld Obama's precedent by again declaring January National Slavery and Human Trafficking Prevention Month. In his declaration Trump highlights funding initiatives aimed at this domestic and international tragedy.

The Bare Stats

Data published by agencies such as the United States Department of Defense and the United Nations Office on Drugs and Crime suggest the staggering impact of human trafficking.

In sum: of the 25 million victims globally, 20 million (all ages) labor in brutal servitude, and five million are subject to rape, prostitution, sham marriages, and all other forms of sexual exploitation.

The total estimated windfall for their oppressors is $150 billion.

Worth Reading

In June 2019, the government released the 527-page "Trafficking in Persons Report" (TIP) with a foreword by Secretary of State Mike Pompeo, who lamented "how depraved this assault on human dignity really is."

Americans who wish to deepen their grasp of this sinister practice in the United States, as well as in countries they intend to visit, are advised to browse the nearly five hundred pages of national profiles in the TIP.

What Can We Do?

Awareness of this crime against humanity is the first step in the right direction.

As we go about our daily business, let's be alert, vigilant, mindful. Let's teach our children to be wary of potential predators. Let's share our concerns with friends, church members, and school officials.

And when we see something suspicious, let's not hesitate to call or text the Human Trafficking Hotline.

Finally, let's support all non-partisan attempts to eradicate this blight from our own nation and the rest of the world, too.

Donald Trump and His Healthcare Lies

January 14, 2020

By Bob Gatty

President Trump is now on a tweet-a-thon claiming that he has saved healthcare coverage for pre-existing conditions, when one of his obsessive priorities since his election has been to wipe out the Affordable Care Act (Obamacare), which guarantees that protection.

Yesterday, I woke up to this tweet from Trump:

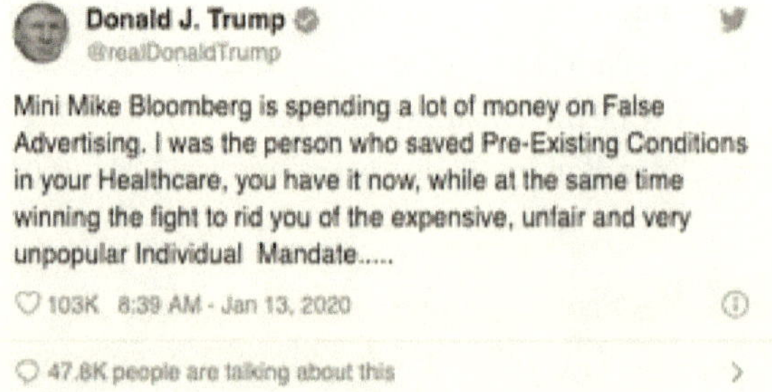

And then, he added:

> ....and, if Republicans win in court and take back the House of Represenatives, your healthcare, that I have now brought to the best place in many years, will become the best ever, by far. I will always protect your Pre-Existing Conditions, the Dems will not!
>
> ♡ 56.9K   8:39 AM - Jan 13, 2020   ⓘ

Really?

The truth is that Trump has been obsessed with undoing every achievement of President Obama and he will stop at nothing until he has accomplished that. Witness his attack on the environment and climate change, for example.

The Enemy of the ACA

But this claim is one of his most outrageous. He is the single biggest enemy of the ACA and that is where protections for pre-existing condition coverage reside. Just last week the Justice Department filed a brief in a lawsuit filed by a group of Republican governors and state attorneys general challenging the healthcare law. The Trump administration backs that lawsuit, which if successful, will result in the entire ACA law being declared unconstitutional.

And yes, Trump supported and signed legislation eliminating the requirement that individuals must purchase health insurance coverage or face penalties at tax time. Indeed, that was unpopular. But it was one of the foundations of the ACA and now the White House argues that by doing that Congress has made the entire law invalid.

Indeed, the law is in jeopardy because of that lawsuit. In mid-December a federal judge in Texas struck down the ACA saying the individual mandate is unconstitutional and the rest of the law cannot stand without it. Now, a New Orleans appeals court is waiting for additional information, but has indicated skepticism about the mandate. If the Texas ruling is sustained, Democratic governors are bound to appeal and the issue is likely to land in the U.S. Supreme Court, which now has a Trumplican majority.

The GOP to the Rescue?

What about Trump's statement that if Republicans regain control of Congress indicates they would provide the "best ever" healthcare coverage with protections for pre-existing conditions?

Just look at their record. Remember when the late Sen. John McCain, his head showing stitches from brain surgery, bravely stood up in the Senate chamber and gave thumbs down to the GOP effort to kill the ACA? They had no plan ready to replace Obamacare at that time, and millions of Americans would have lost their coverage. That has not changed.

Why is Trump doing this now?

Clearly, it's because he wants to go on the offensive and counter certain Democratic charges that he's responsible for ending healthcare for millions of Americans should the court case that he and his GOP pals support ultimately succeed.

It's what he does. He creates a crisis then blames it on others. This time millions of Americans face the very real certainty of losing their health insurance coverage, and it will be entirely the fault of Trump and the GOP -- despite Trump's tweets.

Politically, this tactic is bound to backfire. Currently, Democratic presidential candidates are focused on debating the pros and cons of Medicare for All. But if this court case succeeds, the focus of the 2020 presidential campaign will shift to the broader issue of healthcare overall, and which party -- and candidate -- to trust with getting it right.

Republicans and Trump who will have been responsible for ending coverage for millions of Americans -- including coverage for pre-existing conditions?

Or Democrats who fought for the ACA, defended the ACA, have spent months debating how to make healthcare in the U.S. even better, and will have a strong and effective healthcare plan in place heading into the fall election campaign?

My bet is that Trump's healthcare lies will not hold up when tested in that campaign.

Nutritious Food: Another Trump Obama Target

January 18, 2020

By Bob Gatty

The Trump administration yesterday took action to dilute school lunch nutritional standards pushed by former First Lady Michelle Obama, allowing schools to offer less healthy foods to students, despite staggering rates of childhood obesity in the U.S.

The proposal to lay waste to one of the former first lady's cornerstone achievements just happened to come on her birthday. Anybody believe that was just a coincidence?

In yet another effort by President Trump to undo key achievements of the Obama administration, Agriculture Secretary Sonny Perdue said the new rules were needed because school kids are throwing away the healthier foods they are being served and there is just too much waste.

"Schools and school districts continue to tell us that there is still too much food waste and that more common-sense flexibility is needed to provide students nutritious and appetizing meals" he told The New York Times. "We listened and now we're getting to work."

Yea, they listened alright. They listened not to nutritionists trained in child health, but to the food and snack industries which vigorously fought the Obama rules.

However, we can call BS on Perdue's claim because USDA's owns research analyzing the effects of the Obama regulation that requires more fruits and leafy green vegetables in school lunches and restricting snacks proves that claim is just so much garbage. USDA's own 2019 "School Nutrition and Meal Cost Study" said there was no dramatic change in the amount of food waste as a result of the Obama rules, and that there was better participation in school meal programs as a result.

The watering down of the school lunch program comes as the Centers for Disease Control (CDC) reports that the prevalence of obesity in children and adolescents aged 2-19 years is 18.5 percent, affecting about 13.7 million children and adolescents.

Other key CDC childhood obesity facts:

1. Obesity prevalence was 13.9% among 2- to 5-year-olds, 18.4% among 6- to 11-year-olds, and 20.6% among 12- to 19-year-olds.

2. Hispanics (25.8%) and non-Hispanic blacks (22.0%) had higher obesity prevalence than non-Hispanic whites (14.1%).
3. Non-Hispanic Asians (11.0%) had lower obesity prevalence than non-Hispanic blacks and Hispanics.

Low Income Kids Hurt

Vox points out that for many low-income children, school is the only opportunity to access a nutritious meal. It said that for the 30 million students who depend on free and low-cost school lunches subsidized by the federal government, the relaxed nutrition standards could be "hugely detrimental."

Vox added that "the Healthy, Hunger-Free Kids Act was a game-changing way of providing low-income students with healthy meals — by relaxing these rules, the Trump administration is exacerbating a system where only those who can afford to eat healthy will be able to do so."

Research from the Food Research and Action Center says that the Trump plan could result in childhood obesity rates rising even further.

Dr. Rachel Borton, director of the Family Nurse Practitioner online program at Bradley University, argued in an op-ed for The Hill that poor eating in childhood can have lasting effects by forming poor eating habits.

"If those students don't have access to the nutritious options provided by the school, they may turn to low cost, processed foods that are high in calories but sparse in nutrients. Immediate effects of this type of diet include weight gain and poor physical health," Borton wrote. "Long-term impacts range from increased risk of obesity, heart disease, diabetes, and a slew of other unfortunate health outcomes."

Thanks, Trump administration. Another example of your selling out the American people to satisfy your big business supporters, and to take another stab at President Obama.

Fighting for Stella

By Susan Hutchinson

January 31, 2020

I'm thinking of my friend Stella today. I was in the same grade school class in Chicago with her brother Emilio. Emilio passed away a decade ago from brain cancer and Stella is now fighting liver cancer.

But cancer is not all she is battling. She does not have enough money to pay for the high cost of the hospital, doctors and the treatments she needs to stay alive.

In one of the world's wealthiest countries, people like Stella must find ways to pay the high cost of long-term medical care, so, Vince, her husband, posted on Facebook yesterday that he is selling his collectible records and his guitars to pay medical costs.

Image if you had to sell off your prized possessions just to get money so your wife can continue medical treatments that will save her life. Or maybe you know someone who has already had to do this.

Vince also has created a Facebook fundraising page to try to raise the money for Stella's care, but after two months, donations aren't even close to what they need.

Medical Bankruptcy

Every year millions of people in the U.S. find themselves far short of the money needed to pay the high cost of necessary medical care. Bankruptcy caused by medical expenses affects people who are self or uninsured, but also those with insurance through an employer. A large percentage of people who declare bankruptcy do so because the cost of medical expenses is too much for them to bear, even if they have retirement accounts.

Stella and I grew up in an age before IRA and 401(k) were available. Back then people stayed in the same job for most or all of their lives and if your employer had a pension plan you were lucky. Pensions were a good supplement to the expected Social Security and Medicare that you could count on when you retired. You also saved a little "for a rainy day".

In 2020, for millions of people, especially seniors, that rainy day has turned into a hurricane.

Republicans Want to Make It Even Harder

When Donald Trump ran for president in 2016, he claimed he would not cut Medicare or Social Security. Now that he is in the White House and running for a second term, that old promise has gone by the wayside. Plus, the Affordable Care Act (ACA) has been under attack by Trump and Republicans since it was implemented in 2010. Repeal and replace is now just repeal.

The ACA goes a long way toward helping millions of people get healthcare coverage for themselves and their families, but it is still provided by insurance companies and, just like employer-provided health insurance, premium costs are determined by the choice of annual deductibles and out of pocket maximums.

Consumers can lower their monthly premiums by choosing higher deductibles, which can be upwards of $10,000 or more. Out of pocket maximums usually add $2,000 or more annually. The out of pocket maximum is potentially what someone could pay when a medical catastrophe strikes. Long-term care that carries over into the next year doubles the out of pocket costs as deductibles start over every year.

Medicaid, which covers over 70 million people is also a target for this administration.

You can see why people like Stella struggle when they are faced with suddenly paying for medical care to just to stay alive. But staying alive shouldn't be the only goal when you are sick.

Everyone has the right to a quality of life where they don't have to constantly worry if they can afford rent or to put food on the table because every penny went to pay off medical bills and there was nothing left. Life should have some joy to it, even if it's just little things like holding on to cherished possessions like Vince's records and guitars.

What Can Be Done?

Everyone needs to demand our right to affordable healthcare. This is not just a Democratic issue; it is an American issue. Support the Democratic candidate you think can fix our broken system and stop the madness of out of control insurance companies, medical and prescription drug costs. Then lobby everyone you know to get out and vote so we can become a progressive nation on healthcare, not regressive.

And if you feel the need to pray, pray for Stella and the millions of people like her across America. Pray not just that they survive their life-threatening diseases, but also that they survive the financial burden that goes on for years after the disease has gone into remission.

If you are on Facebook and would like to contribute to Stella's fundraiser, Vince says "every little bit will help".

VFW: Trump Apologize for Disrespecting Injured Troops

January 25, 2020

By Bob Gatty

The Veterans of Foreign Wars (VFW) is demanding that President Trump apologize for downplaying the seriousness of traumatic brain injuries (TBI) suffered by 34 U.S. service members in Iran's missile attacks following the Trump-ordered U.S. assassination of a top Iranian general.

During the World Economic Forum in Davos, Switzerland Trump was asked to explain the discrepancy between his claim that no US military personnel were injured in the January 8 attack on the Al-Asad airbase in Iraq and reports that troops were being treated for injuries resulting from the attack.

"No, I heard they had headaches, and a couple of other things, but I would say, and I can report, it's not very serious" Trump told reporters, adding that compared to soldiers losing limbs in war, traumatic brain injuries are small potatoes.

While the Defense and Veterans Brain Injury Center says most TBI injuries are considered mild (concussions), they can have long-term effects on cognition.

"The VFW expects an apology from the President to our service men and women for his misguided remarks," William "Doc" Schmitz, VFW National Commander, said Friday, following the Pentagon's announcement that 34 US service members have been diagnosed with TBIs from the January 8 Iranian attack.

"And, we ask that he and the White House join with us in our efforts to educate Americans of the dangers TBI has on these heroes as they protect our great nation in these trying times. Our warriors require our full support more than ever in this challenging environment," Schmitz declared.

According to the Pentagon, 17 of the 34 who were injured have returned to duty in Iraq, but nine are still being treated in Germany while eight have been sent to the U.S. for additional treatment.

Apparently, Mr. Macho Man, with his need to bluster and brag about America's might and invisibility in the face of retaliation for the killing of Gen. Qasem Soleimani, felt it necessary to minimize the injuries suffered by U.S. troops when Iran's missiles exploded.

In doing so, he disrespected the men and women in uniform who bravely defend our nation, unlike Trump himself, who weaseled out of the draft with bone spur claims and would run for the hills if ever faced with incoming fire.

Veterans should remember this come the election of November 3, 2020, assuming Trump is still on the ballot.

Health System's Income Skyrockets; Medicaid Cuts Ahead

February 10, 2020
By Bob Gatty

On the same day Kaiser Permanente reported it had nearly tripled its income in 2019, governors of both parties warned that a proposed Trump administration regulation could lead to huge Medicaid cuts, reducing healthcare access for vulnerable, low-income Americans.

While neither of those facts are directly connected, combined they're a microcosm of what is wrong with healthcare in America today and the mindset that currently prevails among Trump and his Republican Congressional supporters.

As some Democratic presidential candidates, such as Elizabeth Warren and Bernie Sanders, rail against the healthcare corporations and insurance industry for ripping off the American people and failing to provide the affordable care and coverage we have a right to expect, Kaiser Permanente is "riding a wave of both strong operating performance and strong investment performance," according to industry publication Modern Healthcare.

The Oakland, CA-based integrated health system reported net income of $7.4 billion, compared to $2.5 billion in 2018.

Meanwhile, the Associated Press reported that an arcane fiscal accountability rule proposed by the Centers for Medicare and Medicaid Services (CMS) could lead to big Medicaid cuts. That's in addition to the administration's plans to turn Medicaid into a block grant program and give states more power over the health plan that's designed to serve low income individuals. That plan could dramatically reduce healthcare availability for millions of low-income individuals.

Under the proposed rule, CMS would tighten federal oversight and approval over complex financing strategies states have used to help pay their share of the $600 billion program, AP reported. Also targeted are certain payments to hospitals that treat many low-income patients. Public comments closed last week amid a chorus of criticism from hospitals, nursing homes, insurers, doctors, and advocates for the poor.

"States may be unable to adequately fund their Medicaid programs, which could lead to unintended consequences that would negatively impact Medicaid beneficiaries across the country," wrote Govs. Kate Brown, D-Ore., and Charlie Baker, R-Mass., in official comments on behalf of National Governors Association.

Here's what these two unrelated reports combined look like to me:

While big business health plans are rolling in the dough, money pouring in from every income source imaginable, investments, fees charged to patients, profits from drugs, whatever, people who can afford it the least -- those with the lowest incomes -- are once again about to get screwed.

Is that the way it should be? I don't think so.

Perhaps this Medicare-for-All idea isn't so wacky after all.

Disrespecting 'the Dignity of Every Human Being'

June 13, 2020

by Bob Gatty

The Trump administration, in finalizing a rule to end nondiscrimination protections for LGBTQ people in health care and health insurance, says it "respects the dignity of every human being."

Just the opposite. That action, which undoes yet another Obama administration initiative, disrespects anyone who does not fit Trump's view of humanity. Ironically, it comes during Gay Pride Month, perhaps intentionally.

"HHS respects the dignity of every human being, and as we have shown in our response to the pandemic, we vigorously protect and enforce the civil rights of all to the fullest extent permitted by our laws as passed by Congress," said Roger Severino, director of the Office for Civil Rights in the Department of Health and Human Services, in announcing that the HHS rule, set to take effect by mid-August, had become final.

Explained NPR.org, the rule deals with nondiscrimination protections contained in the Affordable Care Act, which makes it illegal to discriminate on the basis of "race, color, national origin, sex, age or disability in certain health programs and activities." In 2016, an Obama-era rule explained that protections regarding "sex" include those based on gender identity, which it defined as "male, female, neither, or a combination of male and female."

But when the Trump administration proposed the new rule last June, Severino said, "We're going back to the plain meaning of those terms, which is based on biological sex."

Under the new rule, a transgender person could be refused care for a checkup at a doctor's office, Lindsey Dawson, associate director of HIV policy at the Kaiser Family Foundation told NPR. A transgender man could be denied treatment for ovarian cancer, or a hysterectomy not being covered by an insurer — or costing more when the procedure is related to someone's gender transition.

"We know that LGBTQ people experience discrimination at disproportionately higher rates when seeking medical care which, even before the COVID-19 pandemic, led to devastating health outcomes," said Sasha Buchert, Senior Attorney and Co-Director of Lambda Legal's Transgender Rights Project.

"The Trump administration has enshrined its discriminatory interpretation into the HHS rule book but that does not – and cannot – actually change the law. However, this is enough to cause confusion and hurt our communities, especially transgender people and people of color who already face elevated rates of discrimination in health care settings. This rule change serves no other purpose than to target and discriminate against LGBTQ people," Bucher said. "The cruelty is the point."

"Today's rule is a tragically failed public health policy and just flat out illegal," said Omar Gonzalez-Pagan, Senior Attorney and Health Care Strategist. "We will be challenging the rule because at a time when the entire world is battling a dangerous pandemic, which in the United States has infected more than 2,000,000 people and killed more than 116,000, it is critical for everyone to have ready access to the potentially life-saving health care they need. LGBTQ people need to know that they continue to have rights and Lambda Legal will fight back. If you experience discrimination when seeking health care because of your sexual orientation, gender identity or HIV status you should contact us immediately."

It should be no surprise that the Office for Civil Rights at HHS would take such action under Severino. He joined the Trump administration from the conservative think tank, Heritage Foundation, where he wrote a paper on gender protections in Section 1557.

A devout Catholic, he has made protections of religious freedom a key focus, including the right of doctors to refuse to provide care that contradicts their religious or moral beliefs.

Until Donald Trump is removed from office, such actions will continue by this administration with its misguided, sexist attitudes about sexuality and humanity.

6

TRASHING THE ENVIRONMENT

Among the many catastrophic actions of the Trump Administration, its attack on the environment is one of the most far-reaching with potentially devastating consequences for years to come. A combination of Trump's blind hatred of former President Obama and his determination to undo every possible Obama achievement, while denying climate change, will jeopardize the future for generations still unborn.

Climate Change, Rick Perry, and How Coal Can Stop Rape

November 3, 2017

By Bob Gatty

Energy Secretary Rick Perry, who clunked his way across the Dancing With the Stars stage after dropping out of the GOP presidential primary last year, now says that coal can somehow reduce sexual assault.

Perry espoused this belief during an energy conference in Washington sponsored by Axios and NBC News yesterday, saying that bringing coal-fired power to people in Africa would help save lives. Then, he said:

"But also, from the standpoint of sexual assault, when the lights are on, when you have light that shines, the righteousness, if you will, on those types of acts," Perry said. "So, from the standpoint of how you really affect people's lives, fossil fuels is going to play a role in that. I happen to think it's going to play a positive role."

So, coal can shine the light of "righteousness" on someone who is about to commit sexual assault? Reminds me of the Sunday School song, "This little light of mine, I'm gonna let it shine...don't let Satan blow it out, this little light of mine."

Perry apparently loves coal and is a true believer in Trump's promise to bring coal mining jobs back, even though technology and the advent of much cleaner sources of power have largely made it obsolete.

Perry also said during the energy forum that he still does not believe humans are the main drivers of climate change. "I think the science is out," he said.

Well, that's interesting, Mr. Genius Secretary of Energy, because the science is in.

Your own administration -- 13 federal agencies -- just issued a major scientific study declaring, unequivocally, that actions by humans are to blame for our changing climate. It's not what Trump wanted to hear, and it flies in the face if the skeptics within his administration, but it was issued anyway because it is part of a congressionally mandated National Climate Assessment issued every four years. It was developed by hundreds of experts within the government and academia and was peer-reviewed by the National Academy of Sciences. Thus, it is considered the United States' most definitive statement on climate change science.

So, Mr. Brainiac Energy Secretary, if you can bring yourself to read that report -- maybe when you go buddy bye with a nice reading light, perhaps you'll realize that the "light of righteousness" is shining on those who are trying to save this planet, not those who, out of ignorance, greed, or political expedience -- or all three -- would slowly destroy it.

Tales of Another Swamp Rat

April 18, 2018
By Bob Gatty
Yesterday, President Trump signed a new executive order designed to make it harder for states to protect the environment, all in the name of getting out of the way of corporations that want to build new projects that could harm the environment.

Since Trump has spent the first year of his administration wiping out environmental protections one after another and continues to deny the science of climate change, why is this surprising?

The executive order issued as instructions to his pal, Scott Pruitt, administrator of the Environmental PROTECTION Agency (EPA), is intended to change the way the EPA determines whether states are meeting federal air-quality standards.

The measure imposes stricter deadlines for EPA approval of state plans and changes the way air pollutants are measured.

The Washington Post quoted John Walke, who directs the clean air program at the Natural Resources Defense Council, as saying that the executive order prescribes measures "intended to allow more air pollution, or abbreviated air quality reviews that risk more air pollution, or both."

The order, which was signed with no public announcement and has had limited media coverage, could have far-reaching implications on the nation as Trump and Pruitt continue their attack on Obama-era initiatives to protect the environment and combat climate change.

I found the reference to the executive order near the end the Post's article detailing Pruitt's arrogant rip-offs of the taxpayers in his travels and other ridiculous activities, such as demanding construction of a $43,000 soundproof phone booth for his office -- just another example of how Trump, rather than "draining" the Washington swamp, has filled it with rats and snakes.

The article was based on allegations by an EPA whistleblower, Kevin Chmielewski, who served as deputy chief of staff for operations at the Environmental Protection Agency until last month. He is now alleging that Pruitt engaged in spending excesses and questionable ethics decisions, which he has outlined in detail.

That action prompted five Congressional Democrats to detail his accusations in a six-page letter that revealed stays in boutique hotels that exceeded federal spending caps, frequent trips home to Oklahoma charged to taxpayers, and costly flights on Delta Air Lines so he could maximize his frequent-flier miles.

In a letter to Pruitt, the lawmakers declared, "The new information provided by Mr. Chmielewski, if accurate, leaves us certain that your leadership at EPA has been fraught with unethical and potentially illegal actions on a wide range of consequential matters that you and some members of your staff directed." The lawmakers requested a long list of documents from the agency.

According to The Post, Trump originally intended to sign his executive order with Pruitt in attendance, but that plan was shelved after the latest ethics charges against the EPA boss became public.

Guarding EPA's Pruitt Costs Millions as He Trashes Environment

May 25, 2018

By Bob Gatty

The cost of protecting Scott Pruitt, the EPA dirtbag administrator who is carrying out Trump's policies of dismantling protections of our environment, totals nearly $3.5 million over the past year.

That amount has paid for the salaries ($2,726,719) of 19 agents who protect Pruitt around the clock plus more than $763,000 on travel for Pruitt's detail, which accompanied him to Morocco and Italy, as well as to his Oklahoma home and personal events, like the Rose Bowl and Disneyland.

This report from CNN Politics notes those costs far exceed the cost of protecting his predecessors over the past nine years. Pruitt's security costs are about double what was spent the prior year, when salary costs were $1.4 million, and travel costs for the security detail reached $312,000.

I don't know about you, but I object to my tax dollars being paid to protect Pruitt, who was imbedded by Trump into the EPA to pretty much destroy it. He has set about, diligently, in doing just that.

Many other Americans also object as is evident in the hostile way Pruitt is treated when he travels, so hostile, in fact, that the EPA says he must fly first class to keep him away from the riffraff who don't like his efforts to eliminate protections for clean air and clean water.

Here's how EPA explains it:

"Administrator Pruitt has faced an unprecedented amount of death threats against him and to provide transparency EPA will post the costs of his security detail and pro-actively release these numbers on a quarterly basis," EPA spokesman Jahan Wilcox said in a statement. "Americans should all agree that members of the President's cabinet should be kept safe from violent threats."

Well, CNN reports that many members of Congress question just how serious those "death" threats might be, noting that many come from social media postings and comments from fellow passengers.

In another article last month, CNN reported that Pruitt's moves -- some of which have been challenged in court -- represent an attempt to fundamentally restructure the EPA's role in Washington and are a sharp rebuke of the environmental legacy of former President Barack Obama.

Some of Pruitt's key moves include:

- Pretending the dangers of climate change do not exist.
- Rolling back car emissions standards.
- Proposing to overhaul initiatives on coal ash.
- Withdrawing regulations on 'major sources' of pollution.
- Suspending the clean water rule.
- Withdrawing from the Clean Power Plan.
- Trying to suspend Obama-era methane rule.
- Encouraging Trump to withdraw US from Paris climate accord.

I think they should give him one security agent and that the agent and Pruitt should be required to fly in coach as do most of the taxpayers who pay for their salaries and their travel expenses.

Thought Trump was going to empty the swamp? From my point of view, he's simply replaced Obama's people with a bunch of rats, Pruitt at the head of the pack.

Selling of our National Treasures for the Sake of Greed

July 3, 2018
By Bob Gatty

A Canadian mining firm is planning to mine for minerals on land that was protected as a national monument until Donald Trump came to power. The land in question was previously part of the Grand Staircase-Escalante National Monument in Utah.

So, as we celebrate the July 4th holiday, let's remember that one of the national treasures that made America great for many, many years has been our national parks and national monuments, beautiful, unspoiled land that is unlike any other place on earth.

Oh, say can you see? Oh, I see it, huge mining equipment plowing through this hallowed land. And it's all because of greed. Is this how Trump is Making America Great Again?

Last December, he removed nearly half of the Grand Staircase-Escalante from protection, as well as part of the Bears Ears National Monument, also in Utah. It was the largest reversal of national monument protections in U.S. history.

Glacier Lake Resources Inc., a Vancouver-based copper and silver mining firm, has acquired the Colt Mesa deposit, an approximately 200-acre parcel of land located about 35 miles southeast of Boulder, Utah, NPR reports.

Because it was nationally protected, the area was previously off limits to development and mining. In a press release the company noted that the deposit "recently became open for staking and exploration after a 21- year period moratorium."

According to Saf Dhillon, president and CEO of Glacier Lake Resources, the company's extraction of minerals would have little impact on tourism and the environment. Glacier Lake Resources says it has conducted sampling that confirmed the presence of several minerals, including cobalt.

President Bill Clinton established the Grand Staircase-Escalante National Monument in 1996, then the largest national monument in the country. No longer.

President Trump also has slashed the Bears Ears National Monument by about a million acres — to roughly 15 percent of its original size.

Trump issued an executive order in April 2017 instructing Interior Secretary Ryan Zinke to review any national monument created since 1996. Trump said the review would return control of the land "to the people, the people of all of the states, the people of the United States."

So, we the people get to see our national treasures sold off to satisfy Trump's unending thirst for the almighty dollar. What will be next? The Grand Canyon?

Wake up, America. This man is ruining our country.

The Environment: Greed Remains in Control

July 20, 2018

By Bob Gatty

In another example of unvarnished greed being in control in Washington, the Trump administration is continuing its assault on America's environment by stripping the longstanding Endangered Species Act (ESA) from provisions intended to protect wildlife.

The proposal, announced jointly by the Interior and Commerce departments, which are charged with protecting endangered wildlife, would end the practice of extending protections to species regardless of whether they are listed as endangered or threatened. If the proposal is approved, protections for threatened plants and animals would be made on a case-by-case basis, The Washington Post reports.

In its announcement, complete with the pretty picture of the federally endangered Nihoa Millerbird above, the Fish and Wildlife service said: "The Service proposes to remove its blanket rule under section 4(d) of the ESA that automatically conveys the same protections for threatened species as for endangered species.

"This change will not affect the protections for species currently listed as threatened but will ensure that species listed as threatened in the future receive the protections tailored to the species' individual conservation needs."

The Trump administration also wants the U.S. Fish and Wildlife Service and National Oceanic and Atmospheric Administration to strike language that guides officials to ignore economic impacts when determining how wildlife should be protected.

In other words, economic impacts will now be considered when determining wildlife protection when construction projects and the like are undertaken. That means money -- greed -- will rule. Yes, sometimes it seems almost silly to block a badly needed highway because it would disturb the nesting grounds of some imperiled species, but where does it end? What rules? In the case of the Trump administration, the answer is clear and easy: Greed.

"These regulations are the heart of how the Endangered Species Act is implemented. Imperiled species depend on them for their very lives," said Jamie Rappaport Clark, who was director of the Fish and Wildlife Service under President Bill Clinton, according to The Post. Clark is now president and chief executive of Defenders of Wildlife, a nonprofit advocacy group.

"These proposals would slam a wrecking ball into the most crucial protections for our most endangered wildlife," said Brett Hartl, government affairs director at the Center for Biological Diversity. "If these regulations had been in place in the 1970s, the bald eagle and the gray whale would be extinct today. If they're finalized now, (Interior Secretary Ryan) Zinke will go down in history as the extinction secretary."

The proposed changes will be posted to the Federal Register in a matter of days. The Trump administration has invited public comment on the rules, which will be open for 60 days on regulations.gov after they are posted.

This new policy is a continuation of the attack on the environment that was launched almost immediately by Trump and his lieutenants. Many of the actions roll back Obama-era policies that aimed to curb climate change and limit pollution, while others threaten to limit federal funding for science and the environment.

EPA's Clean Car Rollback: An Unhealthy, Unnecessary Plan

August 7, 2018
By Bob Gatty
The Trump administration's plan announced last week to weaken the 2020-2026 auto emissions and mileage requirements has been blasted by 10 major health and medical organizations, and now we learn that even the auto industry, which had lobbied for relief, apparently thinks it goes too far.

To be effective in 2020, the proposal would eliminate the requirement that new cars and light trucks increase average fuel efficiency every year. Instead, it would freeze the fuel-economy standard at about 29 miles per gallon until 2025 -- compared to the Obama administration's requirement that new cars and trucks average about 43 miles per gallon by that same year.

Trump says it will make cars cheaper and save jobs.

In addition, the plan by the Environmental Protection (?) Agency (EPA) and the National Highway Traffic Safety Administration (NHTSA), would prohibit states from establishing higher standards than those imposed by the feds.

Once again, the Trump administration's priorities are infinitely clear. Support industry and to hell with healthy air, clean water and the well-being of the inhabitants of this planet.

"This proposal from EPA and NHTSA would dismantle fair, achievable pollution limits with a track record of success, limits that will help protect Americans from the life-threatening health impacts of climate change. The proposal would also preempt the ability of states to protect the health of their residents by curbing greenhouse gas emissions from vehicles. If these vehicle standards are weakened, the nation loses a crucial tool to fight climate change," said a statement issued by these health and medical groups:

- The American Lung Association
- Allergy & Asthma Network
- Alliance of Nurses for Healthy Environments
- American Public Health Association
- Asthma and Allergy Foundation of America
- Center for Climate Change and Health
- Children's Environmental Health Network
- Health Care Without Harm
- National Association of County and City Health Officials
- National Environmental Health Association

"Today's announcement reaches beyond efforts to weaken cleaner cars standards at the federal level—it also threatens states' right to limit dangerous vehicle pollution and take more aggressive steps to protect their residents," the statement said.

"This action hampers not only California's ability to protect the health of its citizens, but also that of a dozen other states that have driven nationwide progress in reducing tailpipe pollution, including Connecticut, Delaware, Maine, Maryland, Massachusetts, New Jersey, New York, Oregon, Pennsylvania, Rhode Island, Vermont and Washington.

"Rolling back these standards is another step backward from the essential fight to avoid the worst impacts of climate change. From degraded air quality due to higher temperatures to increased risk from wildfires, climate change poses serious threats to all Americans, especially to the most vulnerable, including children, older adults and those living with chronic diseases," the heath groups' statement declared.

Industry: A Step too Far

The administration's plan even has the auto industry itself concerned, according to this article in The Atlantic.

"With today's release of the administration's proposals, it's time for substantive negotiations to begin," said Gloria Bergquist, a spokeswoman for the Auto Alliance, which represents the major U.S. auto companies, in a statement. In other words, the industry wasn't really looking for an outright freeze.

"We urge California and the federal government to find a commonsense solution that sets continued increases in vehicle efficiency standards while also meeting the needs of America's drivers," the statement said.

Bottom line? The Trump administration is proposing weaker auto clean air and fuel efficiency standards than even the industry wants, while at the same time putting everyone's health at risk.

Brilliant.

A Killer Environmental Strategy

August 21, 2018
By Bob Gatty

President Trump and his buddies in the administration today rolled out yet another new initiative that is part of his killer environmental strategy, one that sounds the death knell on clean air and clean water and makes a joke out of efforts to at least slow the devastating impact of climate change.

And while that was happening, I was at the recycling center trying to do what I can to limit the amount of trash our household contributes to the landfill, which one day is going to run out.

There, I saw an elderly woman get out her pickup truck, grab her four-footed cane in one hand and a couple of cans in the other, then hobble over to the huge container where cans and bottles are to be deposited, and toss them in.

Then, she slowly made her way back to her truck, grabbed a couple more cans, and took them over to the container. I watched as she made several trips to do this, and finally, asked her if she needed help. She looked at me with a quizzical look and said, "No, sonny, I've got this."

First time in a long while anyone called me "sonny".

So, as I drove away, I wondered what she thinks of Trump's determination to ruin our environment to satisfy his West Virginia coal mining supporters and the big corporations who have been lobbying to roll back the Obama administration's environmental protections.

All of this comes, of course, after Trump's consistent actions that demonstrate that he holds environmental initiatives in utter disdain. Bringing asbestos back. Deriding wind energy. Initiating tariffs that devastate solar. And the latest, promoting "clean coal."

His own Environmental Protection Agency (EPA) projects that if finalized, its new regulation could lead to between 470 and 1,400 premature deaths each year compared to the Obama-era rule.

The woman at the recycling center probably will not be affected directly by Trump's policies -- after all, she appeared to be in her late 80s, if not older. But if she has kids, grandkids and great grandkids, they will.

Speaking of climate change, this Washington Post article graphically outlines how rising seas caused by climate change are depressing property values in some coastal communities projected to one day be under water. Although that should cause the Trump team to take notice -- after all, money is at stake -- they will poopoo it because they deny climate change is real.

Greed. That's what drives this administration, this presidency, and in the end, it will only serve to Make America Polluted Again. And, its killer environmental strategy may well have a long-term, devastating impact on the future of our country and those who come after us.

Science Scuttled at EPA; Report Warns of Environmental Disaster

September 29, 2018

By Bob Gatty

As a government report warned of a coming climate change disaster, it was revealed that the Environmental Protection Agency (EPA) plans to scuttle the Office of Science Advisor, created to counsel the E.P.A. administrator on scientific research on which health and environmental regulations are based.

The warning was buried in a 500-page report by the National Highway Traffic Safety Administration (NHTSA), written to justify freezing federal fuel-efficiency standards for cars and light trucks built after 2020.

The study, reported by The Washington Post, said that on its current course, the earth will warm a disastrous seven degrees by the end of this century.

Said The Post:

A rise of seven degrees Fahrenheit, or about four degrees Celsius, compared with preindustrial levels would be catastrophic, according to scientists. Many coral reefs would dissolve in increasingly acidic oceans. Parts of Manhattan and Miami would be underwater without costly coastal defenses. Extreme heat waves would routinely smother large parts of the globe.

But the administration did not offer this dire forecast, premised on the idea that the world will fail to cut its greenhouse gas emissions, as part of an argument to combat climate change. Just the opposite: The analysis assumes the planet's fate is already sealed.

In other words, since human activity has already doomed the earth's atmosphere, we might as well just ride it out and make as much money as possible.

Apparently the same logic was used at the EPA to get rid of the Office of Science Advisor, which works to ensure that the highest quality science is integrated into the agency's policies and decisions, reported The New York Times. Since climate change isn't real, why do we need scientific advice?

The action is just the latest at the agency to diminish the role that science plays in its policy decision making. According to Science Advisor Dr. Jennifer Orme-Zavaleta, dissolution of the office was just a matter of being more efficient by eliminating redundancies and duplication of effort.

Both of these developments occurred this past week, clearly indicating the Trump administration's blatant disregard for the truth about climate change and its hellbent determination to reduce federal regulations with which businesses must comply -- whether they are needed or not.

So, what if parts of Manhattan and Miami would be flooded or extreme heat waves would routinely smother large parts of the globe if temperatures rise an average seven degrees by the end of the century, as predicted.

Who cares?

Nobody in the Trump administration will be around to see it, so what the hell. Let's just not worry about it. Wouldn't want the auto or fossil fuel industries to take a hit, would we?

When these people are finished, what kind of country -- what kind of world -- will be left for our kids and grandkids?

◆◆◆

Should the World be Subjected to Trump's 'Gut'?

November 27, 2018

By Bob Gatty

President Trump is making sweeping decisions that literally effect the future of the world, not based on facts, not based on science, but based on his "gut."

On Monday, he dismissed a study produced by 13 federal agencies in his administration and more than 300 leading climate scientists, warning of the potentially catastrophic impact of climate change.

"I don't believe it," he said.

And because he simply doesn't believe the scientifically based assessments of his own agencies and hundreds of top climate scientists, the U.S. continues to take action that not only reverse the climate change advances of the Obama administration, but actually worsens the situation.

In my opinion, it's all based on Trump's own stubbornness, his ego, and greed. He's right and everyone else is wrong -- always.

Actually, I thought perhaps the report, issued on Black Friday when most Americans were too busy to pay attention, might give Trump pause because it warns of serious economic consequences of climate change. Economic. That means money. And that's what Trump likes, so you'd think he'd at least be concerned about that.

The report, the second of four such annual studies commissioned by Congress, concludes that the world's temperature is rising and that evidence shows that human actions play a role. It concludes that the changing climate "is transforming where and how we live and presents growing challenges to human health and quality of life, the economy, and the natural systems that support us."

It warns of "substantial damages to the US economy, environment, and human health and well-being over the coming decades."

The report predicts climate change will result in hundreds of billions lost, with farms being hardest hit, and that factors like air quality, disease transmission by insects, food and water will "increasingly threaten the health and well-being of the American people."

While not cited in the report, the recent devastating wildfires in California have been at least partially attributed to factors resulting from climate change -- extremely hot and dry conditions. Trump's reaction, though, was, "naw, all you gotta do is a better job of raking the leaves."

Guess that's what his gut told him.

No worries, though, says Trump of the climate report.

"I don't believe it," so there is no need to take steps to curtail auto emissions or industrial pollution. Just a waste of money for all concerned. Just keep on burning that "beautiful, clean coal."

Today, in an interview with the Washington Post, Trump said, "As to whether or not it's man-made and whether or not the effects that you're talking about are there, I don't see it."

But Wait, There's More

Climate change isn't the only area where Trump's decisions are ruled by his gut.

In the Washington Post interview, Trump blasted Federal Reserve Chairman Jerome H. "Jay" Powell, whom he nominated earlier this year, for raising interest rates and blamed that action and other Fed policies for the recent tanking of the stock market and GM's announcement that it was laying off 15 percent of its workforce,

"I'm doing deals, and I'm not being accommodated by the Fed," Trump said. "They're making a mistake because I have a gut, and my gut tells me more sometimes than anybody else's brain can ever tell me."

So, if Trump had his way U.S. economic policy would be driven by his gut, not by sound economic principles.

Really? Is this how such important decisions should be made? Decisions that affect every American, indeed, virtually every citizen of the world?

Frankly, I don't think so.

Dirty Money, Dirty Air

August 13, 2019

By Bob Gatty

As the U.S. Environmental Protection Agency issues a report outlining the remarkable achievements of the 49-year-old Clean Air Act, the Trump administration is taking steps to relax federal requirements that have contributed to those environmental improvements over the years.

Trump says those weaker regulations are necessary to help polluting companies generate more profits, so in the future if our air and water become more polluted -- dirtier -- those enhanced profits could only be described as "dirty money."

The EPA report says that six key pollutants -- ground-level ozone (smog), particulate matter (soot or smoke), carbon monoxide, lead, sulfur dioxide, and nitrogen dioxide -- declined 73 percent since the Clean Air Act was enacted in 1970.

"This progress occurred while the U.S. economy continued to grow, Americans drove more miles and population and energy use increased," the EPA report says, adding that "Today Americans breath cleaner air and face lower risks of adverse health effects" as a result of the Clean Air Act.

"These are remarkable achievements that should be recognized, celebrated, and replicated around the around the world," said acting EPA Administrator Andrew Wheeler on a conference call with reporters. "A 73% reduction in any other social ill, such as crime, disease, or drug addiction would lead the evening news."

Yes, that certainly is great news and worthy of celebration. Then why, on God's green earth, would the Trump administration seek to undercut the very reasons for those remarkable gains?

Here's a quick summary from USA Today of what they are up to:

- In December, then-EPA Administrator Scott Pruitt issued a memo reducing the chances an energy plant will have to abide by stricter air quality standards if it initially miscalculates its future pollutant emissions.

- In January, Pruitt issued a memo repealing a Clinton-era policy known as "once in, always in." The change means industrial facilities deemed "major" sources of air pollution can once again be reclassified as "minor" polluters and, therefore, escape tough clean air regulations.

- In April, President Trump issued a directive, instructing the EPA to work with states that have metro areas which fail to attain clean air standards by giving them additional "flexibility" to meet them. The president's primary aim, the directive states, is "promoting domestic manufacturing and job creation."

- And within days, the administration is expected to formally lay out a plan revisiting strict fuel-economy standards for American light trucks and cars that had been set in motion under President Barack Obama. Environmentalists believe the plan will call at the very least for a lowering of the standard, which calls for yearly increases in fuel efficiency until it hits 54.5 mpg by the end of 2025.

Today, a coalition of 22 states and nine cities sued to block the Trump administration's plans to ease restrictions on coal-burning power plants. Remember how Trump promised to bring back "clean coal?" Guess this is part of that plan.

The lawsuit contends that the EPA had no basis for weakening a regulation established under President Obama (now we know the real reason, right?) that established national limits on carbon dioxide pollution from power plants.

Called the Clean Power Plan, that rule required states to reduce CO2 emissions by 2022, close heavily polluting plants and replace those energy sources with natural gas or renewable energy. CO2 emissions are a major contributor to global warming, but then that's just a hoax, right. Those nasty gases don't really trap the sun's heat, despite what science says. Nope. That's just the figment of a bunch of wacky liberals' imagination.

As a result, we may see yet another result of Trump's effort to pack the Supreme Court with conservative justices. As this legal fight could end up being decided in those hallowed chambers, an adverse result could permanently weaken the nation's ability to combat factors that contribute to global warming -- to say nothing of our ability to keep the air and water free from harmful pollutants.

Maybe you don't care about this. But your children and grandchildren should because that is the environment they will inherit.

Weather Report

August 31, 2019

By Steve Hamelman

As Hurricane Dorian nears Florida, a theologically minded person is apt to recall the tendency of 17th-century Puritans to read nature as a compilation of texts containing messages that signified God's purpose in the world.

Hundreds of years after the Puritans interpreted every big and little natural fact as a divine lesson, the meteorological data amassed by CNN, the Weather Channel, and all the weather-apps on the Web do not necessarily discourage non-scientific speculation of what a hurricane might signify today.

Politically, for instance.

President Donald Trump has levied his share of destruction against the United States of America, most of it in the form of abusing, dismantling, or obliterating people he doesn't like and policies he doesn't respect. As in: "Lock her up!" "Send them back!" "Good people on both sides!" "Break the law, finish the wall!"

He's a political hurricane whose destructive gyrations never make the turn out to sea, where normal storms eventually dwindle to a feeble dot. His incessant churning gives Americans no chance to clean up the debris left in his wake, rebuild democratic values, and move forward with hope into an uncertain future.

Donald Trump: an ever-renewing category five, constantly fueled by the warm Republican waters lapping up against the doors of the White House and seeping into the Oval Office—a kind of insolent typhoon which, after crawling up the coast tearing up all civility in the body politic, crawls right back down again to pick off any survivors.

So forceful are the winds that emerge from his mouth, his tweeting fingers, and his surrogates and partners in mayhem (Graham, McConnell, Carlson, Conway, ad nauseum) that Donald Trump resembles something that nature itself has never produced: a south/north cyclone also capable of travelling east/west, then back across the continent, over and over in a cyclical path threatening to level anything sane and decent in its path.

Treaties, reputations, historical facts, the Constitution—Americans, take cover!

That's one view, anyway.

And maybe it's a bit much. But still, the analogy stands. After all, what will remain of the American landscape by the end of Donald Trump's reign?

The question is not rhetorical, since it's possible that 14 months from now a Democratic candidate will supplant the President, thereby saving us from four more years of damage. Of the 10 candidates who remain, however, does any single one compare to a weather event that, while tumultuous, cleanses the air rather than ravages the land?

Warren, Biden, Sanders, Harris—of these four frontrunners, Sanders is stylistically and ideologically the most stormy and therefore the most likely to send moderates of both parties running for cover.

Warren combines passion and intelligence, interspersing her speeches with lightning bolts of indignation, while Harris, in flashes of turbulence, reveals intense moral clarity. That leaves Joe Biden, who meanders along like a front that may not pack enough electrical charge to effect atmospheric change.

These four, along with six other hopefuls, swirl around each other like warm waters and warm air finding common cause in the Atlantic Ocean. They swirl, a pattern begins to emerge, and soon, with political spin picking up speed as next November approaches, an eye with a well-funded wall of support will form, and the chosen candidate's voice will grow bigger and stronger and impossible to ignore.

But this candidate will not resemble a hurricane in the everyday sense of the term. He or she will not be a force of wrack and ruin. The contender will have too much heart, too much empathy, and too much progressive character to do anything but transform the United States of America with policies that help all survivors of Hurricane Donald salvage what remains of the American way of life.

Hoping not only that the point of this analogy—the Puritans would have called it a conceit (elaborate metaphor)—is clear, but also that my weather report for Democratic resurgence is accurate, I send my best wishes to all my fellow Americans, no matter what their party affiliation or affinities, who are at this moment in the path of Hurricane Dorian.

Climate Change: Listen to the Teenagers

September 16, 2019

By Bob Gatty

Most American teenagers are convinced that humans are changing the Earth's climate and fear it will harm them personally as well as their generation, according to a new Washington Post-Kaiser Family Foundation poll.

Increasingly, teenagers are staging walkouts from school, demonstrating, and speaking out, warning adults that what they are doing is literally threatening their future.

An inspiration for many is Greta Thunberg, 16, who staged a year-long "strike" in front of the Swedish Parliament and sailed across the Atlantic in a carbon-neutral sailboat to draw attention to the crisis.

As the United Nations prepares for its September 23 Climate Action Summit, thousands of teenagers are planning to skip school to demand more aggressive actions to protect the planet.

While some may cynically say, "Oh, those kids will use any excuse to get out of school," these teens are serious. They realize that the future of the earth is at stake, that generations before them have irresponsibly caused global warming threatening our planet.

"People feel very guilty when a child says, 'You are stealing my future.' That has impact," Thunberg told The Washington Post. "We have definitely made people open their eyes."

All of this comes amid an atmosphere of denial by the Trump administration and its Republican supporters in Congress, as action after action seeks to reverse the safeguards and actions established by previous administrations, especially that of Barack Obama.

The major Democratic candidates for president uniformly have put forth proposals to deal with the climate change crisis, and that is good. Meanwhile, there is no telling how much more damage will be imposed upon us -- and generations to come -- by the climate change deniers who are now in power.

"Climate change is the defining issue of our time and now is the defining moment to do something about it," declares the UN's website announcing the Climate Action Summit. "There is still time to tackle climate change, but it will require an unprecedented effort from all sectors of society."

The Summit is intended to accelerate actions to implement the Paris Agreement on Climate Change, from which President Trump unilaterally withdrew the United States. It will showcase "a leap in collective national political ambition" to combat climate change, the UN's announcement says, adding that it will "send strong market and political signals and inject momentum in the 'race to the top' among countries, companies, cities and civil society that is needed to achieve the objectives of the Paris Agreement and the Sustainable Development Goals."

Of course, today the United States, led by Trump, is engaged in a "race to the bottom," one that follows an irresponsible path that threatens the future for those teenagers who are engaged in protest, their younger brothers and sisters, and those still unborn.

Will Trump's Hate Destroy Our Earth?

November 30, 2019
By Bob Gatty
Since his election, President Trump has systematically set out to undo just about every consequential achievement by the man he hates, Barack Obama, and the world will be forced to live with the consequences for decades to come.

As this CNN article by Drew Kann reports, Trump's rollback of regulations designed to limit global warming is one of the clearest ways he has sought to erase a cornerstone of Obama's legacy.

But it's not just Obama's actions that Trump attacks. He's also used environmental law to attack California, home state of his Congressional nemesis House Speaker Nancy Pelosi and Rep. Adam Schiff, who led the impeachment hearings by the House Intelligence Committee.

Trump's actions, from withdrawing from the Paris climate accord to relaxing power plant emission controls, come as the earth experienced record heat in July, as Greenland's massive ice sheet melts at an alarming rate, and as warming sea waters deplete fish populations and threatens the very livelihood of people as far away as Angola.

The Washington Post reports today that The gradual disappearance of fish is a death knell for Tombwa, an Angola town of 50,000 that has little else. Fish are suffocating in oxygen-depleted waters, huge foreign trawlers are grabbing what's left, and the water is heating up far more rapidly here than almost anywhere else on the planet.

Kann's CNN report noted that last fall the world's top climate scientists warned that global carbon emissions must be cut within a decade if the earth is to avoid the worst consequences of the climate crisis droughts wildfires and food shortages that will affect millions of people around the globe.

What has Trump done so far?

- Weakened fuel economy standards.
- Replaced the Clean Power Plan with the much weaker Affordable Clean Energy rule.
- Opened public lands and offshore waters to oil and gas drilling.
- Pulled out of the Paris climate agreement.
- Loosened methane emission restrictions.
- Delayed ratification of hydrofluorocarbon treaty.

"He is locking in permanent, irreversible damage to our environment through his irresponsible environmental policies, including his efforts to block progress on climate change," Dr. Michael E. Mann, distinguished professor of atmospheric science at Penn State University and the director of the Penn State Earth System Science Center, told CNN.. "Once we go beyond key tipping points -- the melting of the major ice sheets -- there is no going back."

Regardless of what happens to Trump, impeachment or defeat in the 2020 election, the earth will suffer the consequences of his actions, born of hate, vindictiveness and stupidity. Heaven forbid he is reelected. The consequences of his destructiveness would be unimaginable.

Trump Assaults the Environment – Again

January 9, 2020

By Bob Gatty

President Trump today continued his unrelenting attack on the environment with proposed changes to rules that for 50 years have helped prevent industry from raping the natural world in which we all live -- and that help guard against climate change.

Wrapped up in promises that the changes will speed progress on needed infrastructure improvements, the proposed rules would weaken protections provided in the National Environmental Policy Act (NEPA), signed by President Nixon, which requires federal agencies to conduct environmental impact statements before major construction projects can begin.

Trump told reporters that the changes would allow highways to be built in "a small fraction of the time," adding, "We will not stop until our nation's gleaming new infrastructure has made America the envy of the world again. It used to be the envy of the world and now we're like a third-world country. It's really sad."

Especially ominous were the words of Interior Secretary David Bernhardt, who said, "The proposal affects virtually every significant decision by the federal government that affects the environment."

That should give us comfort? We should cheer that?

The end result of the changes would reduce community control over local building projects by redefining what constitutes a "major federal action" to exclude privately financed projects with minimal government funding or involvement.

Court challenges are fully expected but remember what Trump and the Republicans have done to our federal courts, stacking them with dozens of conservative jurists. So, what will the future hold?

Pipelines, offshore drilling, highways -- maybe even Trump's beleaguered Wall on the Southern Border -- could be expedited if environmental impact statements, which often take years to complete, no longer are required. The new proposal would require government agencies to finish their most complex reviews within two years.

Added Bernhadt, "The consequences of the government being stuck in place are far-ranging." He cited the lengthy process for approving new schools on Native American reservations, upgrading visitor centers at national parks and giving ranchers approval for grazing on public lands.

"The list goes on and on and on. The reality is that the needless red tape has, over time, lowered the expectations of American exceptionalism and excellence. And that is backwards."

It is "backwards" to limit the potential damage of pipeline leaks or the destructive environmental impact of strip mining? And it is "backwards" to eliminate requirements that a proposed coal mine or oil drilling operation must consider whether that action would contribute to climate change? That's exactly what this proposal would do.

What is "backwards" is the Trump administration's penchant for returning to the good old days, when things were simple and uncomplicated; where untreated waste water could be discharged into our rivers and streams, where factory smokestacks can spew cancer-causing emissions without control, where huge construction projects can wipe out fields and forests without concern except for the satisfaction of greed.

That will be one of the legacies of Donald J. Trump. The unfettered satisfaction of greed.

Giving Up on Climate Change

February 17, 2020
By Bob Gatty
A 74-year-old Canadian recently wrote in a Huffington Post article that he and his 64-year-old wife have decided that climate change is unstoppable, so the best they can do is to move someplace where they will be least affected so they can live out their remaining days in peace.

"At 64 and 74 years of age, my wife and I believe there's a good chance that we'll be gone before coastal cities are flooded, the ice caps have melted, and the planet descends into a "Mad Max" dystopia," wrote Barry Rueger. "We would like to think that this isn't what the future has in store, but the intransigence of almost all governments to actually slow carbon emissions leaves little doubt that things are unlikely to turn around."

It's easy to understand Rueger's point of view as such natural disasters as the horrible fires in Australia, melting icecaps and glaciers, and the increasingly warm temperature of the earth, are threatening the planet. And yet, Donald J. Trump, the president of the United States, scoffs at the scientific evidence and even denies the reports of scientists and other experts within his own administration.

The National Oceanic and Atmospheric Administration (NOAA) within Trump's Commerce Department puts it this way:

"Impacts from climate change are happening now. These impacts extend well beyond an increase in temperature, affecting ecosystems and communities in the United States and around the world. Things that we depend upon and value — water, energy, transportation, wildlife, agriculture, ecosystems, and human health — are experiencing the effects of a changing climate."

It's as if Trump and his legion of climate deniers are making climate change disappear simply by making references and reports about it go away.

Nevertheless, two federally funded websites, Climate.gov and CLEANet.org, have managed to survive. Teachers use both websites to create lessons on everything from increasing CO2 levels to threatened biodiversity to the potential of solar power.

Climate.gov, a function of NOAA, says this on its website:

"NOAA Climate.gov provides science and information for a climate-smart nation. Americans' health, security, and economic well-being are closely linked to climate and weather. People want and need information to help them make decisions on how to manage climate-related risks and opportunities they face."

Said NBC News in its report, "The durability of Climate.gov and CLEANet.org websites shows that — even under the administration of a president who once denied climate change as a "hoax" — mainstream views of global warming can survive and even thrive."

Of course, the big question is for how long.

The Trump budget proposal for FY 2021 calls for significant reductions to environmental programs across the federal government, including a 26 percent cut to the Environmental Protection Agency (EPA) that would eliminate 50 EPA programs, slash research and development, and even end funding for the Energy Star rating system, which helps consumers purchase energy efficient electronics and appliances. If the program is to survive, it will have to rely on fees paid by businesses to participate.

Chip away, chip away, chip away. Deny, deny, deny.

Youth Rise Up

Young Greta Thunberg, the Swedish teenager, rocked the United Nations with her scolding of the world's leaders for failing her generation on climate change and sparked worldwide climate change protests. She was named Time Magazine's Person of the Year in 2019 and Trump went ballistic, tweeting that she has "anger management issues."

And all the while, the fires rage, the earth continues to warm, the ice caps melt, the crops dry up, water supplies are threatened, coastal communities face floods, and people like the Ruegers are simply hoping their planet will survive at least until they are gone.

But what about those who are younger and the generations to follow? Is it any wonder today's young voters are terrified of the future and aggressively embrace candidates who pledge to effectively combat climate change and preserve the planet?

Denying that climate change exists will not make things better. Erasing those two words -- "climate change" -- from government programs, documents and websites will not cool the earth, irrigate the crops, quell the fires, or ease the devastation of tornadoes and hurricanes. It will not save the planet for people yet to come.

No, we cannot give up on climate change. No matter what. And that makes November 3, 2020 a day that will live in infamy -- one way or the other.

◆◆◆

Want Mercury in Your Water? Trump's EPA Will Oblige

February 18, 2020
By Bob Gatty
The U.S Environmental Protection Agency (EPA) plans to roll back an Obama-era regulation that among its benefits protects kids from brain damage even before they are born.

The regulation involved is designed to limit harmful pollutants, like mercury, from power plants. The Trump administration wants it watered down to help the coal industry, even though that could put our health at risk.

Ironically, the electric power industry, which originally opposed the regulation when the Obama administration first launched it in 2011, now opposes the EPA's rollback, saying they've already complied, and the result has been far fewer pollutants being emitted by power plants.

The rule at issue is the Mercury and Air Toxics Standards, which targets a neurotoxin that can affect the IQ and motor skills of children, even in utero. And, it has worked because between 2006 when states started curbing mercury from coal plants and 2016 when the regulation took full effect, emissions declined by 85 percent.

The Trump administration's action is intended to help Trump's favorite industry, coal, whose executives have lobbied for the changes as the regulation prompted the nation's utilities to switch away from coal fired plants to other fuels, such as natural gas.

Of course, there are political ramifications here -- as usual.

Coal producing states, such as West Virginia, are critical to Trump's hopes for reelection and you can bet he will be bragging about how he's ended Obama's "War on Coal" in his red-hat rallies in coal country.

The EPA's plan is part of a broad effort by the administration to overhaul how the government calculates the health benefits of cleaner air, an effort sought by the coal industry. EPA plans to declare that it is not "appropriate or necessary" for the government to limit harmful pollutants from power plants -- even though the utility companies all have complied with those Obama-era standards.

Technically, the existing restrictions on mercury will be kept in place, but under the watered-down regulation, the government no longer will be able to count collateral benefits, like reducing soot and smog, when it sets limits on toxic air pollutions.

"They've unsheathed an incredibly sharp sword," University of Chicago professor Michael Greenstone, an energy and environmental economist, told The Washington Post. "And there's no reason that sword can't be used to roll back other regulations that have produced extraordinarily large benefits for American society."

The Post also noted that Trump's regulation has been stuck at the White House where staffers are trying to figure out which cost impact estimates to use. But expect it to happen soon as Trump puts the heat on, so he has plenty of accomplishments to brag about in the coming campaign.

That's some accomplishment -- rolling back anti-pollution rules that keep kids from suffering brain damage, even before they are born.

◆◆◆

Oil, Oil Everywhere

April 21, 2020

By Chris Waldron

In the famous Samuel Taylor Coleridge poem, "The Rime of the Ancient Mariner", a lone sailor is adrift on the ocean, surrounded by water, yet he suffers from dehydration. Unable to drink the saltwater from the ocean, he laments, "Water, water everywhere but not a drop to drink".

Such is the case with the petroleum producing companies as oil prices plunged into negative territory for the first time since recording began in 1983. A combination of a production war between Russia and Saudi Arabia that flooded the market with oil combined with an historic drop in demand due to the Coronavirus pandemic have resulted in the worst oil crisis since the 1973 Arab Oil Embargo.

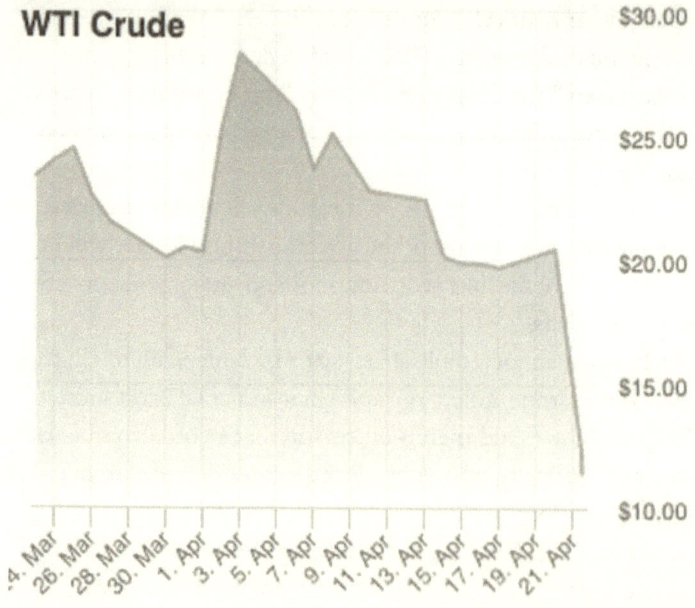

Some of us are old enough to remember the long gas lines and rationing that the oil embargo caused. The result of Middle East tensions, the oil embargo served as punishment on the United States by the Organization of Petroleum

Exporting Countries (OPEC) for America's support of Israel in the ongoing Middle East conflict. It caused a stock market crash and alerted Americans to their fragile reliance on oil exports.

Basically, they had use over a barrel (pun intended).

Similarly, there was the oil crisis of 2003-2008, when a high demand for oil and gasoline led to a dramatic rise in prices, as high as $4 a gallon in some places.

As a result, oil companies began receiving government subsidies to ramp up production and increase oil exploration. Fracking, the process of releasing trapped oil and natural gas from shale, and offshore drilling have led to America becoming the world's number one oil producer.

Now we are in a completely opposite situation. Oil reserves, meant to prevent a crisis similar to the 1973 embargo, are at an all-time high, yet there is little demand. Countries are left with barrels of oil, but no market for them.

The current situation caused the stock market to plunge yet again as another offshoot of the Coronavirus pandemic threatened another part of the economy. Shale oil companies, who specialize in fracking, as well as offshore drilling facilities, could be shut down due to the tremendous drop in demand.

While this is seen as a negative for the economy, environmentalists are surely cheering. Fracking has caused untold damage to the environment as the water used to release the trapped oil has made its way into nearby wells and drinking water, while the opposition to offshore drilling and its impact on marine life has been well documented.

So, the collapse of the oil industry may not be all bad news. It can result in more environmental protections and spur on the long-delayed process of finding alternative energy sources.

7

BLUNDERS IN FOREIGN AFFAIRS

Donald Trump's "America First" foreign policy sounds great to his patriotic base of supporters, but it's isolating our country from our allies even as he befriends dictators and establishes policies that only serve to benefit America's enemies. He is creating a world far more dangerous than the one he inherited from President Obama. Trump's successors will have much to do as he – or she – seeks to restore America's standing in the world.

At the Edge of the Apocalypse

January 25, 2018
By Bob Gatty
The world's "Doomsday Clock" is now set at two minutes to midnight, the closest we have ever come to the end of humanity. It's a sad -- and scary -- commentary on the inability of leading nations to steer a path towards peace rather than drawing ever closer to nuclear war.

That's the grim assessment of the Bulletin of Atomic Scientists, which moved the clock forward, citing "the failure of President Trump and other world leaders to deal with looming threats of nuclear war and climate change."

Bulletin officials Lawrence M. Krauss and Robert Rosner explained the decision to move the clock forward in an op-ed published today by The Washington Post. Krauss, chair of the Bulletin of the Atomic Scientists Board of Sponsors, is director of the Origins Project and foundation professor of the School of Earth and Space Exploration and Physics Department at Arizona State University. Rosner, chair of the Bulletin of the Atomic Scientists Science and Security Board, is a distinguished service professor in the Departments of Astronomy & Astrophysics and Physics at the University of Chicago.

They pointed out that "days after Donald Trump took the oath of office, the Bulletin of the Atomic Scientists reset the Doomsday Clock to 2½ minutes to midnight, in part because of destabilizing comments and threats from America's new commander in chief."

"One year later, they wrote, "we are moving the clock forward again by 30 seconds, due to the failure of President Trump and other world leaders to deal with looming threats of nuclear war and climate change. The Science and Security Board for the Bulletin of the Atomic Scientists assesses that the world is not only more dangerous now than it was a year ago; it is as threatening as it has been since World War II. In fact, the Doomsday Clock is as close to midnight today as it was in 1953, when Cold War fears perhaps reached their highest levels."

Yes, the "Doomsday Clock" is only symbolic and it doesn't mean that when the clock strikes 12 tonight that the apocalypse will come crashing down upon planet earth and we will all be annihilated. Nevertheless, the chilling message in this symbolic gesture must not be ignored.

"To call the world nuclear situation dire is to understate the danger — and its immediacy," Krauss and Rosner wrote. "North Korea's nuclear weapons program appeared to make remarkable progress in 2017, increasing risks for itself, other countries in the region and the United States." The nuclear rhetoric between Trump and North Korean leader Kim Jong Un, does not help, they implied.

They cited other potential flash points around the world, including continuing tensions between the U.S. and Russia, and that Pakistan and India have continued to build arsenals of nuclear weapons. "And in the Middle East, uncertainty about continued U.S. support for the landmark Iranian nuclear deal adds to a bleak overall picture," they wrote.

While climate change poses a less immediate danger to the world, Krauss and Rosner warned that "avoiding catastrophic temperature increases in the long run requires urgent attention now." They said the global response has failed to effectively meet the challenge and warned that the Trump administration's policy of ignoring the crisis adds to the "perilous security situation" faced by the world.

Tell me again, Trump voters, how this Makes America Great Again?

Putin: With Friends Like That...

March 1, 2018

By Bob Gatty

During his campaign for the Presidency, Donald Trump bragged that he would have a great relationship with Vladimir Putin and Russia. Yesterday, Putin announced a new nuclear-capable missile that would be impervious to any U.S. missile defense system.

Wow! What a great job, DJT. Not only do you have North Korea's Rocket Man threatening the U.S. with nuclear weapons, now you have Russia doing the same thing! Great job!

Guess you're finding out that being President of the United States is just a little bit different than being the p-----y groping star of a reality TV show or the ogling owner of the Miss Universe pageant. What you do and what you say actually has real consequences -- in fact, it's so consequential that it could affect the future of the world.

In this latest announcement, Putin said Russia had successfully tested nuclear-propulsion engines that would allow nuclear-tipped cruise missiles and underwater drones to travel for virtually unlimited distances and evade traditional defenses.

Moreover, Putin warned that Moscow would consider a nuclear attack, of any size, on one of its allies to be an attack on Russia and that would lead to an immediate response. Putin did not say which countries he considers allies.

What a friend you have in Putin, Donald! As the old saying goes, with friends like that, who needs enemies?

Thing is, right now Trump is under intense investigation by special prosecutor Robert Mueller for his, and his campaign's, ties to Russia and how that might have fixed the election to unexpectedly send Trump to the White House.

There's no doubt Russia did meddle in that election, using fake social media postings to turn voters towards Trump and away from Democrat Hillary Clinton and perhaps actually changing votes. (Remember when Trump said the election would be rigged?) It probably was -- in his favor.

Now, the same thing is in danger of happening in the upcoming mid-term elections. In fact, In mid-February, leading US intelligence officials warned that Russia intends to interfere in those elections.

"There should be no doubt that Russia perceives its past efforts as successful and views the 2018 U.S. midterm elections as a potential target for Russian influence operations," Dan Coats, the Director of National Intelligence, said during the Senate Intelligence Committee's annual worldwide-threats hearing.

Just this week, Adm. Michael Rogers, who leads US Cyber Command, told lawmakers that Trump has not directed him to strike Russia's cyber operations, meaning that Putin has yet to see any serious repercussions for his country's actions. Worse, there are almost no substantive measures in place to prevent Russia from meddling in the upcoming 2018 midterm elections.

I guess Trump really does want to have a great relationship with Putin and Russia. How's that strategy working, Mr. President?

French President Macron: 'No Planet B'

April 26, 2018

By Bob Gatty

Yesterday, in a historic speech to a joint session of the U.S. Congress, French President Emmanuel Macron warned against President Trump's "America First" policies, pulling out of the existing Iran nuclear deal, and ignoring the dangers of climate change. "There is no Planet B," he declared.

Macron's speech followed a day of touchy-feely imagery and conversations at the White House, during which Macron was honored at a glittering state dinner. All of that pomp and circumstance led Trump to tweet that Macron's speech before Congress would be "great" and he couldn't wait to hear it.

Wonder how he felt when Macron took a swipe at his populist nationalist philosophy and "America First" mantra. "We can choose isolationism, withdrawal and nationalism," said Macron. "This is an option. It can be tempting to us as a temporary remedy to our fears. But closing the door to the world will not stop the evolution of the world. It will not douse but inflame the fears of our citizens."

Unlike Trump, it was clear that this young French president has thought about the future -- or what could be the future -- in a world that must contend with Trump's determination to walk out on international agreements on climate, trade, and nuclear proliferation, insisting that others must carry the load.

"Other powers with the strongest strategy and ambition will then fill the void we would leave empty," warned Macron. "Other powers will not hesitate once again to advocate their own model to shape the 21st century world order."

And then, he said, "Personally, if you ask me, I do not share the fascination for new strong powers, the abandonment of freedom and the illusion of nationalism."

No 'Planet B'

As to the environment, Macron declared "We are killing our planet. Let us face it: There is no planet B."

"We must find a smoother transition to a lower carbon economy," Macron said. "Because what is the meaning of our life, really, if we work and live destroying the planet while sacrificing the future of our children? ... On this issue, it may happen we have disagreements between the U.S. and France, it may happen, like in all families. That for me is a short-term aggravation. In the long run, we will have to face the long-term realities... together."

"Let us work together in order to make our planet great again and create new jobs and new opportunities while safeguarding our earth," he declared. (Wonder where he got that from!)

Macron also jabbed Trump's trade policies. "We need a free and fair trade for sure," Macron said, adding, "a commercial war opposing allies is not consistent with our mission, with our history, with our current commitments for global security."

He called for differences on trade imbalances and over capacity to be managed through the World Trade Organization, precisely the opposite of Trump's threats of tariffs that have rattled our allies abroad.

There was more, and most of his speech was met with cheers from lawmakers attending. Wonder if Trump thought that speech was as "great" as he expected.

Trump's Right: It IS a 'Disgrace'

January 14, 2019

By Bob Gatty

President Trump denied today that he has ever "worked for Russia" and said it is a "disgrace" that he should be asked if he ever did.

Trump is right. It's a disgrace that our president would ever even be suspected of working for America's arch enemy, to the point that a legitimate news reporter would feel obliged to ask such a question.

But that's the situation in America today and Donald Trump has no-one to blame but himself.

It was Trump, not "crooked Hillary" or anyone else, whose actions in the firing of former FBI Director James Comey were so suspicious that the agency launched an investigation to determine if the President of the United States was colluding with or being influenced by the enemy.

That investigation, which Trump has ridiculed and derided, was continued by Special Counsel Robert Mueller III, whose work is widely viewed to be nearing a conclusion with a report expected to be presented to the Justice Department perhaps as early as next month.

It was Trump, not "crooked Hillary" or anyone else, who met with Vladimir Putin, kicked his aides out of the room and demanded the transcript from the interpreter, swearing that individual to secrecy. Today, Trump said that meeting was "no big deal," that he meets one-on-one with world leaders "all the time."

Does he demand the transcripts of those meetings? Is any record kept of what is said?

So, what are we to make of those facts? Why would Trump excuse other U.S. officials and his aides from the meeting so he could talk with Putin privately, and then demand the transcript so it could not be leaked? What does he have to hide?

Yes, Mr. President, it is a disgrace, indeed, that our country has a leader who is so untrustworthy that millions of our citizens are convinced that you have betrayed America for whatever reason, whether it's your unending and insatiable greed, your desire to be a strongman leader like Putin, your ego, blackmail -- or maybe a combination of all of those things.

So now, with this ridiculous fight over your wall, which you promised your anti-immigrant supporters, you have shut down a big chunk of our government with ever-growing consequences. People are missing their paychecks. Farmers are missing their government support checks so they can't plant their fields. SNAP recipients are in danger of being unable to purchase food. Airport security personnel, Coast Guard personnel, even border security personnel are not being paid. Contractors, many of them small companies, are getting stuck and not being paid. Food isn't being inspected. The list goes on and on and on.

Why? Is it really about your pledge to "keep America safe?" Or is it about your need to divert attention away from all of these investigations and revelations regarding Russia?

You are right, Mr. President. It is a disgrace. But the disgrace is you.

◆◆◆

U.S. Intelligence Chiefs Naïve?

January 30, 2019
By Bob Gatty
President Trump says U.S. intelligence chiefs are "naive" in their assessments of Iran, ISIS and North Korea, obviously unhappy that they contradicted him yesterday in a closed-door session with members of the Senate Intelligence Committee.

Where does he get that idea? From his gut? Or from wishful thinking? I put my money on the guys who make a living doing this stuff, not a rich egomaniac who hopes to be the world's biggest big shot.

Here's what Trump tweeted after the meeting about Iran, in case you didn't see it:

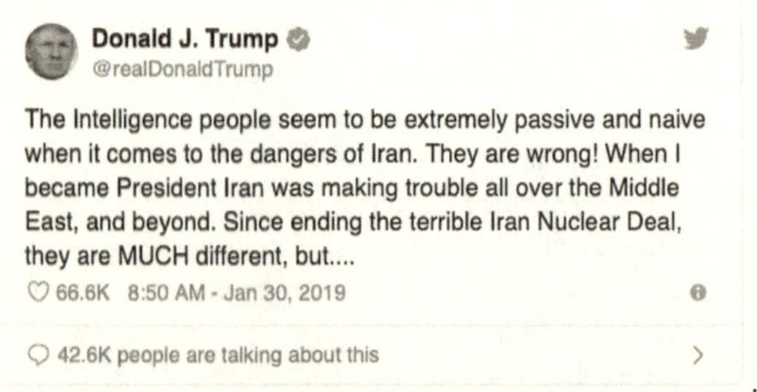

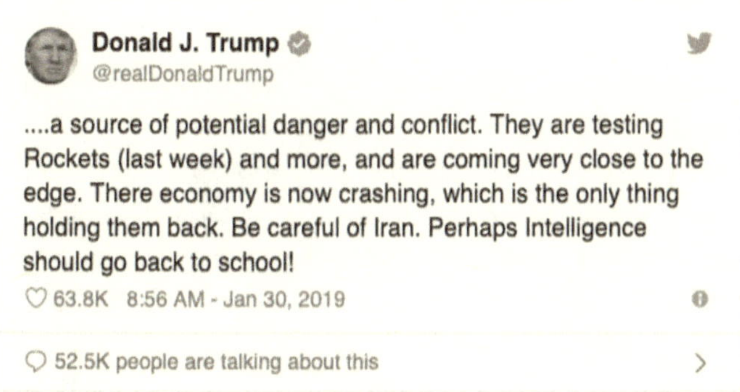

Trump also said the Islamic State's control in parts of Iraq and Syria "will soon be destroyed" and there is a "decent chance of denuclearization" in North Korea.

The New York Times reported that on Tuesday, top intelligence officials -- all appointed by Trump -- said Iran is currently not trying to make a nuclear bomb and appears to be complying with a 2015 nuclear agreement, even after Mr. Trump promised last year to withdraw from it.

Of course, that deal was negotiated by the Obama administration, so nothing more needs to be said.

On Syria, intelligence officials said the Islamic State would go on "to stoke violence" with thousands of fighters there and in Iraq, and with 12 networks around the world. They also said North Korea was unlikely to permanently shed its nuclear weapons, contradicting Trump's prediction he says is based on the "best" relationship ever between North Korea and the U.S.

You know, Trump received a "great letter" from Kim Jong Un, so that seals the deal.

The fact that this man has access to America's launch codes is scary as hell.

Come on, #MuellerTime...what are you waiting for?

Trump, the Would-be Dictator

August 23, 2019

By Bob Gatty

This morning Donald J. Trump, the reality show president, posted a notice on Facebook and on his favorite, channel, Twitter, that American companies "are hereby ordered to immediately start looking for an alternative to China, including bringing your companies HOME and making your products in the USA."

Since when can the president of the United States ORDER American companies to do his bidding? Where does that come from? What authority?

Who and what will he ORDER next? I shudder to think. Trump is completely delusional and anyone who follows him blindly is as well.

What happened following his announcement? Within 45 minutes the stock market plunged nearly 400 points, stalling, at least temporarily, a slow climb back from previous scares caused by this unhinged occupant of the White House. And by the close? Down 628 points.

Why? Presumably because investors are worried -- and rightly so -- about the long-term implications of Trump's continuing trade war with China. What will he do next? It's anybody's guess.

What is remarkable, although not surprising, is the response by many of those who follow his Facebook page:

Greg Knight: As expected after president trump announced we don't need China and for companies To look elsewhere for their supply chains, The Stock Market went down. I lost money! I don't care. I'll gladly pay more for things made elsewhere or not buy things I don't need. I support this decision. 1000%. Day traders and anti-trumpers can sell Their stocks all day long. We will win in true end. Wars cost money, at least this war won't cost our amazing service member lives. Fight on President Trump!

Eric Ochanji II: Finally, the world finds a man who can tell China off. China is crippling my country. This is beautiful!

Pete Kruml: Fantastic. The US can't be held hostage by China, and we have a president willing to stand his ground and not bend like so many others have. It's all about our country, our people, our IP. Go Trump Go!!!.

But then, there were these from some people who at least think:

Brian Thomas Auker: We've never had a president this ignorant about international economics.

Trump needs to ease up on the amphetamines and start listening to his advisors.

Krassenstein Brothers: You don't get it... You have WAY MORE to LOSE in this than China's leadership. You are up for re-election in 14 months. China knows this and won't back down. You are going to spiral the world economy into a massive recession driven by currency devaluation and trade wars.

So, once again, America's economy and our own financial security are being toyed with by an egomaniac who thinks he can turn our precious democracy into an autocracy. Sorry, Mr. Reality Show MC, you are mistaken. Our Constitution was designed to protect us from the likes of you.

But unless Congress grows some cojones and acts, what disasters await us until November 2020? I shudder to think.

◆◆◆

Betrayal

October 18, 2019
By Chris Waldron
Picture this: It's December 8th, 1941 and President Roosevelt announces we have signed a treaty with Japan to end hostilities in the Pacific. We have ceded Hawaii and withdrawn to our continental borders. Can't happen you say? Actually, it IS happening, right before our very eyes.

By abandoning our allies, the Kurds, the Trump administration has given free license to Russia, reinvigorated ISIS and abandoned our role as protectors of Democracy as outlined in the Truman Doctrine. We have, in essence, allowed our country to have its policies dictated by our enemies.

What did this  "ceasefire" accomplish?

Turkey was able to gain access to territory it long sought while destroying those who opposed them. They agreed to a five-day "pause", yet they continue to attack fleeing Kurds, while ISIS prisoners are left unguarded and free to return to their terrorist activities.

It displayed to the world that the Trump administration, once again, will refuse to honor its international commitments just as it did when it abandoned the Iran Nuclear Deal. It displayed a betrayal of our allies and destroyed any sense of trust that any country could have in America's future treaties.

Trump supporters bristle when I compare his behavior to Adolph Hitler, but who else has the same historical profile? Stalin? Mao? Like Hitler, Trump prizes loyalty to self over country. His rabid base believes his lies even when facts stare them in the face, the same way the Nazis swallowed Hitler's propaganda over the casualty reports coming in from the various fronts of World War II.

But perhaps I am making the wrong comparison. Instead of Hitler, perhaps Trump would more aptly be compared to Neville Chamberlain, the British Prime Minister who declared "Peace in our time" after he granted Hitler the right to annex part of Czechoslovakia in order to avoid war in Europe. Trump is making the same claims in allowing Turkey and Russia to claim dominance in the Middle East.

Trump's justification for US withdrawal from Syria is based on his assertion that he is fulfilling a campaign promise to bring American troops home. This would be a bit more believable if he didn't simultaneously agree to send thousands of troops to Saudi Arabia; the same country whose leaders are implicated in the murder of an American journalist and was home to a majority of the 9/11 hijackers.

Following the 9/11 attacks, the world stood behind America in a unified front against terrorism and Al Qaeda. They defended us because we abided by our treaties and fulfilled our international obligations. Given the current situation, the world would be hard pressed to defend us again.

The world will remember this act of betrayal.

◆ ◆ ◆

Loose Lips

By C J Waldron

October 27, 2019

An ISIS terrorist is dead. Kudos to Donald Trump, the intelligence community, the United States military and the countries and others who assisted us in this effort. This was a decidedly dangerous individual whose continued existence was a major threat to everyone. His demise should definitely be applauded.

And then there was the announcement and the typical self-congratulatory proclamations where things went awry.

The statement began simply enough, with Trump making his typical dead-pan delivery as he focused on what was on the teleprompter. It didn't take long before he predictably drifted off the prepared text and began a rambling account of the terrorist leader's last moments. He also went into explicit detail as to the operations and methods used to track and ultimately find ISIS leader Abu-Bakar al-Baghdadi, describing how he was "whimpering and crying" and begging for his life before detonating an explosive device he wore when his capture was inevitable.

Trump continued to ramble on, praising a reporter who gave him favorable coverage and complimenting his own intelligence while at the same time making certain he thanked Russia and other foreign countries for their assistance while giving a passing nod to the Kurds whose participation in this effort may never be known.

Trump expressed surprise and admiration for these efforts and the efforts of the Delta Force soldiers who led the operation. Many of these things could have been obvious if he bothered to read his intelligence briefings.

In his announcement and the rambling Q & A that followed, Trump continued to reveal information about methods that are usually classified. True, he has the right to declassify anything he sees fit, and he's had no problem doing so in the past, as he did in an Oval Office meeting with Russian officials, yet by revealing methods and practices, Trump put future operations at risk.

In his vivid description of the terrorist's final moments, Trump has created a rallying cry for the recruitment of future ISIS fighters. His insulting and degrading commentary will no doubt be used to gain more followers and foment further hatred of Americans both here and abroad.

During World War II, there was a concerted effort to keep American tactics secret, lest some hostile power gain access to them. It was summarized in the phrase "Loose lips sink ships" and other equally ominous warnings, to keep silent about our efforts. What Trump did in his announcement today was completely abandon this practice by revealing specific details of the raid and taking a self-congratulatory victory lap that will surely infuriate our enemies.

What should have been a great victory over terrorism may turn out to be another motivation for a 9/11-style attack on American soil.

◆◆◆

The Laughing-Stock Buffoon

December 4, 2019
By Bob Gatty
So, President Trump became the butt of jokes between top world leaders at the NATO summit near London, prompting him to stalk away and start calling people names.

Wasn't it Trump who said in a 2014 tweet that "We need a President who isn't a laughing stock to the entire world?" In that tweet, he added, "We need a truly great leader, a genius at strategy and winning. Respect!"

Well, la de da.

Barack Obama has the admiration and respect of virtually every free nation in the world. In fact, the man who Trump absolutely despises and who he tried to obsessively discredit and still tries to undo his legacy, has been the "Most Admired Man" in the World for 11 years.

Donald Trump? Not so much.

The Canadian Prime Minister, the French President, and the British Prime Minister were captured on video mocking Trump's performance during a NATO meeting, during which Canada's Justin Trudeau was heard saying White House aides were agog at his behavior.

The video circulated widely on social media today and is shared above.

During that conversation, Canada's Justin Trudeau said to the others, "You just watched his team's jaws drop to the floor." Later. Trudeau said his comment was in reference to Trump's announcement during their bilateral meeting that the upcoming G7 summit will be hosted at Camp David.

Trump's reaction?

He called Trudeau "two-faced." Then, to soften things a bit, he added, ""honestly with Trudeau, he's a nice guy."

Trump criticized Trudeau because Canada does not currently meet NATO's 2% defense spending target.

"The truth is I called him out on the fact that he's not paying 2% and I guess he's not very happy about it," Trump said. "I can imagine he's not that happy, but that's the way it is."

Well, the way it is, actually, is that America has a buffoon who is a world laughingstock as our president. He stalks out of meetings when he doesn't get his way, and like the schoolyard bully, resorts to calling people names. He whines and complains and says no president has ever had it so bad. We had a seven-year-old visitor over Thanksgiving who is more mature than this man.

In fact, a Trump trademark is calling people nasty names when he disagrees or doesn't like them. Or feels threatened by them. He demeans at every opportunity.

Now, some of those who have been his target -- Rep. Adam Schiff (D-CA) for example --may just have the last laugh. He calls Schiff "Pencil Neck" and "Shifty Schiff."

Now, Schiff chaired the House Intelligence Committee's impeachment hearings and authored the 300-page report recommending Trump's impeachment on charges of obstruction of justice and bribery, among others.

How's that for revenge?

The Assassination of Qasem Soleimani: Actions Have Consequences

January 3, 2020
By C J Waldron
Donald Trump ordered the assassination of a foreign government official on sovereign soil. That much is clear. What is also clear is that he, and others in his administration, failed to consider the consequences such an action would cause.

What was his motivation behind carrying out this deliberately hostile gesture now?

While I'm no fan of conspiracy theories, it is no secret that Trump has told multiple lies on a daily basis. With that being said, how can we be certain that he isn't lying now to ensure his re-election?

Trump has made no secret of his love of hostile dictators who regularly use violence to suppress those who oppose them.

There is Saudi Arabia, with its de facto leader Crown Prince Mohammad bin Salman. The suppression of any opposition and civil liberties has led to sham trials and multiple executions and even the murder of American journalist Jamal Khashoggi, yet this administration continues to cozy up to the crown prince as it promotes genocide in Yemen. The close relationship between the crown prince and Trump son-in-law Jared Kushner casts a further cloud on this unusual partnership.

There is Turkey, with its dictatorial leader, President Recip Erdogan. When protests against his rule were organized, he declared a state of emergency, suspending many civil rights. He also was the beneficiary of the US withdrawal from Syria, which allowed him to systematically seize lands from the Kurdish population.

Israel has long been a staunch ally, yet is led by a man, Benjamin Netanyahu, who is currently under indictment for fraud and bribery as he suppresses the rights of the Palestinian population while refusing to consider the two-state solution that many consider the only path to peace in the Middle East. Trump's recognition of Jerusalem as its capital has long been a hotly disputed issue, yet Trump rolled over on this quicker than the time it takes to tie your shoes. Again, son-in-law Jared Kushner was at the center of this action, as he was placed in charge of the Middle East peace plan; a plan that, when presented to Arab leaders, was laughed at.

Long-time adversary North Korea has been the center of a very odd international relationship. What began as a childish war of words quickly evolved into a decidedly one-sided love affair as Trump repeatedly rewarded murderous dictator Kim Jong-un with the place on the world stage he craved while threatening nuclear annihilation to those who oppose him. Kim's human rights' violations include the murder of his uncle and that of US citizen Otto Warmbier, yet Trump continues to maintain a positive relationship with this murderous dictator.

And then there is Russia and its ruthless leader Vladimir Putin. Putin makes no secret that he will deal with those who oppose him most harshly, leading President Obama to kick Russian diplomats out of the United States when Putin's agents were implicated in the murder of Russian expatriates living up in the United Kingdom. Putin also admitted to being behind election meddling in the 2016 race, and is implicated in spreading the debunked conspiracy theory that is the nexus for the current impeachment hearings, yet Trump still has such admiration for Putin that he said he would accept an invitation to travel to Russia even while he's currently under investigation.

What does this have to do with the current situation? Under each of these situations, Trump ignored the advice of multiple intelligence agencies, yet now he is attempting to use them to back up his murder of a foreign national. He is also mirroring the actions of several brutal regimes to justify this. Meanwhile, he is continuing his staunch partisanship by refusing to include Congressional Democrats in the process.

No matter what, his base will continue to support him, even if it results in the deaths of young Americans in a war, he began to support his re-election. Trump has shown a propensity to use any means necessary to achieve his goals. It wouldn't be much of a stretch to consider that he had a foreign leader murdered to guarantee his next term. Yet, this is the very act he accused President Obama of attempting during his 2012 re-election campaign.

Like I said, I'm no fan of conspiracy theories, but this is definitely food for thought.

Trump & American Imperialism

January 13, 2020
By C J Waldron
Imperialism (n): the policy of extending a country's power or influence through diplomacy or military force

Imperialism has its definite appeal to Donald Trump. Since his inauguration, he has sought to use his powerful position as means of disrupting the governments of Venezuela, Iran, Iraq, Syria and the Ukraine, among others. The assassination of a top Iranian government official is the latest example of Trump's desire to return America to an imperial power.

America is no stranger to imperial rule. Indeed, 4 million people, including Puerto Rico, Guam and American Samoa currently live under the auspices of the United States government with no representation. But it is the attempt to exercise its influence over foreign governments that is so troubling.

Its history, dating back to 1867, with the purchase of Alaska, often known as Serward's Folly, is a part of the American landscape. Since then,

America has sought to exert its influence over Spain, the Philippines, Panama and numerous other countries.

During the latter half of the 20th century, American leaders from Truman to Bush Sr. have used methods, both overt and covert, to destabilize governments that they saw as not being receptive to the American way.

In Vietnam, America supported the assassination of its president while supporting the installment of one who would support the American war effort and not pursue peace with their Communist counterparts .

In Nicaragua, the United States engaged in a "dirty war" with anti-American rebels on numerous occasions.

And in Iran, the installation of a pro-American ruler has resulted in our current political turmoil.

Indeed, it would appear that a return to an imperial power is exactly what Donald Trump seeks as he courts strongmen like the rulers of Russia, Turkey and North Korea. And it is these types of actions that will likely draw the attention of democracies around the world, as they await his next move.

The world waits…and it worries.

Danger

By C J Waldron

We are indeed living in dangerous times. Never have I been so afraid of the future of our country than under this current "regime". We are witnessing the devolution of America. Rights and privileges that I came to accept as natural rights have been eroded by an administration that is denying that America deserves a place on the world stage by alienating our allies.

I grew up hearing about the assassination of JFK. I studied his methods and admired his handling of the Cuban Missile Crisis.

I found LBJ to be a weak successor to Kennedy's legacy and questioned his handling of Vietnam. Yet, I admired his approach to Civil Rights and his advancement of social programs through his Great Society.

As I grew closer to drafting age, I became even more politically aware. When Nixon was elected, and he caused the war in Vietnam to explode, I wondered how I could become more involved. I followed the Watergate hearings with rapt attention. I breathed a sigh of relief when he resigned.

Ford was a weak president, being the only resident of the White House not to be elected. His immediate pardon of Nixon sealed his fate, and his bumbling became fodder for late night comics.

Carter was unsuited for the office. He was chosen because of the intense backlash against Republicans but was not a strong leader. His handling of the Iran Crisis was evidence of this. His efforts after he left office cemented his place in history.

Reagan was hailed as "the Great Communicator". He used his skills as an actor to get his message out to the people, while surviving numerous scandals and an assassination attempt. He witnessed the downfall of the Soviet Union and the fall of the Berlin Wall. He also ruined the economy by providing tax breaks to the rich.

George H W Bush was a career diplomat. Despite this, he failed to live up to the "legacy" that he inherited from Reagan. The invasion of Iraq after it seized neighboring Kuwait doomed his chance at re-election.

Clinton rose on a Blue Wave of enthusiasm. Despite scandal after scandal, he managed to wipe out the deficit and create a surplus, making the United States economy the envy of the world. He survived impeachment and sailed to re-election.

George W Bush was not elected by popular vote, so was an intensely unpopular president. He took the surplus he inherited and squandered it into a huge deficit by again providing tax breaks to the wealthy while allowing Wall Street to run amok. As a result, he plunged the country into the Great Recession. He only won re-election through his handling of the country in the aftermath of 9/11. He also involved us in two seemingly endless conflicts in Iraq and Afghanistan.

Barack Obama did indeed "inherit a mess". Using his astute political acumen, he was able to guide our country out of the Great Recession while enduring the hatred of white supremacists who refused to accept him as their president. He easily won re-election and will be remembered as one of the greatest leaders our country has known.

That brings us to the current occupant of the Oval Office. Like W, he did not win the popular vote. Also, like W, he is intensely unpopular, yet has a fervently loyal base that backs his every move and defends his every lie.

Which brings me to my point: We live in dangerous times. Religion is seeking to overrun reason. Defenders of the Second Amendment are seeking to run roughshod over those seeking to protect their First Amendment rights. Protests over police brutality are being distorted and misrepresented as a disrespect for America. The opinions of brutal dictators are being accepted over American Intelligence agencies. The administration is abandoning its allies while embracing these regimes. The message emboldened on the Statue of Liberty has been replaced by a "Keep Out" sign.

While the economy continues to chug along, trade wars and tax breaks for the wealthy remain a threat as the rich get richer while the rest of America struggles to survive. History tells us that it is only a matter of time before it all comes to a screeching halt.

My advice to everyone: Be afraid. Be VERY afraid!

Pact Buster-in-Chief

May 23, 2020
By Steve Hamelman
Donald Trump continues to take America down the road to isolationism, putting our nation in jeopardy of losing support from the rest of the free world. Pulling out of the Open Skies Treaty, is just the latest example.

Among its original signatories in March 1991 were all of America's allies in NATO, as well as some long-time adversaries. A few countries, like Russia, were slow to ratify, so it didn't go into effect until 2002.

As of today, 35 countries belong to this treaty, whose purpose is to maintain international peace by allowing certified surveillance aircraft of participating countries to fly over and observe each other's military installations and activity without fear of reprisal.

The original goal was to decrease tensions and to increase transparency among nations, notably the treaty's two biggest rivals, Russia and the United States.

In practice Russia would permit, upon request, and at specified intervals, a pre-approved American plane to observe military operations/facilities throughout Russia's vast lands, and vice versa—and so on and so forth with all participating countries. Conflict created by clandestine operations, or by unverified suspicion of arms build-ups, would evaporate.

And, thus, it stood for three decades.

President Donald Trump has now added Open Skies to his pile of trashed alliances and treaties.

International Repercussions

Let us assume Trump's reason for pulling out—Russia's chronic violation of the treaty—is true. (Not incidentally, Russia accuses the United States of the same thing.) And let us also assume that from a technological perspective this kind of aerial surveillance is outdated anyway.

Such concessions do not offset the harm done by withdrawing.

There is the obvious problem, as reported on May 21 by David Sanger in The New York Times:

"Mr. Trump's decision, rumored for some time, is bound to further aggravate European allies, including those in the North Atlantic Treaty Organization, who are also signatories to the treaty [emphasis added]."

Similarly, John Hudson and Paul Sonne in The Washington Post write:

"A withdrawal from the Treaty on Open Skies risks driving another wedge between the United States and its European allies, some of which urged the United States to remain in the pact [emphasis added]."

A classic case of throwing the baby out with the bathwater!

Trump and Secretary of State Mike Pompeo seem unable or unwilling to acknowledge that crucial allies, whose patience has been sorely tested time and time again by the MAGA man, must bear the brunt of their unilateral decision.

For as Sanger points out, "Russia will almost certainly respond by also cutting off their [other signatories'] flights, which the allies use to monitor troop movements on their borders—especially important to the Baltic nations."

Trump has left 30-odd allies in the lurch, just as he left the Kurds in the lurch when the United States pulled out of Syria, leaving our anti-Isis comrades to fend for themselves against Turkey, the remnants of Isis, and other enemies.

Oblivious

When it comes to Russia, Donald Trump's inconsistencies endanger national security. How exactly does one make America great again by making decisions that actually empower Russia?

Trump gave, and continues to give, Russia a free pass on U.S. election interference. With shame we recall the spectacle of 45 mortifying himself and the entire nation at the U.S./Russian summit in Helsinki in July 2018. Contradicting his own national intelligence advisors and overwhelming evidence, he instead sucked up to Vladimir Putin: "He just said it's not Russia. I will say this: I don't see any reason why it would be."

With Open Skies, the repercussions of not giving Russia a pass will be felt by 30 innocent countries who wish to keep the pact intact.

Trump and his State Department are oblivious to the harm done, in the first example, to democracy, and in the second example to global peace through collaboration.

In other words, Trump's solution is far worse than the problem.

WHO's Next?

We see Trump using the same my-way-or-the-highway tactic with the World Health Organization (WHO). Trump claims WHO has been too easy on China, which Trump has repeatedly demonized not only for being Covid-19's ground-zero, but also for failing to release details about the pandemic in a timely manner.

But instead of using diplomacy to resolve differences with China, he punishes WHO.

This humanitarian agency can no longer depend on 900 million U.S. dollars donated biennially.

And once again, this will be at best a pyrrhic victory for our myopic president.

For one thing, other members of WHO will be left to face the huge shortfall, thereby soiling our reputation around the planet. In turn, China will fill the income and image-gap caused by America's failure to live up to its obligations or to lead the world through a global crisis.

Moreover, the other work done by WHO (Earth to Donald Trump: Covid-19 is not the only disease studied by WHO's scientists) in its 150 field offices will be hit hard.

Finally, the president's attempt to shift blame onto others—WHO, China, the Democrats—won't disguise the fact that his garbled responses to the coronavirus ("We think we have it very well under control," "We're in great shape," "We're going to be pretty soon at only five people," "One day, it's like a miracle, it will disappear") was shackled from the outset by an administration equal parts unprepared and incompetent.

Game Over

But is anyone really surprised anymore by Trump's blinkered behavior?

He and his advisers have had plenty of practice throwing allies under the bus. Previously axed by this administration has been America's membership in the Trans-Pacific Partnership, the Paris Climate Accord, the Iran Nuclear Treaty, and UNESCO.

Hugely significant pacts: tossed aside, shattered, and abandoned rather than renegotiated for the benefit of all parties, including, for succeeding generations, the United States itself.

When it comes to treaties and pacts and partnerships, Trump is like a combination of spoiled brat and addicted gambler who, losing a hand

because of another player's alleged cheating, sweeps all the cards and dice off the table, kicks it over, and storms out, leaving someone else to clean up the mess.

But someday our allies may refuse to pick up after us.

Someday, we may return to the table only to find no one there willing to play another round with the United States of America.

EPILOGUE

Former Vice President Joe Biden says "we can, and we must, restore the soul of our nation."

He is right. Under the presidency of Donald John Trump, America's "soul" has become darkened as he has systematically and deliberately sought to divide us as a people, encouraging racism, hate, and suspicion one against another.

It has been a mean presidency prosecuted by an insecure, vicious, vindictive man who has little regard for the people he has sworn to protect and defend.

The preceding pages have chronicled many of those acts, but there will be many more to come. Just this morning as I write this, I see the headline "Trump administration asks Supreme Court to invalidate Obamacare." The filing came the same day the government reported that nearly 500,000 people who lost their health insurance during the pandemic gained Affordable Care Act (ACA) coverage.

House Speaker Nancy Pelosi (D-CA) said the administration's late-night request was "an act of unfathomable cruelty" during the pandemic.

Of course, she is correct. But it was an act that typified the mentality of this president, his hatred for his predecessor, Barack Obama, the father of the ACA, a hatred that has guided many of Trump's most harmful actions throughout his presidency.

Don Kohn, the chairman of the Horry County, SC, Democratic Party is fond of saying that the November 3 election will be "the most consequential election of our lifetime."

Indeed, that is true. Never, it seems, have the stakes been so high. Yes, we must "restore the soul of our nation."

Afterword

The preceding pages offer a virtual play-by-play of the tragedy of the Donald Trump presidency as it has unfolded since his election. We pick up the story beginning in September 2017 when the Not Fake News.biz blog was launched, running until today, June 26, 2020.

These past two-plus years have been a time of historic discord in America, marked by the failure of Donald J. Trump, the reality television personality who was elected president in November 2016, to effectively respond to the responsibilities of the presidency and to lead our nation effectively through these difficult times.

We, the writers at Not Fake News.biz, have chronicled many of these developments and offered our perspective as these historic events have unfolded. We will continue to do so, "From the Outside, Looking in."

As always, we invite you to become a regular reader, subscriber or member of Not Fake News and to listen to our podcast and view our videos on YouTube.

So, stay in the loop by visiting notfakenews.biz and signing up either as a subscriber or member. And check out The Forum, where Members can post their own commentary. Don't worry, it's all free. You can check out our videos here, too -- just click on the Videos tab.

If you enjoy listening instead, check out NFN Radio News podcasts, which offer narrations of our blogs, often with bonus commentary and interviews with experts and newsmakers. You can also just click on the Podcast tab on our home page.

We hope you enjoyed Volume 1 of *Hijacked Nation.* Please see Volume 2 for the following chapters:

8	Immoral Immigration
9	An Impeached President
10	Politics in the Age of Trump
11	The Coronavirus Pandemic

Acknowledgements

My thanks to all of our loyal Not Fake News readers and listeners on podcast, NFN Radio News. Your encouragement and support keep us going as we seek to shed some light on the major developments that continue to shape our nation.

I also want to express my appreciation to all of the writers who have contributed to Not Fake News since its inception -- Cecelia Blalock, Lauren Kligman, Helen Bass, Joe Picatello -- in addition to the contributing authors whose blogs are included in this book -- Stacy Fitzgerald, Stacie Pearman, Susan Hutchinson, and Stephen Hamelman. Your contributions enrich our content at Not Fake News and are much appreciated.

The co-author of this book, C J (Chris) Waldron is incredible. His insight into the issues and his determination to use his talents to help affect needed changes are evident in his blogs. Chris pulls no punches and refuses to quit, which is one reason we get along. Our job, he says, "is to preserve American ideals until America came to its senses." Thank you, Chris, for your friendship and your dedication to Not Fake News. Let's hope we are celebrating big time on November 4!

Finally, to my wife, Jackie, my thanks for putting up with my Not Fake News obsession. I even talked her into doing that silly Bob & Jackie Show on YouTube. She's funny and engaging, and I hope I can talk her into a few more episodes. --Bob Gatty

From Our Readers
Praise for Not Fake News

Bob Gatty's experience and perspective make him the perfect guy to start "Not Fake News." He began as a newsman, becoming a state capital bureau chief for United Press International. He served as the top staffer for two U.S. Congressmen, worked for a variety of DC lobbying organizations, and ran his own editorial services company. Bob knows his way around DC, understands the intricacies of politics at the national, state, and local levels, and has a solid perspective on business.

When Bob no longer could take Donald Trump's berating of the news media, and his constantly labeling stories, journalists, and major news outlets as "fake news," he launched a new blog site, Not Fake News.biz. His purpose was to call out Trump for his misdirections, lies, and exaggerations as he deliberately tries to mislead and divide the American people.

That was in September of 2017. Now Bob and an outstanding team of like-minded volunteer writers, including co-author Chris Waldron, is producing a contemporary history of political developments with, as he says, "just a little lean to the left." Apparently, he and his team have struck a chord with these blogs as their popularity continues to grow and expand, reaching readers around the world. "Not Fake News" is just what its name says. Read it and rely on it. I, for one, look forward to my Not Fake News "fix" every day.

Now, this book, with its politically focused blogs categorized into chapters by topic, pulls together that contemporary history and is must reading for anyone who is concerned about the future of our democracy under this president. – *Scott Ramminger, retired trade association CEO, now a successful jazz and blues songwriter and musician, Nashville, TN.*

I look forward to reading blogs from Not Fake News on a daily basis. This is 100 percent real news with bloggers presenting excellent thought-provoking political commentary. I have learned many things I would not have otherwise known from reading such informative and intelligently written blogs. I love the ability to leave my own comments and engage in ongoing conversation with the bloggers and to be an interactive part of Not Fake News. -- *Debbie Winkler CABC, CPDT, Director, Humane Domain, Sykesville, MD.*

NFN writers always find an interesting way to put the daily political news into context that impacts me on an emotional level. I look forward to my daily dose of this blog to see a new perspective on the events of this crazy political year. -- *Don Kohn, chairman, Horry County, SC, Democratic Party.*

Not Fake News is a refreshing daily antidote to the drama of current affairs. It's informative, insightful and humor when fitting. The writers are terrific and pull no punches when it comes to calling out Donald Trump, who is a catastrophe in the White House and a danger to the world. I look forward to receiving it in my inbox every day. -- *Bob Friedman, retired food industry executive, Chicago, IL.*

Not Fake News has been a welcome addition to my readings on political matters. Chris Waldron writes with thoroughness and accuracy, and also with passion and commitment about his hopes for a more perfect democracy in a time when democracy itself is under attack at home and abroad.

Thank you, Chris, and the other contributors for not only expressing the frustrations of so many of us, but also for using the power of the written word to advocate for positive change during a critical time in our country's history. -- *Patricia Bucci Johnson Devine, retired high school English teacher and reading instructor, Schenectady, NY.*

I have been following Not Fake News for quite some time and have truly learned so much from Chris Waldron on the subject of politics. Whenever I have doubts or concerns, I know I can turn to Not Fake News blogs and always find the true answers. It's always honest and well researched. I look forward to reading and staying up to date with this site. Thank you, Not Fake News, for always being there! Cheers! -- *Ali Price, retail manager and animal rights activist, Marion, OH.*

www.ingramcontent.com/pod-product-compliance
Lightning Source LLC
Chambersburg PA
CBHW031053250726
48655CB00004B/1422